A. H. Louie
More Than Life Itself
A Synthetic Continuation in Relational Biology

CATEGORIES

Edited by

Roberto Poli (Trento)

Advisory Board

John Bell (London, CA)
Mark Bickhard (Lehigh)
Heinrich Herre (Leipzig)
David Weissman (New York)

Volume 1

A. H. Louie

More Than Life Itself

A Synthetic Continuation in Relational Biology

ontos
verlag

Frankfurt I Paris I Lancaster I New Brunswick

Bibliographic information published by the Deutsche Nationalbibliothek

The Deutsche Nationalbibliothek lists this publication in the Deutsche
Nationalbibliografie; detailed bibliographic data are available in the
Internet at http://dnb.d-nb.de.

North and South America by
Transaction Books
Rutgers University
Piscataway, NJ 08854-8042
trans@transactionpub.com

United Kingdom, Ireland, Iceland, Turkey, Malta, Portugal by
Gazelle Books Services Limited
White Cross Mills
Hightown
LANCASTER, LA1 4XS
sales@gazellebooks.co.uk

Livraison pour la France et la Belgique:
Librairie Philosophique J.Vrin
6, place de la Sorbonne; F-75005 PARIS
Tel. +33 (0)1 43 54 03 47; Fax +33 (0)1 43 54 48 18
www.vrin.fr

©2009 ontos verlag
P.O. Box 15 41, D-63133 Heusenstamm
www.ontosverlag.com

ISBN 978-3-86838-044-6

2009

Printed on acid-free paper
FSC-certified (Forest Stewardship Council)
This hardcover binding meets the International Library standard

Printed in Germany
by buch bücher dd ag

To my *lignum vitae* and *arbor scientiae*,
my genealogical and academic ancestors
on whose shoulders I stand

In 518 BC, Pythagoras journeyed west, and had a comprehensive interview with the prominent ruler Leon of Phlius while both were attending the Olympic Games. Prince Leon was most impressed by Pythagoras's range of knowledge and asked in which of the arts he was most proficient. Pythagoras replied that, rather than being proficient in any art, he regarded himself as being a "philosopher". Prince Leon had never heard this term before — it had been newly coined by Pythagoras —and asked for an explanation.

Pythagoras said: "Life may well be compared with these pan-Grecian Games. For in the vast crowd assembled here, some are led on by the hopes and ambitions of fame and glory, while others are attracted by the gain of buying and selling, with mere views of profit and wealth. But among them there are a few, and they are by far the best, whose aim is neither applause nor profit, but who come merely as spectators through curiosity, to observe what is done, and to see in what manner things are carried on here.

"It is the same with life. Some are slaves to glory, power and domination; others to money. But the finest type of man gives himself up to discovering the meaning and purpose of life itself. He, taking no account of anything else, earnestly looks into the nature of things. This is the man I call a lover of wisdom, that is, a philosopher. As it is most honourable to be an onlooker without making any acquisition, so in life, the contemplation of all things and the quest to know them greatly exceed every other pursuit."

— free translation of anecdote recorded in
Marcus Tullius Cicero (*c.* 45 BC)
Tusculanae Questiones
Liber Quintus, III: 8–9

Contents

Praefatio
Unus non sufficit orbis

In my mentor Robert Rosen's iconoclastic masterwork *Life Itself* [1991], which dealt with the epistemology of life, he proposed a Volume 2 that was supposed to deal with the ontogeny of life. As early as 1990, before *Life Itself* (i.e., 'Volume 1') was even published (he had just then signed a contract with Columbia University Press), he mentioned to me in our regular correspondence that Volume 2 was "about half done". Later, in his 1993 Christmas letter to me, he wrote:

> ...I've been planning a companion volume [to *Life Itself*] dealing with ontology. Well, that has seeped into every aspect of everything else, and I think I'm about to make a big dent in a lot of old problems. Incidentally, that book [*Life Itself*] has provoked a very large response, and I've been hearing from a lot of people, biologists and others, who have been much dissatisfied with prevailing dogmas, but had no language to articulate their discontents. On the other hand, I've outraged the "establishment". The actual situation reminds me of when I used to travel in Eastern Europe in the old days, when everyone was officially a Dialectical Materialist, but unofficially, behind closed doors, nobody was a Dialectical Materialist.

When Rosen died unexpectedly in 1998, his book *Essays on Life Itself* [published posthumously in 2000] was in the final stages of preparation. But this collection of essays is *not* 'Volume 2', as he explained in its Preface:

> Thus this volume should be considered a supplement to the original volume. It is not the projected second volume, which deals with ontogenetics rather than with epistemology, although some chapters herein touch on ideas to be developed therein.

We see, therefore, that the "projected second volume" was then still a potentiality. I have, however, never seen any actualization of this 'Volume 2', and no part of its manuscript has ever been found.

Rosen did, nevertheless, leave behind a partially completed manuscript tentatively entitled "Complexity". This was a work-in-progress, with only a few sections (mostly introductory material) finished. It may or may not be what he had in mind for the projected second volume of *Life Itself*. My opinion is that it is not. To me, its contents are neither sufficiently extent nor on-topic enough for it to be a more-than-half-done Volume 2 on the ontogeny of life. In the years since, I had begun an attempt to extend the manuscript into *Life Itself Volume 2*, but this effort of raising his orphan, as it were, was abandoned for a variety of reasons — one of them was that I did not want to be Süssmayr to Mozart's *Requiem*.

The book that you are now reading, *More Than Life Itself*, is therefore *not* my completion of the anticipated Volume 2 of Robert Rosen's *Life Itself*, and has not incorporated any of his text from the "Complexity" manuscript. It is entirely my own work in the Rashevsky-Rosen school of relational biology. The inheritance of Nicolas Rashevsky (1899–1972) and Robert Rosen (1934–1998), my academic grandfather and father, is, of course, evident (and rightly and unavoidably so). Indeed, some repetition of what Rosen has already written first (which is worthy of repetition in any case) may occasionally be found. After all, he was a master of *les mots justes*, and one can only rearrange a precise mathematical statement in a limited number of ways. As Aristotle said, "When a thing has been said once, it is hard to say it differently."

The crux of *relational biology*, a term coined by Nicolas Rashevsky, is

"Throw away the matter and keep the underlying organization."

The characterization of life is not what the underlying physicochemical *structures* are, but by its entailment *relations*, what they *do*, and to what *end*. In other words, life is not about its material cause, but is intimately linked to the other three Aristotelian causes, formal, efficient, and final. This is, however, not to say that structures are not biologically important: structures and functions are intimately and synergistically related. Our slogan is simply an emphatic statement that we take the view of 'function dictates structure' over 'structure implies function'. Thus *relational biology* is the operational description of our endeavour, the characteristic name of our approach to our subject, which is *mathematical biology*. Note that 'biology' is the noun and 'mathematical' is the adjective: the study of living organisms is the subject, and the abstract deductive science that is mathematics is the tool. Stated otherwise, biology is the final cause and mathematics is the efficient cause. The two are indispensable ingredients, indeed complementary (and complimentary) halves of our subject. Relational biology can no more be done without the mathematics than without the biology. Heuristic, exploratory, and expository discussions of a topic, valuable as they may be, do not become the topic itself; one must distinguish the science from the meta-science.

The Schrödinger question "What is life?" is an abbreviation. A more explicitly posed expansion is "What distinguishes a *living system* from a non-living one?"; alternatively, "What are the defining characteristics of a natural system for us to perceive it as being alive?" This is the epistemological question Rosen discusses and answers in *Life Itself*. His answer, in a nutshell, is that an *organism* — the term is used in the sense of an 'autonomous life form', i.e., any living system — admits a certain kind of relational description, that it is 'closed to efficient causation'. (I shall explain in detail these and many other somewhat cryptic, very Rosen terms in this monograph.) The epistemology of biology concerns what one learns about life by looking at the living. From the epistemology of life, an understanding of the relational model of the inner workings of what is alive, one may move on to the ontogeny of life. The ontology of biology involves the existence of life, and the creation of life out of something else. The ontogenetic expansion of Schrödinger's question is "What makes a natural system alive?"; or, "What does it take to fabricate an organism?" This is a hard question. This monograph *More Than Life Itself* is my first step, a *synthesis* in every sense of the word.

With the title that I have chosen for the book, I obviously intend it to be a *continuation* of Robert Rosen's conception and work in *Life Itself*. But (as if it needs to be explicitly written) I am only Robert Rosen's student, not Robert Rosen himself. No matter how sure I am of my facts, I cannot be so presumptuous as to state that, because I know my mentor-colleague-friend and his work so well, what I write is what he would have written. In other words, I cannot, of course, claim that I speak for Robert Rosen, but in his absence, with me as a 'torch-bearer' of the school of relational biology, my view will have to suffice as a surrogate.

But surrogacy implicitly predicates nonequivalence. My formulations occasionally differ from Rosen's, and this is another reason why I find it more congenial to not publish my *More Than Life Itself* as 'Volume 2 of Robert Rosen's *Life Itself* '. I consider these differences *evolutionary* in relational biology: as the subject develops from Rashevsky to Rosen to me, each subsequent generation branches off on the *arbor scientiae*. Any errors (the number of which I may fantasize to be zero but can only hope to be small, and that they are slight and trivially fixable) that appear in this book are, naturally, entirely mine. The capacity to err is, in fact, the real marvel of evolution: the processes of metabolism-repair-replication are ordained from the very beginning to make small mistakes. Thus through mutational blunders progress and improvements are made. The Latin root for 'error', the driving force of evolution, is *erratio*, which means roving, wandering about looking for something, quest.

In complex analysis (the theory of functions of a complex variable), *analytic continuation* is a technique used to extend the domain of a given holomorphic (*alias* analytic) mapping. As an analogue of this induction, I use the term *synthetic continuation* in the subtitle of this monograph that is the song of our *synthetic* journey. Analytic biology attempts to model specific fragments of natural phenomena; synthetic biology begins with categories of mathematical objects and morphisms, and seeks their realizations in biological terms. Stated otherwise, in relational biology, mathematical tools are used synthetically: we do not involve so much in the making of particular models of particular biological phenomena, but rather invoke the entailment patterns (or lack thereof) from certain mathematical theories and interpret them biologically. Nature is the realization of the simplest conceivable mathematical ideas. I shall have a lot more to say on analysis versus synthesis in this monograph.

Someone once said to Rosen: "The trouble with you, Rosen, is that you keep trying to answer questions nobody wants to ask." [Rosen 2006]. It appears that his answers themselves cause even more self-righteous indignation in some people, because the latter's notions of truth and Rosen's answers do not coincide. Surely only the most arrogant and audacious would think that the technique they happen to be using to engage their chosen field is the be-all and end-all of that subject, and would be annoyed by any alternate descriptions, Rosen's or otherwise. One needs to remember that the essence of a complex system is that a single description does not suffice to account for our interactions with it. Alternate descriptions are fundamental in the pursuit of truth; plurality spices life.

"One world is not enough."

Uncritical generalizations about what Rosen said are unhelpful. For example, according to Rosen, one of the many corollaries of being an organism is that it must have noncomputable models. The point is that *life itself* is not computable. This in no way means that he somehow implies that computable models are useless, and therefore by extension people involved with biological computing are wasting their time! There are plenty of useful computing models of biological processes. The simple fact is that computing models (an indeed any models whatsoever) will be, by definition, *incomplete*, but they may nevertheless be fruitful endeavours. One learns a tremendous amount even from partial descriptions.

Along the same vein, some impudent people take great offence in being told by Rosen that their subject area (*e.g.* the physics of mechanisms), their 'niche', is *special* and hence *nongeneric*. Surely it should have been a compliment! An algebraic topologist, say, would certainly take great pride that her subject area is indeed not run-of-the-mill, and is a highly specialized area of expertise. I am a mathematical biologist. I would not in my wildest dream think that mathematics can provide *almost all* (in the appropriately mathematical sense) the tools that are suitable for the study of biology. A mathematical biologists is a specialist in a very specialized area. There is nothing wrong in being a specialist; what is wrong is the reductionistic view that the specialization is in fact general, that all (or at least all in the 'territory' of the subject at hand) should conform to the specialization. Why is being nongeneric an insult? Are some people, in their self-aggrandizement, really pretentious enough to think that the subject they happen to be in would provide answers to *all* the questions of life, the universe, and everything?

Rosen's revelations hit particular hard those who believe in the 'strong' Church-Turing thesis, that for every physically realizable process in nature there exists a Turing machine that provides a complete description of the process. In other words, to them, *everything* is computable. Note that Rosen only said that life is not computable, not that artificial life is impossible. However one models life, natural or artificial, one cannot succeed by computation alone. Life is not definable by an algorithm. Artificial life does not have to be limited to what a computing machine can do algorithmically; computing is but one of a multitude of available tools. But for the 'strong' Church-Turing thesis believers, they would have the syllogism

> Rosen says life is not computable.
> Everything is computable.
> Therefore Rosen says artificial life is impossible.

Compare and contrast this to Alan Turing's psychotic syllogism, a *non sequitur* that is so iconic of his demise

> Turing believes machines think.
> Turing lies with men.
> Therefore machines cannot think.

The following is a diagram of the modelling relation. (I shall have a lot more to say about it in Chapter 4.)

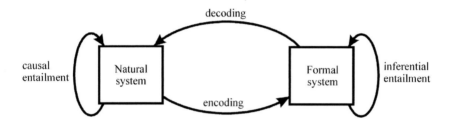

Natural systems from the external world generate in us our percepts of 'reality'. While causal entailments *themselves* may be universal truths, *perceived* causal entailments are *not*. All we have are our own *observations, opinions, interpretations,* our individual *alternate descriptions* of 'reality' that are our personal *models* of 'truth'. Causal entailments are interpreted, not proven.

A mathematical proof is absolute; it is categorically more than a scientific 'proof' (and a judicial 'proof') of 'beyond a reasonable doubt'. A scientific theory can never be proven to the same absolute certainty of a mathematical theorem. This is because a scientific 'proof' is merely considered 'highly likely based on the evidence available'; it depends on observation, experimentation, perception, and interpretation — all of which are fallible, and are in any case approximations of truth. Sometimes the minimized doubt later turns out to be errors, and paradoxically, in the same spirit of 'errors drive evolution', the inherent weakness in scientific proofs leads to scientific revolutions, when, 'based on new evidence', 'proven' theories are refined, updated, surpassed, or replaced.

Modelling is the art of bringing entailment structures into congruence. The essence of an art is that it rests on the heuristic, the unentailed, the intuitive leap. The encoding and the decoding arrows in the modelling relation diagram are themselves unentailed. Theoretical scientists are more artists than artisans. Natural Law assures them only that their art is not in vain, but it in itself provides not the slightest clue how to go about it. There is no right or wrong in art, only similarities and differences, the congenial and the uncongenial.

Among the four arrows in the diagram of the modelling relation, only inferential entailment may be *proven* in the rigorous mathematical sense. Absolute statements about the truth of statements validated by proofs cannot be disputed. Rosen proved the theorems that he stated in *Life Itself*, although his presentations are not in the orthodox form of definition-lemma-theorem-proof-corollary that one finds in conventional mathematics journals and textbooks. His book is, after all, not a text in pure mathematics. While the presentation may be 'Gaussian', with all scaffolding removed, there are nevertheless enough details in Rosen's prose that any reasonably competent mathematician can 'fill in the blanks' and rewrite the proofs in full, if one so wishes. But because of the unorthodox heuristic form, people have contended Rosen's theorems. Since the dispute is over form rather than substance, it is not surprising that the contentions are mere grumbles, and no logical fallacies in the theorems have ever been found. A common thread running in many of the anti-Rosen papers that I have encountered is the following: they simply use definitions of terms different from Rosen's, whence resulting in consequences different from Rosen's, and thereby concluding that Rosen must be wrong! I shall in the present monograph recast Rosen's theorems in as rigorously mathematical a footing as possible, using the algebraic theory of lattices. It is an interesting exercise in itself, but it is most unlikely to convert any skeptics with their preconceived ideas of truth.

The other three arrows in the modelling relation diagram — causal entailment, encoding, and decoding — all have intuitive elements in their art and science. As such, one if so inclined may claim that another's interpretations are *uncongenial*, but cannot conclude that they are *wrong*: there are no *absolute truths* concerning them.

Rosen closed his monograph *Anticipatory Systems* with these words:

> For in a profound sense, the study of models is the study
> of man; and if we can agree about our models, we can
> agree about everything else.

Agree with our models and partake our synodal exploration. Else agree to disagree, then we shall amicably part company.

In the Preface of *Life Itself*, Rosen identified his intended readership by quoting from Johann Sebastian Bach's *Clavierübung III*:

> Denen Liebhabern,
> und besonders denen Kennern von vergleichen Arbeit,
> zur Gemüths Ergezung...

> [Written for those who love,
> and most especially those who appreciate such work,
> for the delight of their souls...]

Let me add to that sentiment by quoting a couplet from a Chinese classic:

勞者自歌
非求傾聽

> [The diligent one sings for oneself,
> not for the recruitment of an audience.]

The same readers who took delight in *Life Itself* should also enjoy this *More Than Life Itself*. Be our companions on our journey and join us in our songs.

A. H. Louie
22 February, 2009

Nota bene

Many references in this monograph are drawn from Robert Rosen's Trilogy:

- [*FM*] *Fundamentals of Measurement and Representation of Natural Systems* [1978]

- [*AS*] *Anticipatory Systems: Philosophical, Mathematical, and Methodological Foundations* [1985a], and

- [*LI*] *Life Itself: A Comprehensive Inquiry into the Nature, Origin, and Fabrication of Life* [1991].

Additional references are in

- [*NC*] "Organisms as Causal Systems which are not Mechanisms: an Essay into the Nature of Complexity" [1985b] and

- [*EL*] *Essays on Life Itself* [2000].

My thesis

- [*CS*] "Categorical System Theory" [1985]

contains much of the background material on the category theory of natural and formal systems. (See the Bibliography for publication details of these references.) Familiarity with our previous work is not a prerequisite; it would, however, make simpler a first reading of this monograph. I strive to make it as self-contained as possible, but because of the subjects' inherent complexity, the entailment patterns of the many concepts cannot be rendered unidirectional and sequential. Some topics I present herein depend not only upon material on previous pages but also upon material on following pages. So in a sense this monograph is an embodiment of a relational diagram in graph-theoretic form, a realization of the branches and cycles of the entailment patterns.

In this book I assume that the reader is familiar with the basic facts of *naive set theory*, as presented, for example, in Halmos [1960]. Set theory from the naive point of view is the common approach of most mathematicians (other than, of course, those in mathematical logic and the foundations of mathematics). One assumes the existence of a suitable universe of sets (*viz.* the universe of *small* sets) in which the set-theoretic constructions, used in contexts that occur naturally in mathematics, will not give rise to paradoxical contradictions. In other words, one acknowledges these paradoxes, and moves on. This is likewise the position I take in this monograph. In the Prolegomena I present some set-theoretic and logical preliminaries, but more for the clarity of notations than for the concepts themselves. For example, the relative complement of a set A in a set B may be variously denoted as $B \sim A$, $B - A$, $B \backslash A$, etc.; I use the first one.

I often used the language of *category theory* as a metalanguage in my text. The definitive reference on this branch of abstract algebra is Mac Lane [1978]. I give a concise summary in the Appendix of those category-theoretic concepts that appear in my exposition.

Prolegomenon
Concepts from Logic

The principle that can be stated
Cannot be the absolute principle.
The name that can be given
Cannot be the permanent name.

— Lao Tse (6th century BC)
Tao Te Ching
Chapter 1

In principio...

0.1 Κοιναι εννοιαι α   Book I of Euclid's *Elements* begins with a list of twenty-three definitions and five postulates in plane geometry, followed by five *common notions* that are general logical principles. Common Notion 1 states

"Things equal to the same thing are also equal to one another."

Equality is a primitive: such proclamation of its self-evident property without proof is the very definition of *axiom*. Thus formally begins mathematics...

It may be argued that *equality* is the most basic property in any mathematical subject. In set theory, equality of sets is formulated as the

0.2 Axiom of Extension *Two sets are equal if and only if they have the same elements.*

Subset

I shall assume that the reader has a clear intuitive idea of the notions of a *set* and of *belonging to a set*. I use the words 'set', 'collection', and 'family' as synonyms. The elementary operations that may be performed with and on sets are used without further comments, save one:

0.3 Definition If A and B are sets and if every element of A is an element of B, then A is a *subset* of B.

The wording of the definition implies that there are two possibilities: either $A = B$, or B contains at least one element that is not in A, in which case A is called a *proper subset* of B. It has been increasingly popular in the mathematical literature to use $A \subseteq B$ as notation, seduced by the ordering relation $\leq$. This usage, unfortunately, almost always ends here. $\subseteq$-users rarely use the then-consistent notation $A \subset B$, analogous to $<$, to mean proper subset, but often resort to the idiosyncratic $\subsetneq$ instead. The few exceptions that do employ $\subset$ to mean 'proper subset' invariably lead to confusion, because of the well-established standard notation

(1) $\qquad A \subset B$

for '*either* $A = B$ *or* A is a proper subset of B'. The notation I use in this book is this standard which is inclusive of both senses of the containment of set A in set B. Sometimes $A \subset B$ is reversely described as 'B is a *superset* of A'.

If A and B are sets such that $A \subset B$ and $B \subset A$, then the two sets have the same elements. It is equally obvious *vice versa*. The Axiom of Extension 0.2 may, therefore, be restated as the

0.4 Theorem *Two sets A and B are equal if and only if $A \subset B$ and $B \subset A$.*

On account of this theorem, the proof of set equality $A = B$ is usually split into two parts: first prove that $A \subset B$, and then prove that $B \subset A$.

Conditional Statements and Variations

0.5 Conditional Many statements, especially in mathematics, are of the form '*If p, then q.*' We have already encountered some in this prologue. These are called *conditional statements*, and are denoted in the predicate calculus of formal logic by

$$(2) \qquad p \to q.$$

The if-clause p is called the *antecedent* and the then-clause q is called the *consequent*. Note that the conditional form (2) may be translated equivalently as 'q *if* p.' So the clauses of the sentence may be written in the reverse order, when the antecedent does not in fact 'go before', and the conjunction 'then' does not explicitly appear in front of, the consequent.

If the antecedent is true, then the conditional statement is true if the consequent is true, and the conditional statement is false if the consequent is false. If the antecedent is false, then the conditional statement is true regardless of whether the consequent is true or false. In other words, the conditional $p \to q$ is false if p is true and q is false, and it is true otherwise.

0.6 I Say What I Mean

"Then you should say what you mean," the March Hare went on.

"I do," Alice hastily replied; "at least — at least I mean what I say — that's the same thing, you know."

"Not the same thing a bit!" said the Hatter. "Why, you might just as well say that 'I see what I eat' is the same thing as 'I eat what I see'!"

"You might just as well say," added the March Hare, "that 'I like what I get' is the same thing as 'I get what I like'!"

"You might just as well say," added the Dormouse, which seemed to be talking in his sleep, "that 'I breathe when I sleep' is the same thing as 'I sleep when I breathe'!"

"It is the same thing with you," said the Hatter, and here the conversation dropped, and the party sat silent for a minute,...

— Lewis Carroll (1865)
Alice's Adventures in Wonderland
Chapter VII A Mad Tea Party

Alice's "I do" is the contention "I say what I mean". This may be put as the conditional statement

"If I mean it, then I say it.".

which is form (2), $p \to q$, with p = 'I mean it' and q = 'I say it'. It is equivalent to the statement

"I say it if I mean it.".

The conditional $p \rightarrow q$ may also be read as 'p *only if* q'. Alice's statement is then

"I mean it only if I say it.".

The adverb 'only' has many nuances, and in common usage 'only if' is sometimes used simply as an emphasis of 'if'. But in mathematical logic 'only if' means 'exclusively if'. So 'p *only if* q.' means 'If q does not hold, then p cannot hold either.' In other words, it is logically equivalent to 'If not q, then not p.', which in the predicate calculus is

(3) $\neg q \rightarrow \neg p$

(where $\neg$ denotes *negation*, the logical *not*). The conditional form (3) is called the *contrapositive* of the form (2). The contrapositive of Alice's "I mean it only if I say it." (= "If I mean it, then I say it.") is the equivalent conditional statement

"If I do not say it, then I do not mean it.".

0.7 I Mean What I Say   The conditional form

(4) $q \rightarrow p$

is called the *converse* of the form (2), and the equivalent contrapositive of the converse, *i.e.* the conditional form

(5) $\neg p \rightarrow \neg q$,

is called the *inverse* of the original form (2). A conditional statement and its converse or inverse are *not* logically equivalent. For example, if p is true and q is false, then the conditional $p \rightarrow q$ is false, but its converse

$q \to p$ is true. The confusion between a conditional statement and its converse is a common mistake. Alice thought "I mean what I say." (*i.e.* the converse statement "If I say it, then I mean it.") was the same thing as "I say what I mean." (the original conditional statement "If I mean it, then I say it."), and was then thoroughly ridiculed by her Wonderland acquaintances.

0.8 Biconditional The conjunction

$$(6) \qquad (p \to q) \wedge (q \to p)$$

(where $\wedge$ is the logical *and*) is abbreviated into

$$(7) \qquad p \leftrightarrow q,$$

called a *biconditional statement*. Since $q \to p$ may be read 'p if q' and $p \to q$ may be read 'p only if q', the biconditional statement $p \leftrightarrow q$ is 'p if and only if q', often abbreviated into 'p iff q'. If p and q have the same truth value (*i.e.* either both are true or both are false), then the biconditional statement $p \leftrightarrow q$ is true; if p and q have opposite truth values, then $p \leftrightarrow q$ is false.

Mathematical Truth

"Pure mathematics consists entirely of such asseverations as that, if such and such a proposition is true of *anything*, then such a such another proposition is true of that thing. It is essential not to discuss whether the first proposition is really true, and not to mention what the anything is of which it is supposed to be true. ... If our hypothesis is about *anything* and not about some one or more particular things, then our deductions constitute mathematics. Thus mathematics may be defined as the subject in which we never know what we are talking about, nor whether what we are saying is true."

> — Bertrand Russell (1901)
> *Recent work on the principles of Mathematics*

In mathematics, theorems (also propositions, lemmata, and corollaries) assert the truth of statements. Grammatically speaking, they should have as their subjects the statement (or the name of, or some other reference to, the statement), and as predicates the phrase 'is true' (or 'holds', or some similar such). For example, the concluding Rosen theorem in Section 9G of *LI* is

0.9 Theorem *There can be no closed path of efficient causation in a mechanism.*

(The word 'mechanism' has a very specific meaning in the Rosen lexicon:

0.10 Definition A natural system is a *mechanism* if and only if all of its models are simulable.

I shall have a lot more to say on this in Chapter 8.) Theorem 0.9 should be understood as

0.9' Theorem *'There can be no closed path of efficient causation in a mechanism.' is true.*

Or, what is the same,

0.9' Theorem *Theorem 0.9 is true.*

But, of course, this Theorem 0.9' really means

0.9'' Theorem *Theorem 0.9' is true.*

Or, equivalently,

0.9″ Theorem *"Theorem 0.9 is true." is true.*

This "statement about a statement" idea may, alas, be iterated *ad infinitum*, to

0.9 $^\omega$ Theorem ⸺ " " " " *"Theorem 0.9 is true." is true* " *is true* " *is true* " *is true* " ⸺ .

Lewis Carroll wrote about this hierarchical 'reasoning about reasoning' paradox in a witty dialogue *What the Tortoise said to Achilles* [1895]. Efficiency and pragmatism dictate the common practice that the predicate is implicitly assumed and hence usually omitted. A theorem, then, generally consists of just the statement itself, the truth of which it asserts.

0.11 Implication An *implication* is a *true* statement of the form

(8)   " ' $p \rightarrow q$ ' is true."

It is a statement about (the truth of) the conditional statement

(9)   ' $p \rightarrow q$ '.

The implication (8) is denoted in formal logic by

(10) $p \Rightarrow q$,

which is read as ' p *implies* q '. When a conditional statement is expressed as a theorem in mathematics, *viz.*

Theorem *If p, then q.*

it is understood in the sense of (8), that it is an implication.

The difference between $\rightarrow$ and $\Rightarrow$, *i.e.* between a conditional statement and an implication, is that of syntax and semantics. Note that $p \rightarrow q$ is just a proposition in the predicate calculus, which may be true or false. But $p \Rightarrow q$ is a statement *about* the conditional statement $p \rightarrow q$, asserting that the latter is a true statement. In particular, when $p \Rightarrow q$, the situation that p is true and q is false (which is the only circumstance for which the conditional $p \rightarrow q$ is false) *cannot* occur.

0.12 Modus tollens Since a conditional statement and its contrapositive are equivalent, when $p \rightarrow q$ is true, $\neg q \rightarrow \neg p$ is also true. The contrapositive inference

$$(11) \qquad (p \Rightarrow q) \Rightarrow (\neg q \Rightarrow \neg p)$$

is itself an implication, called *modus tollens* in mathematical logic.

Most mathematical theorems are stated, or may be rewritten, as implications. The Rosen Theorem 0.9, for example, is $p \Rightarrow q$ with $p =$ 'N is a mechanism' and $q =$ 'there is no closed path of efficient causation in N', where N is a natural system. Stated explicitly, it is the

0.13 Theorem *If a natural system N is a mechanism, then there is no closed path of efficient causation in N.*

The equivalent contrapositive implication $\neg q \rightarrow \neg p$ is the

0.14 Theorem *If a closed path of efficient causation exists in a natural system N, then N cannot be a mechanism.*

0.15 Equivalence A true statement of the form

$$(12) \qquad \text{``'} p \leftrightarrow q \text{' is true.''},$$

which asserts the truth of a biconditional statement, is called an *equivalence*. It is denoted as

(13) $p \Leftrightarrow q$,

and is read as 'p and q are *equivalent*'. It is clear from the definitions that the equivalence (13) is equivalent to the conjunction

(14) $p \Rightarrow q$ and $q \Rightarrow p$.

When $p \Leftrightarrow q$, either both p and q are true, or both are false.

When a biconditional statement is expressed as a theorem in mathematics, *viz.*

Theorem   *p if and only if q.*

it is understood in the sense of (12) that the biconditional statement $p \leftrightarrow q$ is in fact true, that it is the equivalence $p \Leftrightarrow q$.

0.16 Definition   A *definition* is trivially a theorem — by definition, as it were. It is also often expressed as an equivalence, *i.e.*, with an 'if and only if' statement. See, for example, Definition 0.10 of 'mechanism'.

Occasionally a definition may be *stated* as an implication (*e.g.* Definition 0.3 of 'subset'), but in such cases the converse is *implied* (by convention, or, indeed, by definition). Stated otherwise, a definition is always an equivalence, whether it is expressed as such or not, between the term being defined and the defining conditions. Definition 0.3 is the implication $p \Rightarrow q$ where p = 'every element of A is an element of B' and q = 'set A is a *subset* of set B'. But since this is a definition, implicitly entailed is the converse $q \Rightarrow p$:

0.3' Definition If a set A is a *subset* of a set B then every element of A is an element of B.

So the definition is really

0.3'' Definition A set A is a *subset* of a set B *if and only if* every element of A is an element of B.

Note that this implicit entailment is *not* a contradiction to the fact, discussed above in 0.7, that a conditional statement is not logically equivalent to its converse. The propositions $p \to q$ and $q \to p$ will always remain logically distinct, and in general the implication $p \Rightarrow q$ says nothing about $q \Rightarrow p$. The previous paragraph only applies to definitions, and its syntax is

(15)
> '*If* $p \Rightarrow q$ *is a definition,*
> then also $q \Rightarrow p$,
> whence $p \Leftrightarrow q$.'

Necessity and Sufficiency

0.17 Modus ponens The law of inference

(16) 'If $p \Rightarrow q$ and p is true, then q is true.'

is called *modus ponens*.

This inference follows from the fact that when $p \Rightarrow q$, $p \to q$ is true; so the situation that p is true and q is false (the only circumstance for which the conditional $p \to q$ is false) cannot occur. Thus the truth of p predicates q. Incidentally, modus ponens is the 'theorem' that begins the propositional canon in Lewis Carroll's *What the Tortoise said to Achilles*

[1895]. Note that the truth of $p \to q$ is required for the truth of p to entail the truth of q. In a general (not necessarily true) conditional statement $p \to q$, the truth values of p and q are independent.

Because of its inferential entailment structure (that the truth of p is sufficient to establish the truth of q), the implication $p \Rightarrow q$ may also be read 'p is *sufficient* for q'. Contrapositively (hence equivalently), the falsehood of q is sufficient to establish the falsehood of p. In other words, if q is false, then p cannot possibly be true; *i.e.* the truth of q is necessary (although some additional true statements may be required) to establish the truth of p. Thus the implication $p \Rightarrow q$ may also be read 'q is *necessary* for p'. The equivalence $p \Leftrightarrow q$ (*i.e.* when 'p iff q' is true so that p and q predicate each other) may, therefore, be read 'p is *necessary and sufficient* for q'.

0.18 Membership The concepts of necessity and sufficiency are intimately related to the concept of subset. Definition 0.3" is the statement

(17) $\qquad A \subset B$ iff $\forall x\,(x \in A) \Rightarrow (x \in B)$.

Stated otherwise, when A is a subset of B (or, what is the same, B *includes* A), membership in A is sufficient for membership in B, and membership in B is necessary for membership in A. Similarly, the Axiom of Extension 0.2 is the statement

(18) $\qquad A = B$ iff $\forall x\,(x \in A) \Leftrightarrow (x \in B)$;

i.e. membership in A and membership in B are necessary and sufficient for each other.

The major principle of set theory is the

0.19 Axiom of Specification   For any set U and any statement $p(x)$ about x, there exists a set P the elements of which are exactly those $x \in U$ for which $p(x)$ is true.

It follows immediately from the Axiom of Extension that the set P is determined uniquely.   To indicate the way P is obtained from U and $p(x)$, the customary notation is

(19) $P = \{x \in U : p(x)\}.$

The '$p(x)$' in (19) is understood to mean " '$p(x)$' is true" (with the conventional omission of the predicate); it may also be read as 'x has the property p'.

For example, let **N** be the set of all natural systems, and let $s(N) =$ 'all models of N are simulable'.   Then one may denote the set of all mechanisms **M** (*cf.* Definition 0.10)] as

(20) $\mathbf{M} = \{N \in \mathbf{N} : s(N)\}.$

When the 'universal set' U is obvious from the context (or inconsequential), it may be dropped, and the notation (19) abbreviates to

(21) $P = \{x : p(x)\}.$

As a trivial example, a set A may be represented as

(22) $A = \{x : x \in A\}.$

0.20 Implication and Inclusion   Statement (17) connects set inclusion with implication of the membership property. Analogously, if one property implies another, then the set specified by the former is a subset of the set specified by the latter (and conversely). Explicitly, if x has the property p

14

implies that x has the property q, *i.e.* if $\forall x\, p(x) \Rightarrow q(x)$, then $P = \{x : p(x)\}$ is a subset of $Q = \{x : q(x)\}$ (and conversely):

(23) $P \subset Q$ iff $\forall x\, p(x) \Rightarrow q(x)$.

The equivalence (23) may be read as $P \subset Q$ if and only if p is sufficient for q, and also $P \subset Q$ if and only if q is necessary for p.

For example, let **N** be the set of all natural systems, let $t(N) =$ 'there is no closed path of efficient causation in N', and let

(24) $\mathbf{T} = \{N \in \mathbf{N} : t(N)\}$.

Let **M** be the set of all mechanisms as specified in (20). Theorem 0.9 (the proof of which is the content of Chapter 9 of *LI*, and is given an alternate presentation later on in Chapter 8 of this monograph) is the statement

(25) $\forall N \in \mathbf{N}\; s(N) \Rightarrow t(N)$,

whence equivalently

(26) $\mathbf{M} \subset \mathbf{T}$.

Complements

"I think that it would be reasonable to say that no man who is called a philosopher really understands what is meant by the complementary descriptions."

— Niels Bohr (1962)
Communication 1117

"Some believe the Principle of Complementarity, but the rest of us do not."

— Anonymous

0.21 Definition The *relative complement* of a set A in a set B is the set of elements in B but not in A:

(27) $B \sim A = \{x \in B : x \notin A\}.$

When B is the 'universal set' U (of some appropriate universe under study, *e.g.* the set of all natural systems **N**), the set $U \sim A$ is denoted A^c, *i.e.*

(28) $A^c = \{x \in U : x \notin A\},$

and is called simply the *complement* of the set A. An element of U is either a member of A, or not a member of A, but not both. That is, $A \cup A^c = U$, and $A \cap A^c = \varnothing$.

The set specified by the property p, $P = \{x : p(x)\}$, has as its complement the set specified by the property $\neg p$; *i.e.*

(29) $P^c = \{x : \neg p(x)\}.$

In the predicate calculus, there are these

0.22 Laws of Quantifier Negation

(30) $\neg \forall x\, p(x) \Leftrightarrow \exists x\, \neg p(x)$
(31) $\neg \exists x\, p(x) \Leftrightarrow \forall x\, \neg p(x)$

The negation of the statement $s(N) =$ '*all* models of N are simulable' is thus $\neg s(N) =$ '*there exists* a model of N that is *not* simulable' This characterizes the collection of natural systems that are *not* mechanisms as those that have at least one nonsimulable model.

The predicate calculus also has this trivial tautology:

0.23 Discharge of Double Negation

(32) $\neg\neg p \Leftrightarrow p$

The negation of the statement $t(N) =$ 'there is no closed path of efficient causation in N' is therefore $\neg t(N) =$ 'there exists a closed path of efficient causation in N'. The equivalent contrapositive statement of (25) is hence

(33) $\forall N \in \mathbf{N} \, \neg t(N) \Rightarrow \neg s(N),$

which gives the

0.24 Theorem   *If there exists a closed path of efficient causation in a natural system, then it has at least one model that is not simulable (whence it is not-a-mechanism).*

I shall explore the semantics of Theorems 0.9, 0.13, 0.14, and 0.24 (instead of just their sample syntax used in this prologue to illustrate principles of mathematical logic) in Chapter 8 *et seq.*

Neither More Nor Less

0.25 Nominalism

"I don't know what you mean by 'glory'," Alice said.

Humpty Dumpty smiled contemptuously. "Of course you don't — till I tell you. I meant 'there's a nice knock-down argument for you'!"

"But 'glory' doesn't mean 'a nice knock-down argument'," Alice objected.

"When *I* use a word," Humpty Dumpty said, in a rather scornful tone, "it means just what I choose it to mean — neither more nor less."

"The question is," said Alice, "whether you *can* make words mean so many different things."

"The question is," said Humpty Dumpty, "which is to be master — that's all."

— Lewis Carroll (1871)
Through the Looking-Glass,
and What Alice Found There
Chapter VI Humpty Dumpty

Humpty's point of view is known in philosophy as *nominalism*, the doctrine that universals or abstract concepts are mere names without any corresponding 'reality'. The issue arises because in order to perceive a particular object as belonging to a certain class, say 'organism', one must have a prior notion of 'organism'. Does the term 'organism', described by this prior notion, then have an existence independent of particular organisms? When a word receives a specific technical definition, does it have to reflect its prior notion, the common-usage sense of the word? Nominalism says no.

0.26 Semantic Equivocation A closely related issue is a fallacy of misconstrual in logic known as *semantic equivocation*. This fallacy is quite common, because words often have several different meanings, a condition known as *polysemy*. A polysemic word may represent any one of several concepts, and the semantics of its usage are context-dependent. Errors arise when the different concepts with different consequences are mixed together as one. For a word that has a technical definition in addition to its everyday meaning, non sequitur may result when the distinction is blurred.

Confusion often ensues from a failure to clearly understand that words mean "neither more nor less" than what they are defined to mean, not what they are perceived to mean. This happens even in mathematics, where terms are usually more precisely defined than in other subjects. The most notorious example is the term 'normal', which appears in numerous mathematical subject areas to define objects with specific properties. In almost all cases (*e.g.* normal vector, normal subgroup, normal operator), the normal subclass is nongeneric within the general class of objects; *i.e.* what is defined as 'normal' is anything but normal in the common-usage sense of 'standard, regular, typical'.

While it is not my purpose in this monograph to dwell into nominalism and semantic equivocation themselves, they do make occasional appearances in what follows as philosophical and logical undertones.

0.27 Structure 'Extreme' polysemous words, those having two current meanings that are opposites, are called *amphibolous*. For example, the word 'structure', which means 'a set of interconnecting parts of a thing' (its Latin root is *struere*, to build), has antonymous usage in biology and mathematics: 'concrete' in one, and 'abstract' in the other.

In biology, 'structure' means *material* structure, the constituent physicochemical parts. In our subject of relational biology, our slogan is 'function dictates structure'. Entailment relations within living systems are their most important characteristics.

In mathematics, on the other hand, 'structure' (as in *set-with-structure*) in fact means the *relations* defined on the object. A *structure* on a set is a collection of nullary, unary, binary, ternary ... operations satisfying as axioms a variety of identities between composite operations. Thus a partially ordered set (which I shall introduce in Chapter 1) is a set equipped with a binary operation $\leq$ having certain specified properties. A group is a set equipped with a binary (the group multiplication), a nullary (the unit element), and a unary (the inverse) operation, which together satisfy certain identities. A topological space's structure is a collection of its subsets (the open sets) with certain prescribed properties. And so forth. It is perhaps this 'relations are structure' concept in mathematics that inspired Nicolas Rashevsky on his foundation of relational biology.

0.28 Function   We should also note the polysemy of the word 'function'. The Latin *functio* means 'performance'. An activity by which a thing fulfils a purpose, the common meaning of 'function', may be considered a performance. This is the word's biological usage, although the teleologic 'fulfils a purpose' sense is regularly hidden. (I shall have much more to say on this later.) A mathematical function may be considered as a set of operations that are performed on each value that is put into it. Leibniz first used the term function in the mathematical context, and Euler first used the notation $f(x)$ to represent a function, because the word begins with the letter f.

Since in mathematics 'function' has a synonym in 'mapping', in this book I shall use *mapping* for the mathematical entity (*cf.* Definition 1.3), and leave *function* to its biological sense.

PART I

Exordium

No one really understood music unless he was a scientist,
her father had declared, and not just a scientist, either, oh,
no, only the real ones, the theoreticians, whose language
was mathematics. She had not understood mathematics
until he had explained to her that it was the symbolic
language of relationships. "And relationships," he had
told her, "contain the essential meaning of life."

> — Pearl S. Buck (1972)
> *The Goddess Abides*
> Part I

Equivalence relation is a fundamental building block of epistemology. The first book of the Robert Rosen trilogy is *Fundamentals of Measurement and Representation of Natural Systems* [*FM*]. It may equally well be entitled 'Epistemological Consequences of the Equivalence Relation'; therein one finds a detailed mathematical exposition on the equivalence relation and its linkage to *similarity*, the pre-eminent archetypal concept in all of science, in both the universes of formal systems and natural systems.

Equivalence relation is also a fundamental building block of mathematics. The concept of equivalence is ubiquitous. Many of the theorems in this book depend on the fact that the collection of equivalence relations on a set is a mathematical object known as a *lattice*. In this introductory Part I, I present a précis of the algebraic theory of lattices, with emphasis, of course, on the topics that will be of use to us later on. Some theorems will only be stated in this introduction without proofs. Their proofs may be found in books on lattice theory or universal algebra. The standard reference is *Lattice Theory* written by Garrett Birkhoff, a founder of the subject [Birkhoff 1967].

1

Praeludium:
Ordered Sets

Mappings

1.1 Definition
(i) If X is a set, the *power set* PX of X is the family of all subsets of X.
(ii) Given two sets X and Y, one denotes by $X \times Y$ the set of all *ordered pairs* of the form (x, y) where $x \in X$ and $y \in Y$. The set $X \times Y$ is called the *product* (or *cartesian product*) of the sets X and Y.

1.2 Definition   A *relation* is a set R of ordered pairs; i.e. $R \subset X \times Y$, or equivalently $R \in P(X \times Y)$, for some sets X and Y.

The collection of *all* relations between two sets X and Y is thus the power set $P(X \times Y)$.

1.3 Definition   A *mapping* is a set f of ordered pairs with the property that, if $(x, y) \in f$ and $(x, z) \in f$, then $y = z$.

Note the requirement for a subset of $X \times Y$ to qualify it as a mapping is in fact quite a stringent one: most, i.e., *common*, members of $P(X \times Y)$ do not have this property. A mapping is therefore a *special*, i.e., *nongeneric*, kind of relation. But genericity is not synonymous with importance: general relations and mappings are both fundamental mathematical objects of study.

1.4 Definition   Let f be a mapping. One defines two sets, the *domain* of f and the *range* of f, respectively by

(1) $\qquad \operatorname{dom}(f)=\{x:(x,y)\in f \text{ for some } y\}$

and

(2) $\qquad \operatorname{ran}(f)=\{y:(x,y)\in f \text{ for some } x\}.$

Thus f is a subset of the product $\operatorname{dom}(f)\times\operatorname{ran}(f)$. If $\operatorname{ran}(f)$ contains exactly one element, then f is called a *constant mapping*.

Various words, such as 'function', 'transformation', and 'operator', are used as synonyms for 'mapping'. The mathematical convention is that these different synonyms are used to denote mappings having special types of sets as domains or ranges. Because these alternate names also have interpretations in biological terms, to avoid semantic equivocation, in this book I shall — unless convention dictates otherwise — use *mapping* (and often *map*) for the mathematical entity.

1.5 Remark The traditional conception of a mapping is that of something that assigns to each element of a given set a definite element of another given set. I shall now reconcile this with the formal definition given above. Let f be a mapping and let X and Y be sets. If $\operatorname{dom}(f)=X$ and $\operatorname{ran}(f)\subset Y$, whence f is a subset of $X\times Y$, one says that f is a *mapping of X into Y*, denoted by

(3) $\qquad f:X\to Y,$

and occasionally (mostly for typographical reasons) by

(4) $\qquad X \xrightarrow{\;f\;} Y.$

The collection of *all* mappings of X into Y is a subset of the power set $P(X \times Y)$; this subset is denoted Y^X (see A.3, in the Appendix).

To each element $x \in X$, by Definition 1.3, there corresponds a *unique* element $y \in Y$ such that $(x,y) \in f$. Traditionally, y is called the *value of the mapping f at the element x*, and the relation between x and y is denoted by $y = f(x)$ instead of $(x,y) \in f$. Note that the $y = f(x)$ notation is only logically consistent when f is a mapping — for a general relation f, it is possible that $y \neq z$ yet both $(x,y) \in f$ and $(x,z) \in f$; if one were to write $y = f(x)$ and $z = f(x)$ in such a situation, then one would be led, by Euclid's Common Notion 1 (*cf.* 0.0 and also the Euclidean property 1.10(*e*) below), to the conclusion that $y = z$: a direct contradiction to $y \neq z$.

With the $y = f(x)$ notation, one has

(5) $\qquad \operatorname{ran}(f) = \{y : y = f(x) \text{ for some } x\},$

which may be further abbreviated to

(6) $\qquad \operatorname{ran}(f) = \{f(x) : x \in \operatorname{dom}(f)\}.$

One then also has

(7) $\qquad f = \{(x, f(x)) : x \in X\}.$

From this last representation, we observe that when $X \subset \mathbb{R}$ and $Y \subset \mathbb{R}$ (where $\mathbb{R}$ is the set of real numbers), my formal definition of a mapping coincides with that of the 'graph of f' in elementary mathematics.

26

Sometimes it is useful to trace the path of an element as it is mapped. If $a \in X$, $b \in Y$, and $b = f(a)$, one uses the 'maps to' arrow (note the short vertical line segment at the tail of the arrow) and writes

(8) $\qquad f: a \mapsto b.$

Note that this 'element-chasing' notation of a mapping *in no way* implies that there is somehow only one element a in the domain $\mathrm{dom}(f) = \{a\} = X$, mapped by f to the only element b in the range $\mathrm{ran}(f) = \{b\} \subset Y$. a is a symbolic representation of *variable* elements in the domain of f, while b denotes its corresponding image $b = f(a)$ defined by f. The notation $f: a \mapsto b$ is as general as $f: X \to Y$, the former emphasizing the elements while the latter emphasizing the sets. One occasionally also uses the 'maps to' arrow to define the mapping f itself:

(9) $\qquad x \mapsto f(x).$

1.6 Definition   Let f be a mapping of X into Y. If $E \subset X$, $f(E)$, the *image* of E under f, is defined to be the set of all elements $f(x) \in Y$ for $x \in E$; i.e.,

(10) $\qquad f(E) = \{f(x): x \in E\} \subset Y.$

In this notation, $f(X)$ is the range of f.

1.7 Definition   If f is a mapping of X into Y, the set Y is called the *codomain* of f, denoted by $\mathrm{cod}(f)$.

The range $f(X) = \mathrm{ran}(f)$ is a subset of the codomain $Y = \mathrm{cod}(f)$, but they need not be equal. When they are, i.e. when $f(X) = Y$, one says that f is a *mapping of X onto Y*, and that $f: X \to Y$ is *surjective* (or is a *surjection*). Note that every mapping maps onto its range.

1.8 Definition   If $E \subset Y$, $f^{-1}(E)$ denotes the set of all $x \in X$ such that $f(x) \in E$:

(11) $f^{-1}(E) = \{x : f(x) \in E\} \subset X,$

and is called the *inverse image* of E under f. If $y \in Y$, $f^{-1}(\{y\})$ is abbreviated to $f^{-1}(y)$, so it is the set of all $x \in X$ such that $f(x) = y$.

Note that $f^{-1}(y)$ may be the empty set, or may contain more than one element. If, *for each* $y \in Y$, $f^{-1}(y)$ consists of *at most* one element of X, then f is said to be a *one-to-one* (*1-1*, also *injective*) *mapping* of X into Y. Other commonly used names are '$f: X \to Y$ is an *injection*', and '$f: X \to Y$ is an *embedding*'. This may also be expressed as follows: f is a one-to-one mapping of X into Y provided $f(x_1) \neq f(x_2)$ whenever $x_1, x_2 \in X$ and $x_1 \neq x_2$.

If $A \subset X$, then the mapping $i: A \to X$ defined by $i(x) = x$ for all $x \in A$ is a one-to-one mapping of A into X, called the *inclusion map* (of A in X).

If $f: X \to Y$ is both one-to-one and onto, i.e. both injective and surjective, then f is called *bijective* (or is a *bijection*), and that it establishes a *one-to-one correspondence* between the sets X and Y.

While the domain and range of f are specified by f as in Definition 1.4, the codomain is not *yet* uniquely determined — all that is required so far is that it contains the range of f as a subset. One needs to invoke a category theory axiom (see Appendix: Axiom A.1(c1)), and *assigns* to each mapping f a unique set $Y = \text{cod}(f)$ as its codomain.

28

Equivalence Relations

Recall Definition 1.2 that a relation R is a set of ordered pairs, $R \subset X \times Y$ for some sets X and Y. Just as for mappings, however, there are traditional terminologies for relations that were well established before this formal definition. I shall henceforth use these traditional notations, and also concentrate on relations with $X = Y$.

1.9 Definition   If X is a set and $R \subset X \times X$, one says that R is a *relation on* X, and write $x R y$ instead of $(x, y) \in R$.

1.10 Definition   A relation R on a set X is said to be
(r) *reflexive* if for all $x \in X$, $x R x$;
(s) *symmetric* if for all $x, y \in X$, $x R y$ implies $y R x$;
(a) *antisymmetric* if for all $x, y \in X$, $x R y$ and $y R x$ imply $x = y$;
(t) *transitive* if for all $x, y, z \in X$, $x R y$ and $y R z$ imply $x R z$;
(e) *Euclidean* if for all $x, y, z \in X$, $x R z$ and $y R z$ imply $x R y$.

1.11 Definition   A relation R on a set X is called an *equivalence relation* if it is reflexive, symmetric, and transitive; *i.e.* if it satisfies properties (r), (s), and (t) in Definition 1.10 above.

The *equality* (or *identity*) relation I on X, defined by $x I y$ if $x = y$, is an equivalence relation. As a subset of $X \times X$, I is the *diagonal* $I = \{(x, x) : x \in X\}$. Because of reflexivity (r), any equivalence relation $R \subset X \times X$ must have $(x, x) \in R$ for all $x \in X$; thus $I \subset R$. The *universal* relation U on X, defined by $x U y$ if $x, y \in X$, is also an equivalence relation. Since $U = X \times X$, for any equivalence relation R on X one has $R \subset U$.

The equality relation I is Euclidean. Indeed, when $R = I$, the Euclidean property (e) is precisely Euclid's Common Notion 1 (*cf.* 0.0):

"Things equal to the same thing are also equal to one another." One readily proves the following

1.12 Theorem *If a relation is Euclidean and reflexive, it is also symmetric and transitive (hence it is an equivalence relation).*

1.13 Definition Let R be an equivalence relation on X. For each $x \in X$ the set

(12) $[x]_R = \{ y \in X : xRy \}$

is called the *equivalence class of x determined by R*, or the *R-equivalence class of x*. The collection of all equivalence classes determined by R is called the *quotient set* of X under R, and is denoted by X/R; i.e.

(13) $X/R = \{ [x]_R : x \in X \}$.

1.14 All or Nothing By reflexivity (r), one has $x \in [x]_R$ for all $x \in X$. The equivalence classes determined by R are therefore all nonempty, and

(14) $X = \bigcup_{x \in X} [x]_R$.

Also, the members of X/R are pairwise disjoint. For suppose $x, y \in X$ and $[x]_R \cap [y]_R \neq \varnothing$. Choose $z \in [x]_R \cap [y]_R$, whence xRz and yRz. By symmetry (s) and transitivity (t) one has yRx. Now if $w \in [x]_R$, xRw, so together with yRx just derived, transitivity (t) gives yRw, whence $w \in [y]_R$. This shows that $[x]_R \subset [y]_R$. By symmetry (of the argument) $[y]_R \subset [x]_R$, and consequently $[x]_R = [y]_R$.

Stated otherwise, every element of X belongs to exactly one of the equivalence classes determined by R.

1.15 Congruence An equivalence relation is sometimes also called a *congruence*. There is, however, a canonical usage of the latter which provides a nontrivial example of the former.

Let $m > 0$ be a fixed integer. One defines a relation $\bullet \equiv \bullet \pmod{m}$ on the set $\mathbb{Z}$ of integers as follows: for $a, b \in \mathbb{Z}$, one writes

(15) $\qquad a \equiv b \pmod{m},$

and says that a is *congruent modulo m* to b, when the difference $a - b$ is a multiple of m; the fixed positive integer m is called the *modulus* of the relation. It easily follows that $a \equiv b \pmod{m}$ if and only if a and b leave the same remainder upon division by m.

The relation *congruence modulo m* defines an equivalence relation on the set $\mathbb{Z}$ of integers, and it has m equivalence classes, $[0], [1], ..., [m-1]$. One readily verifies the arithmetic rules: if $a \equiv b \pmod{m}$ and $c \equiv d \pmod{m}$, then $a + c \equiv b + d \pmod{m}$ and $ac \equiv bd \pmod{m}$. One may also prove that if $ab \equiv ac \pmod{m}$ and a is relatively prime to m, then $b \equiv c \pmod{m}$.

The quotient set $\mathbb{Z}/\equiv$ of $\mathbb{Z}$ under $\bullet \equiv \bullet \pmod{m}$ is often denoted $\mathbb{Z}_m$. All the rules for addition and multiplication hold for $\mathbb{Z}_m$, so it is in fact a *ring*. It is called the *ring of integers modulo m*, and plays an important role in algebra and number theory. We shall encounter $\mathbb{Z}_m$ again later on in this monograph.

1.16 Definition A pairwise disjoint family of sets the union of which is X is called a *partition* of X. The sets in the disjoint family are the *blocks* of the partition.

Here is a special type of partition that we shall need later:

1.17 Definition A partition is called *singular* if all its blocks consist of single elements except for one block.

We have just seen in 1.14 that the family of equivalence classes determined by an equivalence relation on X is a partition of X. The blocks of the partition that corresponds to the equality relation I are all singleton sets (sets containing exactly one member). In the partition that corresponds to the universal relation U, there is only one block, the set X itself.

Conversely, given a partition of X one may define a relation R by defining two elements of X to be related under R if they belong to the same block. It is trivial to verify that R is an equivalence relation on X, and that its equivalence classes are precisely the blocks of the partition. One thus has:

1.18 Lemma *There is a one-to-one correspondence between the equivalence relations on a set X and the partitions of X.*

The set of all ordered pairs (x, y) with $x, y \in A$ is, of course, simply the product set $A \times A$. So an alternate concise formulation of the above lemma is

1.19 Lemma *A relation R on a set X is an equivalence relation if and only if there is a partition $\mathfrak{A}$ of X such that $R = \bigcup_{A \in \mathfrak{A}} A \times A$.*

Partially Ordered Sets

1.20 Definition A relation R on a set X is called a *partial order* if it is reflexive, antisymmetric, and transitive; i.e. if it satisfies properties (r), (a), and (t) in Definition 1.10 above.

One usually uses the notation $\leq$ instead of R when it is a partial order.

1.21 Definition A *partially ordered set* (often abbreviated as *poset*) is an ordered pair $\langle X, \leq \rangle$ in which X is a set and $\leq$ is a partial order on X.

When the partial order $\leq$ is clear from the context, one frequently for simplicity omits it from the notation, and denote $\langle X, \leq \rangle$ by the underlying set X. Each subset of a poset is itself a poset under the same partial order.

1.22 Definition Let $\langle X, \leq \rangle$ be a poset and $x, y \in X$. If $x \leq y$, one says 'x is *less than or equal to* y', or 'y is *greater than or equal to* x', and write '$y \geq x$'. One also writes '$x < y$' (and '$y > x$') for '$x \leq y$ and $x \neq y$', whence reads 'x is *less than* y' (and 'y is *greater than* x').

The simplest example of a partial order is the equality relation I. The equality relation, as we saw above, is also an equivalence relation, and it is in fact the only relation which is *both* an equivalence relation and a partial order.

The relation $\leq$ on the set of all integers $\mathbb{Z}$ is an example of a partial order. As another example, the *inclusion* relation $\subset$ is a partial order on the power set $\mathcal{P}A$ of a set A.

Morphisms in the category of posets are order-preserving mappings:

1.23 Definition A mapping f from a poset $\langle X, \leq_X \rangle$ to a poset $\langle Y, \leq_Y \rangle$ is called *order-preserving*, or *isotone*, if

(16) $x \leq_X y$ in X implies $f(x) \leq_Y f(y)$ in Y.

(The somewhat awkward symbols $\leq_X$ and $\leq_Y$ are meant to indicate the partial orders on X and Y may be different. With this clearly understood, I shall now simplify the notation for the next part of the definition.) Two posets X and Y are *isomorphic*, written $X \cong Y$, if there exists a bijective map $f : X \to Y$ such that both f and its inverse $f^{-1} : Y \to X$ are order-preserving; i.e.

(17) $x \le y$ in X iff $f(x) \le f(y)$ in Y.

Any poset may be represented as a collection of sets ordered by inclusion:

1.24 Theorem   *Let $\langle X, \le \rangle$ be a poset. Define $f : X \to PX$, for $x \in X$, by*

(18) $f(x) = \{y \in X : y \le x\}$.

Then X is isomorphic to the range of f ordered by set inclusion $\subset$; i.e.
$\langle X, \le \rangle \cong \langle f(X), \subset \rangle$.

1.25 Definition   The *converse* of a relation R is the relation $\breve{R}$ such that $x \breve{R} y$ if $y R x$.

Thus the converse of the relation 'is included in' $\subset$ is the relation 'includes' $\supset$; the converse of 'less than or equal to' $\le$ is 'greater than or equal to' $\ge$. A simple inspection of properties (r), (a), and (t) leads to the

1.26 Duality Principle   *The converse of a partial order is itself a partial order.*

The *dual* of a poset $X = \langle X, \le \rangle$ is the poset $\tilde{X} = \langle X, \ge \rangle$ defined by the converse partial order. Definitions and theorems about posets are dual in pairs (whenever they are not self-dual). If any theorem is true for all posets, then so is its dual.

1.27 Definition   Let $\le$ be a partial order on a set X and let $A \subset X$. The subset A is *bounded above* if there exists $x \in X$ such that $a \le x$ for all

$a \in A$; such $x \in X$ is called an *upper bound* for A. An upper bound x for A is called the *supremum* for A if $x \le y$ for all upper bounds y for A. A subset A can have at most one supremum (hence the article *the*), and if it exists it is denoted by $\sup A$.

The terms *bounded below*, *lower bound*, and *infimum* (notation $\inf A$) are defined analogously. A set that is bounded above and bounded below is called *bounded*.

1.28 The Greatest and the Least   Every element of X is an upper bound for the empty set $\varnothing \subset X$. So if $\varnothing$ has a supremum in X, then $\sup\varnothing$ is an element such that $\sup\varnothing \le y$ for all $y \in X$; such an element (if it exists) is called the *least element* of X, and this is the element $\sup\varnothing = \inf X$.

Dually, $\inf\varnothing$, if it exists, is an element such that $y \le \inf\varnothing$ for all $y \in X$; such an element is called the *greatest element* of X, and this is the element $\inf\varnothing = \sup X$.

Let A be a set and consider the poset $\langle \mathcal{P}A, \subset \rangle$. Each subset $\mathfrak{S} \subset \mathcal{P}A$ (i.e. each family of subsets of A) is bounded above (trivially by the set A) and bounded below (trivially by the empty set $\varnothing$), hence bounded. A subset B of A (i.e. $B \in \mathcal{P}A$) is an upper bound for $\mathfrak{S}$ if and only if $\bigcup_{S \in \mathfrak{S}} S \subset B$, and a lower bound for $\mathfrak{S}$ if and only if $B \subset \bigcap_{S \in \mathfrak{S}} S$. Thus $\bigcup_{S \in \mathfrak{S}} S = \sup\mathfrak{S}$ and $\bigcap_{S \in \mathfrak{S}} S = \inf\mathfrak{S}$. The least element of $\langle \mathcal{P}A, \subset \rangle$ is $\varnothing$, and the greatest element of $\langle \mathcal{P}A, \subset \rangle$ is A.

The greatest and least elements of a poset X are only considered to 'exist' if they are members of X. It is important to note, however, that an upper bound, a lower bound, the supremum, and the infimum (if any exists) for a subset $A \subset X$ are only required to be elements of the original poset X. They may or may not be in the subset A itself. In the example in the previous paragraph, $\bigcup_{S \in \mathsf{S}} S = \sup \mathsf{S}$ and $\bigcap_{S \in \mathsf{S}} S = \inf \mathsf{S}$ are members of PA, but they are not necessarily members of S.

Even in cases where there is no greatest or least element, there may be elements in a poset that have no other elements greater than or less than they are:

1.29 Definition Let $\leq$ be a partial order on a set X and let $A \subset X$. An element $x \in A$ is *maximal* if whenever $y \in A$ and $x \leq y$ one has $x = y$. Stated otherwise, $x \in A$ is maximal if $x < y$ for no $y \in A$. Dually, an element $x \in A$ is *minimal* if whenever $y \in A$ and $y \leq x$ one has $x = y$, or equivalently if $y < x$ for no $y \in A$.

Note that maximal and minimal elements of A are required to be members of A.

The greatest element (if it exists) must be maximal, and the least element (if it exists) must be minimal. But the converse is not true. As an example, let A be the three-element set $\{1,2,3\}$. Its power set is

$$PA = \{\varnothing, \{1\}, \{2\}, \{3\}, \{1,2\}, \{1,3\}, \{2,3\}, A\},$$

partially ordered by $\subset$. The element A is the greatest element (hence a maximal element) of this poset $\langle PA, \subset \rangle$, and the element $\varnothing$ is the least element (hence a minimal element). Now consider $\mathsf{S} \subset PA$ with

$$\mathsf{S} = \{\{1\}, \{1,2\}, \{1,3\}\}.$$

$\langle \mathsf{S}, \subset \rangle$ is a poset in its own right. One has

$$\sup \mathsf{S} = \bigcup_{S \in \mathsf{S}} S = \{1\} \cup \{1,2\} \cup \{1,3\} = \{1,2,3\} = A$$

and

$$\inf \mathfrak{S} = \bigcup_{s \in \mathfrak{S}} S = \{1\} \cap \{1,2\} \cap \{1,3\} = \{1\}.$$

So both $\sup \mathfrak{S}$ and $\inf \mathfrak{S}$ exist in $\mathcal{P}A$, but $\sup \mathfrak{S} \notin \mathfrak{S}$ while $\inf \mathfrak{S} \in \mathfrak{S}$. $\langle \mathfrak{S}, \subset \rangle$ has no greatest element, but both $\{1,2\}$ and $\{1,3\}$ are maximal elements. $\langle \mathfrak{S}, \subset \rangle$ has $\{1\}$ as its least element (which is therefore also a minimal element).

1.30 Theorem *Any (nonempty) finite subset of a poset has minimal and maximal elements.*

PROOF Let $\langle X, \le \rangle$ be a poset and $A = \{x_1, x_2, ..., x_n\}$ be a finite subset of X. Define $m_1 = x_1$, and for $k = 2,...,n$, define

(19)
$$m_k = \begin{cases} x_k & \text{if } x_k < m_{k-1} \\ m_{k-1} & \text{otherwise} \end{cases}.$$

Then m_n will be minimal. Similarly, A has a maximal element. □

1.31 Poset as Category A partially ordered set $\langle X, \le \rangle$ may *itself* be considered as a category, in which the objects are elements of X, and a hom-set $X(x,y)$ for $x,y \in X$ has either a single element or is empty, according to whether $x \le y$ or not. Product in this category corresponds to infimum, and coproduct corresponds to supremum. This is a single-poset-as-a-category, and is completely different from 'the category of all posets and isotone mappings' considered in 1.23 above. Note the analogy to a single-set-as-a-category (i.e. a discrete category) versus the category **Set** of all sets and mappings (see A.2 and A.3).

Totally Ordered Sets

Two elements x and y in a poset are called *comparable* if either $x \leq y$ or $y \leq x$. A poset may contain incomparable elements. (Consider $\langle PA, \subset \rangle$ in the previous example in 1.29, and one has neither $\{1,2\} \subset \{1,3\}$ nor $\{1,3\} \subset \{1,2\}$.) A partial order for which this cannot happen is called a *total order*. Explicitly:

1.32 Definition A poset $\langle X, \leq \rangle$ is said to be *totally* (or *linearly*) *ordered* if [in addition to properties (r), (a), and (t)] all elements are comparable, i.e.

(l)   for all $x, y \in X$, either $x \leq y$ or $y \leq x$.

The term 'totally ordered set' is sometimes abbreviated into *toset*. The relation $\leq$ on the set of all integers $\mathbb{Z}$ is an example of a total order.

1.33 Definition A *chain* in a poset $\langle X, \leq \rangle$ is a subset $A \subset X$ such that $\leq$ totally orders A.

Every subset of a chain is a chain. In chains, the notions of least and minimal element are identical. This is because if $x \in A$ is minimal, whence $y < x$ for no $y \in A$, then by property (l) of Definition 1.32 one must have $x \leq y$ for all $y \in A$, whence x is the least element of A. Dually, in chains, the notions of greatest and maximal element are identical. So in view of Theorem 1.30, one has

1.34 Theorem *Every finite chain has a least element and a greatest element.*

The set $\{1, 2, ..., n\}$ of the first n natural numbers (i.e. positive integers) in its natural order $\leq$ forms a finite chain, called the *ordinal number n*. When totally *unordered* (so that no two different elements are comparable), it forms another poset called the *cardinal number n*.

1.35 Theorem   *Every finite chain of n elements is isomorphic to the ordinal number **n**.*

There is a result about partial orders that has far-reaching consequences in several branches of mathematics. It is

1.36 Zorn's Lemma   *Let X be a nonempty partially ordered set with the property that each nonempty chain in it has an upper bound. Then X has a maximal element.*

It is interesting to note that Zorn's Lemma is equivalent to the

1.37 Axiom of Choice   Given a nonempty family $\mathfrak{A}$ of nonempty sets, there is a mapping f with domain $\mathfrak{A}$ such that $f(A) \in A$ for all $A \in \mathfrak{A}$.

The encyclopaedic treatise on this topic is Rubin & Rubin [1963]. Both Zorn's Lemma and the Axiom of Choice will make their appearance again later on.

2

Principium:
The Lattice of Equivalence Relations

Lattices

2.1 Definition A *lattice* is a nonempty partially ordered set $\langle L, \leq \rangle$ in which each pair of elements x, y has a supremum and an infimum in L. They are denoted by $x \vee y = \sup\{x, y\}$ and $x \wedge y = \inf\{x, y\}$, and are often called, respectively, the *join* and *meet* of x and y.

For any elements x, y of a lattice,

(1) $\qquad x \leq y \iff x \vee y = y \iff x \wedge y = x.$

If the lattice L (as a poset) has a least element 0, then $0 \wedge x = 0$ and $0 \vee x = x$ for all $x \in L$. If it has a greatest element 1, then $x \wedge 1 = x$ and $x \vee 1 = 1$ for all $x \in L$.

It is trivially seen from condition (1), known as *consistency*, that every totally ordered set is a lattice, in which $x \vee y$ is simply the larger and $x \wedge y$ is the smaller of x and y. The poset $\langle PA, \subset \rangle$, of the power set of a set A with the partial order of inclusion, is also a lattice; for any $X, Y \in PA$, $X \vee Y = X \cup Y$ and $X \wedge Y = X \cap Y$.

The families of open sets and closed sets, respectively, of a topological space are both lattices. In these lattices the partial orders, joins, and meets are the same as those for the power set lattice.

The collection of all subgroups of a group G is a lattice. The partial order $\leq$ is set-inclusion restricted to subgroups, i.e. the relation 'is a subgroup of'. For subgroups H and K of G, $H \wedge K = H \cap K$, but $H \vee K$ is the smallest subgroup of G containing H and K (which is generally not their set-theoretic union).

A lattice may also be regarded as a set with two binary operators, $\vee$ and $\wedge$, i.e. the triplet $\langle L, \vee, \wedge \rangle$. Again, for simplicity of notation, we often abbreviate to the underlying set and denote the lattice as L. The two operators satisfy a number of laws that are similar to the laws of addition and multiplication, and these laws may be used to give an alternative definition of lattices.

2.2 Theorem *Let L be a lattice, then for any $x, y, z \in L$,*

(a) [*associative*] $\quad x \vee (y \vee z) = (x \vee y) \vee z, \quad x \wedge (y \wedge z) = (x \wedge y) \wedge z;$

(b) [*commutative*] $\quad x \vee y = y \vee x, \quad x \wedge y = y \wedge x;$

(c) [*absorptive*] $\quad x \wedge (x \vee y) = x, \quad x \vee (x \wedge y) = x;$

(d) [*idempotent*] $\quad x \vee x = x, \quad x \wedge x = x.$

Conversely, if L is a set with two binary operators $\vee$ and $\wedge$ satisfying (a)–(c), then (d) also holds, and a partial order may be defined on L by the rule

(e) $\quad x \leq y \quad$ *if and only if* $\quad x \vee y = y$

[*whence if and only if $x \wedge y = x$*]. *Relative to this ordering, L is a lattice such that $x \vee y = \sup\{x, y\}$ and $x \wedge y = \inf\{x, y\}$.*

We have already seen the duality principle for partial orders in 1.26. As one may deduce from Theorem 2.2, this duality is expressed in lattices by interchanging $\vee$ and $\wedge$ (hence interchanging $\leq$ and $\geq$), resulting in its *dual*. Any theorem about lattice remains true if the join and meet are interchanged.

2.3 Duality Principle *The dual of a lattice is itself a lattice.*

2.4 The Greatest and the Least The greatest element of a poset (if it exists) must be maximal, and the least element (if it exists) must be minimal. I illustrated with an example in 1.29 that the converse is not necessarily true. But for a lattice, one has

Theorem *In a lattice, a maximal element is the greatest element (and hence unique); dually, a minimal element is the least element (and hence unique).*

PROOF Let x_1 and x_2 be two maximal elements. Their join $x_1 \vee x_2$ is such that $x_1 \leq x_1 \vee x_2$ and $x_2 \leq x_1 \vee x_2$ (by definition of $\vee$ as the supremum). Because x_1 is maximal, it cannot be less than another element, so $x_1 \leq x_1 \vee x_2 \implies x_1 = x_1 \vee x_2$; similarly, because x_2 is maximal, $x_2 \leq x_1 \vee x_2 \implies x_2 = x_1 \vee x_2$. Therefore $x_1 = x_2$. Thus there can only be one maximal element.

Now let x be the only maximal element, and y be an arbitrary element of the lattice. One must have $x \leq y \vee x$ by definition of $\vee$; but x is maximal, so $x \leq y \vee x \implies x = y \vee x$, whence $y \leq x$ (by property 2.2(*e*) above). Thus x is the greatest element. □

Note that this theorem does not say a lattice necessarily has the greatest and the least elements, only that *if* a maximal (respectively, minimal) element exists, *then* it is the greatest (respectively, least).

2.5 Inequalities *Let L be a lattice, and let $x, y, z \in L$. Then*

(a) *[isotone] if $x \le z$, then $x \wedge y \le y \wedge z$ and $x \vee y \le y \vee z$;*

(b) *[distributive] $x \wedge (y \vee z) \ge (x \wedge y) \vee (x \wedge z)$ and*

$$x \vee (y \wedge z) \le (x \vee y) \wedge (x \vee z);$$

(c) *[modular] if $x \le z$, then $x \vee (y \wedge z) \le (x \vee y) \wedge z$.*

While any subset of a poset is again a poset under the same partial order, a subset of a lattice need not be a lattice (because $x \vee y$ or $x \wedge y$ may not be members of the subset even if x and y are). So one needs to make the explicit

2.6 Definition A *sublattice* of a lattice L is a subset M which is closed under the operators $\vee$ and $\wedge$ of L; i.e. $M \subset L$ is a sublattice if $x \vee y \in M$ and $x \wedge y \in M$ for all $x, y \in M$.

The empty set is a sublattice, and so is any singleton subset. Let $a, b \in L$ and $a \le b$. The *(closed) interval* is the subset $[a, b] \subset L$ consisting of all elements $x \in L$ such that $a \le x \le b$. An interval $[a, b]$ need not be a chain (Definition 1.33), but it is always a sublattice of L, and it has the least element a and the greatest element b.

Let A be a set and let $*$ be a fixed element of A, called the *base point*. A *pointed subset of A* is a subset X of A such that $* \in X$ (*cf.* Example A.6(ii) in the Appendix). The *pointed power set* $\mathbf{P}_* A$ is the subset of the power set $\mathbf{P}A$ containing all pointed subsets of A; i.e. $\mathbf{P}_* A = \{X \subset A : * \in X\}$. $\mathbf{P}_* A$ is a sublattice of $\mathbf{P}A$.

Note that it is possible for a subset of a lattice L to be a lattice without being a sublattice of L. For example, as we saw above, the collection $\Sigma(G)$ of all subgroups of a group G is a lattice. When G is considered a set (forgetting the group structure), $\mathbf{P}G$ is a lattice with $\vee = \cup$ and $\wedge = \cap$. $\Sigma(G)$ is a subset of $\mathbf{P}G$, but it is not a sublattice of $\mathbf{P}G$.

While $\Sigma(G)$ and PG have the same partial order $\leq\,=\,\subset$ and the same meet operator $\wedge=\cap$, the join operator $\vee$ of $\Sigma(G)$ is not inherited from that of PG.

For another example, let X be a set, whence the power set $P(X\times X)$ is a lattice with $\vee=\cup$ and $\wedge=\cap$. A relation on X is a subset of $X\times X$, so the collection QX of all equivalence relations on X is a subset of $P(X\times X)$. As we shall soon see, QX is again a lattice, but not usually a sublattice of $P(X\times X)$. In particular, the union of two equivalence relations need not be an equivalence relation. QX is another example of a lattice with a join operator different from the standard set-theoretic union.

A morphism in the category of lattices is defined in the obvious structure-preserving fashion:

2.7 Lattice Homomorphism A mapping f from a lattice L to a lattice L' is called a (*lattice*) *homomorphism* if for all $x,y\in L$

(2) $\qquad f(x\vee y)=f(x)\vee f(y)$ and $f(x\wedge y)=f(x)\wedge f(y)$.

A lattice homomorphism preserves the ordering: $x\leq y\Rightarrow f(x)\leq f(y)$. But not every order-preserving mapping (i.e. poset homomorphism) between lattices is a lattice homomorphism.

2.8 Lemma *If f is a homomorphism from a lattice L into a lattice L', then the image $f(L)$ is a sublattice of L'.*

If a lattice homomorphism $f:L\to L'$ is one-to-one and onto, then f is called an *isomorphism* of L onto L', and the two lattices are said to be *isomorphic*. If $f:L\to L'$ is one-to-one, then f is an *embedding*, L and

44

$f(L)$ are isomorphic, and by Lemma 2.8 L has a *representation* (namely $f(L)$) as a sublattice of L'.

2.9 Heyting Algebra   Any *nonempty finite* subset $A = \{a_1, ..., a_n\}$ of a lattice L has, by induction, both a supremum and an infimum, denoted respectively by

$$(3) \qquad \sup A = \bigvee_{i=1}^{n} a_i = a_1 \vee \cdots \vee a_n \ \text{ and } \ \inf A = \bigwedge_{i=1}^{n} a_i = a_1 \wedge \cdots \wedge a_n.$$

Note that brackets may be omitted by associativity, and that the order of the factors is immaterial by commutativity.

For the empty subset, however, the existence of $\sup \varnothing = \inf L$ (least element) and $\inf \varnothing = \sup L$ (greatest element) have to be postulated separately (*cf.* the discussion on finite categorical products in the appendix, A.28 and Lemma A.29). Now let $\langle L, \leq \rangle = \langle L, \vee, \wedge \rangle$ have *all* finite suprema and infima (including those of the empty family, hence L has least element 0 and greatest element 1). Recall (1.31) that a poset $\langle L, \leq \rangle$ may itself be considered as a category, in which the objects are elements of L, and a hom-set $L(x, y)$ for $x, y \in L$ has either a single element or is empty, according to whether $x \leq y$ (alternatively, $x \vee y = y$, $x \wedge y = x$) or not. The category L is cartesian closed (*cf.* A.53). The exponential (*cf.* A.52) $z^y \in L$ defined in the bijection $L(x \wedge y, z) \cong L(x, z^y)$ is uniquely determined as the largest element for which the meet with y is less than or equal to z, i.e., $z^y = \sup\{x \in L : x \wedge y \leq z\}$, whence $x \wedge y \leq z$ iff $x \leq z^y$. A lattice with all finite suprema and infima is called a *Heyting Algebra*, and is a model of the propositional calculus.

2.10 Completeness   An infinite subset of a lattice, however, need not have a supremum or an infimum. (Consider, for example, the lattice $\mathbb{Z}$ of integers totally ordered by $\leq$.) A lattice in which *every* subset has a supremum *and* an infimum is said to be *complete*. This includes the empty subset $\varnothing$. So in particular, a complete lattice L has a least element ($\inf L = \sup \varnothing$) and a greatest element ($\sup L = \inf \varnothing$). It is an interesting fact that for a lattice to be complete, it suffices for every subset to have a supremum (*or* for every subset to have an infimum): the 'other half' of the requirement is automatically entailed.

2.11 Theorem *Let L be a poset in which every subset has a supremum (or in which every subset has an infimum). Then L is a complete lattice.*

One must note carefully that in the hypothesis of this theorem, *every subset* includes the empty subset $\varnothing$, otherwise the conclusion does not follow. For example, in the lattice $\mathbb{N}$ of natural numbers (positive integers) totally ordered by $\leq$, every *nonempty* subset has an infimum (the smallest number in the subset). But $\mathbb{N}$ is not complete, since an infinite subset does not have a supremum. This is not a contradiction to the theorem, because the infimum of the empty set, $\inf \varnothing = \sup \mathbb{N}$, does not exist.

2.12 Examples The power set $\mathsf{P}A$ of any set A is a complete lattice with $\vee = \cup$ and $\wedge = \cap$; so is a pointed power set P_*A.

For a less trivial example, consider the collections $\mathcal{O}$ and $\mathcal{C}$ respectively of open sets and closed sets of a topological space X. We have already encountered them above, as examples of lattices. With $\vee = \cup$ and $\wedge = \cap$, $\mathcal{O}$ and $\mathcal{C}$ are sublattices of $\mathsf{P}X$. But $\mathcal{O}$ and $\mathcal{C}$ are not complete with these operators, because the intersection of an infinite collection of open sets needs not be open, and the union of an infinite collection of closed sets needs not be closed. To make $\mathcal{O}$ and $\mathcal{C}$ complete, $\vee$ and $\wedge$ have to be defined slightly differently. Let A be an arbitrary index set. Let $\{F_a : a \in A\} \subset \mathcal{O}$. Then the operations

$$(4) \qquad \bigvee_{a \in A} F_a = \bigcup_{a \in A} F_a \quad \text{and} \quad \bigwedge_{a \in A} F_a = \left(\bigcap_{a \in A} F_a \right)^{\circ}$$

(where $S°$ denotes the *interior* of the set S) are the join and meet that make $\mathcal{O}$ into a complete lattice. Similarly, for $\{G_a : a \in A\} \subset \mathbf{C}$, the operations

$$(5) \qquad \bigvee_{a \in A} G_a = \left(\bigcup_{a \in A} G_a \right)^- \quad \text{and} \quad \bigwedge_{a \in A} G_a = \bigcap_{a \in A} G_a$$

(where S^- denotes the *closure* of the set S) are the join and meet that make $\mathbf{C}$ into a complete lattice. [Note that when the index set A is finite, the $(\ )°$ and $(\ )^-$ of the definitions are redundant, and these new $\vee$ and $\wedge$ become identical to set-theoretic union and intersection respectively.] This is another example that shows it is possible for a subset of a lattice L to be a lattice without being a sublattice of L. With the operators defined as in (4) and (5), both $\mathcal{O}$ and $\mathbf{C}$ are themselves lattices, and they are both subsets of $P X$. But neither is a sublattice of $P X$, because in each case, the partial order, join, and meet are not *all* identical to the $\subset$, $\cup$, and $\cap$ of $P X$.

The Lattice $\mathbf{Q} X$

Let X be a set and let $\mathbf{Q} X$ denote the collection of all equivalence relations on X. A relation on X is a subset of $X \times X$, so $\mathbf{Q} X$ is a subset of $P(X \times X)$. An equivalence relation as a subset of $X \times X$ has a very special structure (Lemma 1.19), so an arbitrary subset of an equivalence relation is not necessarily itself an equivalence relation. The partial order $\subset$ of set inclusion, *when restricted to* $\mathbf{Q} X$, implies more. When two equivalence relations $R_1, R_2 \in \mathbf{Q} X$ are such that $R_1 \subset R_2$, it means that in fact every R_1-equivalence class is a subset of some R_2-equivalence class. This also means, indeed, that the blocks in the partition defined by R_1 are obtained by further partitioning the blocks in the partition defined by R_2. Stated otherwise, the blocks of R_2 are obtained from those of R_1 by taking set-theoretic unions of them. I shall henceforth use the notation $R_1 \leq R_2$

when $R_1, R_2 \in \mathbf{Q}X$ are such that $R_1 \subset R_2$. An alternate description of $R_1 \leq R_2$ is

2.13 Definition Let R_1 and R_2 be equivalence relations on a set X. One says that R_1 *refines* R_2 (and that R_1 is a *refinement* of R_2) if for all $x, y \in X$,

(6) $\qquad x R_1 y \implies x R_2 y.$

When R_1 refines R_2, i.e. when $R_1 \leq R_2$, one says that R_1 *is finer than* R_2, and that R_2 *is coarser than* R_1.

One may verify that the relation of refinement on $\mathbf{Q}X$ is a partial order. Thus

2.14 Theorem $\langle \mathbf{Q}X, \leq \rangle$ *is a partially ordered set.*

The equality relation I is the least element, and the universal relation U is the greatest element in the poset $\langle \mathbf{Q}X, \leq \rangle$. Stated otherwise, the equality relation I, which partitions X into a collection of singleton sets, is the finest equivalence relation on X; the universal relation U, which has one single partition that is X itself, is the coarsest equivalence relation on X. Contrast this with the fact that $\varnothing$ is the least element in $\langle \mathbf{P}(X \times X), \subset \rangle$, while the largest element is the same $U = X \times X$.

2.15 Definition Let R_1 and R_2 be equivalence relations on a set X. Their *meet* $R_1 \wedge R_2$ is defined as

(7) $\qquad x(R_1 \wedge R_2)y \quad$ iff $\quad x R_1 y$ and $x R_2 y.$

It is trivial to verify that $R = R_1 \wedge R_2$ is an equivalence relation on X, and that R refines both R_1 and R_2, i.e.

(8) $\qquad R \le R_1 \text{ and } R \le R_2,$

and is the coarsest member of $\mathbf{Q}X$ with this property. In other words,

(9) $\qquad R = R_1 \wedge R_2 = \inf\{R_1, R_2\}.$

One also has

2.16 Lemma *The equivalence classes of $R_1 \wedge R_2$ are obtained by forming the set-theoretic intersection of each R_1-equivalence class with each R_2-equivalence class. As subsets of $\mathbf{P}(X \times X)$, $R_1 \wedge R_2 = R_1 \cap R_2$.*

Since the collection of equivalence classes form a partition, the R_1-class and R_2-class that intersect to form $R_1 \wedge R_2$-class are uniquely determined.

The definition of meet may easily be extended to an arbitrary index set A and a collection of equivalence relations $\{R_a : a \in A\}$:

(10) $\qquad x\left(\bigwedge_{a \in A} R_a\right) y \text{ iff } x R_a y \text{ for all } a \in A.$

And one has

(11) $\qquad \bigwedge_{a \in A} R_a = \inf\{R_a : a \in A\}.$

The set-theoretic union of two equivalence relations does not necessarily have the requisite special structure as a subset of $X \times X$ (Lemma 1.19) to make it an equivalence relation. The join has to be defined thus:

2.17 Definition Let R_1 and R_2 be equivalence relations on a set X. Their *join* $R_1 \vee R_2$ is defined as follows: $x(R_1 \vee R_2) y$ iff there is a finite sequence of elements $x_1, ..., x_n \in X$ such that

(12) $x\,R_1\,x_1,\; x_1\,R_2\,x_2,\; x_2\,R_1\,x_3,\; ...,x_n\,R_1\,y.$

One readily verifies that $R = R_1 \vee R_2$ is an equivalence relation on X, and that R is refined by both R_1 and R_2, i.e.

(13) $R_1 \leq R$ and $R_2 \leq R,$

and is the finest member of $\mathbf{Q}X$ with this property. In other words,

(14) $R = R_1 \vee R_2 = \sup\{R_1, R_2\}.$

One concludes from (13) that, as subsets of $\mathbf{P}(X \times X)$, $R_1 \subset R_1 \vee R_2$ and $R_2 \subset R_1 \vee R_2$, whence $R_1 \cup R_2 \subset R_1 \vee R_2$. The set (and relation) $R_1 \vee R_2$ is called the *transitive closure* of the union $R_1 \cup R_2$.

For an *arbitrary* index set A and a collection of equivalence relations $\{R_a : a \in A\}$, the definition of the join $\bigvee_{a\in A} R_a$ (i.e. the transitive closure of the union $\bigcup_{a\in A} R_a$), that corresponds to the binary join in (12), is: $x\left(\bigvee_{a\in A} R_a\right)y$ iff there exist a *finite* sequence of elements $x_1,...,x_n \in X$ and indices $a_1,...,a_n \in A$ such that

(15) $x\,R_{a_1}\,x_1,\; x_1\,R_{a_2}\,x_2,\; x_2\,R_{a_3}\,x_3,\; ...,x_n\,R_{a_n}\,y.$

With the meet and join as defined in 2.15 and 2.17, $\mathbf{Q}X$ is a lattice. In fact,

2.18 Theorem $\mathbf{Q}X$ *is a complete lattice.*

Because of the one-to-one correspondence between equivalence relations and partitions (Lemma 1.18), any sublattice of the lattice of equivalence relations is also called a *partition lattice*.

Mappings and Equivalence Relations

2.19 Definition Given a mapping $f : X \to Y$, one calls two elements $x_1, x_2 \in X$ *f-related* when $f(x_1) = f(x_2)$, and denotes this relation by R_f; i.e.

(16) $\qquad x_1 \, R_f \, x_2 \quad \text{iff} \quad f(x_1) = f(x_2).$

Then R_f is an equivalence relation on X, whence the equivalence classes determined by R_f form a partition of X. f is a constant mapping on each R_f-equivalence class. R_f is called the *equivalence relation on X induced by f*, and f is called a *generator* of this equivalence relation.

The equivalence relation induced on a set X by a constant mapping is the universal relation U (with only one single partition block which is all of X). The equivalence relation induced on a set X by a one-to-one mapping is the equality relation I (with each partition block a singleton set).

Any mapping with domain X induces an equivalence relation on X. It is a very important fact that *all* equivalence relations on X are of this type:

2.20 Theorem *If R is an equivalence relation on X, then there is a mapping f with domain X such that $R = R_f$.*

PROOF Consider the mapping from X to the quotient set of X under R, $\pi : X \to X/R$, that maps an element of X to its equivalence class; i.e.

(17) $\qquad \pi(x) = [x]_R \quad \text{for} \quad x \in X.$

This mapping π is called the *natural mapping (projection)* of X onto X/R, and has the obvious property that $R_\pi = R$. $\qquad \square$

2.21 Lemma   *Let $f : X \to Y$ be a mapping and R_f be the equivalence relation on X induced by f. Then there is a one-to-one correspondence between the quotient set X/R_f and the range $f(X)$.*

PROOF   Let $x \in X$, then $f(x) \in f(X)$. Identify the equivalence class $[x]_{R_f}$ with $f(x)$. This is the one-to-one correspondence between X/R_f and $f(X)$.   □

If one denotes the one-to-one correspondence by $\bar{f} : X/R_f \to f(X)$ and the natural mapping of X onto X/R_f by π_f, then the diagram

(18)

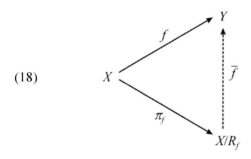

commutes; i.e. for all $x \in X$, $\bar{f}(\pi_f(x)) = f(x)$.   The result also shows that the range of any mapping with domain X may always be identified with a quotient set of X. Via $\bar{f}$, any (algebraic or topological) structure on Y may be pulled to X/R_f, and very often, via π_f back to X. I shall have more to say on this imputation of structure from codomain to domain later (*cf.* injection in 7.37, and metaphorically in terms of the modelling relation in Chapter 4).

2.22 Homomorphism Theorems   Let R be an equivalence relation on X. Any mapping with the quotient set X/R as domain may be *lifted*, via the natural mapping $\pi : X \to X/R$, to give a mapping with X as domain. Explicitly, for $\bar{g} : X/R \to Y$, define $g : X \to Y$ by $g(x) = \bar{g}(\pi(x))$ for $x \in X$:

(19)

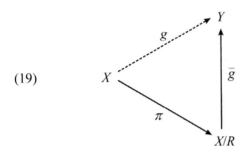

The results of Lemma 2.21 and Remark 2.22 are very general, and appear in many areas in mathematics. For example, the *Fundamental Theorem of Group Homomorphisms* is

Theorem   *Let ϕ be a homomorphism of a group G into a group H with kernel K. Then $G/K \cong \phi(G)$.*

Note that in connection with this theorem there are many important results in group theory. For example, that the kernel K is a normal subgroup of G, that $\phi(G)$ is a subgroup of H, that if ϕ is onto, then $G/K \cong H$, etc. In linear algebra, one has the corresponding

Theorem   *If T is a linear transformation from vector space U into vector space V with kernel W, then $T(U)$ is isomorphic to U/W. Conversely, if U is a vector space and W is a subspace of U, then there is a homomorphism of U onto U/W.*

The reader is invited to discover homomorphism theorems in other categories.

2.23 Definition Let X be a set. An *observable* of X is a mapping with domain X. The collection of all observables of X, i.e. the union of Y^X for all **Set**-objects Y, may be denoted $\bullet^X$.

2.24 Equivalent Observables   We just saw that a mapping f with domain X induces an equivalence relation $R_f \in \mathbf{Q}X$. Dually, equivalence relations on a set X induce an (*algebraic*) *equivalence* relation $\sim$ on the set of all mappings with domain X (i.e. on the set $\bullet^X$ of observables of X), as follows. If f and g are two mappings with domain X, define $f \sim g$ if $R_f = R_g$, i.e. if and only if

(20) $f(x) = f(y) \;\;\Leftrightarrow\;\; g(x) = g(y)$ for all $x, y \in X$.

This means the equivalence relations induced by f and g partition their common domain the same way. Stated otherwise, $f \sim g$ iff f and g are generators of the same equivalence relation in $\mathbf{Q}X$. By definition, an observable cannot distinguish among elements lying in the same equivalence class of its induced equivalence relation. Two algebraically equivalent mappings 'convey the same information' about the partitioning of the elements of X — one cannot distinguish the elements of X further by employing equivalent observables. Succinctly, one has

(21) $\bullet^X/\!\sim \;\cong\; \mathbf{Q}X$.

Note that the algebraic equivalence $f \sim g$ only means that $X/R_f \cong X/R_g$; in other words, there is a one-to-one correspondence between $f(X)$ and $g(X)$, but there may be no relation whatsoever between the *values* $f(x)$ and $g(x)$ for $x \in X$. Indeed, the two mappings f and g may even have codomains that do not intersect. In particular, if their codomains are equipped with metrics, the fact that $f(x)$ may be 'close' to $f(y)$ in $\mathrm{cod}(f)$ says nothing about the closeness between $g(x)$ and $g(y)$ in $\mathrm{cod}(g)$. So in this sense, even equivalent mappings give 'alternate information' about the elements of X, when the codomains are taken into account.

2.25 Qualitative versus Quantitative   An *observable* of X, as I define it, may have any set Y as codomain. The difference between 'qualitative' and 'quantitative' thus becomes in degree and not in kind. Indeed, an observable measures a 'quantity' when Y is a set of numbers [*e.g.* when Y is a subset of $\mathbb{N}$, $\mathbb{Z}$, $\mathbb{Q}$, $\mathbb{R}$, or even $\mathbb{C}$ (respectively the sets of natural numbers, integers, rational numbers, real numbers, and complex numbers), without for now straying into the territories of quaternions and Cayley numbers], and measures a 'quality' when Y is not a 'numerical set'.

Seen in this light, quantitative is in fact a meagre subset of qualitative. The traditional view of reductionism is (among other things) that every perceptual quality can and must be expressible in numerical terms. Consider Ernest Rutherford's infamous declaration "Qualitative is nothing but poor quantitative." For us, the features of natural systems in general, and of biological systems in particular, that are of interest and importance are precisely those that are *unquantifiable*. Even though the codomains of qualitative observables can only be described ostensively, the observables themselves do admit rigorous formal definitions. Rosen has discussed much of this in earlier work. See, for example, *AS, NC, LI, EL*.

Linkage

Let R_1 and R_2 be equivalence relations on a set X.   Recall (Definition 2.13) the partial order of *refinement* in the lattice $\mathbb{Q}X$: $R_1 \leq R_2$ (R_1 *refines* R_2) if

(22) $x R_1 y \implies x R_2 y.$

2.26 Lemma *If R_1 is a refinement of R_2, then there is a unique mapping $\rho : X/R_1 \to X/R_2$ that makes the diagram*

(23)

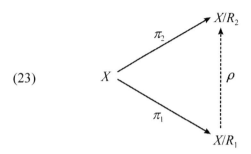

commute.

PROOF Define $\rho\left([x]_{R_1}\right) = [x]_{R_2}$. □

The mapping ρ induces an equivalence relation on X/R_1. By Lemma 2.21, one sees that $(X/R_1)/R_\rho \cong X/R_2$. In other words, when R_1 refines R_2, one may regard X/R_2 as a quotient set of X/R_1.

The refinement relation between two equivalence relations may be defined through their generators:

2.27 Lemma *Let f and g be two mappings with domain X. $R_f \le R_g$ in $\mathbb{Q}X$ if and only if*

(24) $f(x) = f(y) \;\Rightarrow\; g(x) = g(y) \quad$ for all $x, y \in X$.

2.28 Definition If $R \le R_g$ in $\mathbb{Q}X$, then g is called an *invariant of R*.

An invariant of an equivalence relation R is an invariant of every refinement of R. R_g is the largest equivalence relation of which g is invariant. An invariant of R is constant on the equivalence classes of R. An invariant g of R will in general take the same value on more than one R-class; it takes on distinct values on distinct R-classes iff $R = R_g$, i.e., iff g is a generator of R.

If $R_f \leq R_g$, then by Lemma 2.26 there is a unique mapping $h: X/R_f \to X/R_g$ that makes the diagram

(25)
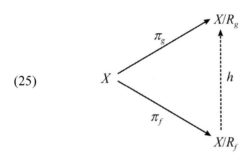

commute. This says the value of g at every $x \in X$ is completely determined by the value of f through the relation

(26) $\qquad g(x) = h(f(x))$.

Thus, in the obvious sense of 'is a function of', one has

2.29 Lemma *If $R_f \leq R_g$ in $\mathfrak{Q}X$, then g is a function of f.*

2.30 Definition Let f and g be observable of X. Let $\pi_f : X \to X/R_f$ and $\pi_g : X \to X/R_g$ be the natural quotient maps. For the R_f-equivalence class $[x]_{R_f} \in X/R_f$, consider the set of R_g-equivalence classes that intersect $[x]_{R_f}$; i.e. consider the set

(27)
$$\pi_g \circ \pi_f^{-1}\left([x]_{R_f}\right) = \left\{[y]_{R_g} \in X/R_g : f(x) = f(y)\right\}$$
$$= \left\{[y]_{R_g} \in X/R_g : [y]_{R_g} \cap [x]_{R_g} \neq \varnothing\right\}.$$

Note that $[x]_{R_g} \in \pi_g \circ \pi_f^{-1}\left([x]_{R_f}\right)$, so the set (27) is necessarily nonempty, containing at least one R_g-equivalence class. One says

(a) g is *totally linked to* f at $[x]_{R_f}$ if the set (27) consists of a single R_g-class;

(b) g is *partially linked to* f at $[x]_{R_f}$ if the set (27) consists of more than one R_g-class, but is not all of X/R_g;

(c) g is *unlinked to* f at $[x]_{R_f}$ if the set (27) is all of X/R_g.

Further, one says that g is *totally linked to* f if g is totally linked to f at each $[x]_{R_f} \in X/R_f$, and that g is *(totally) unlinked to* f if g is unlinked to f at each $[x]_{R_f} \in X/R_f$.

It is immediate from the definition that $R_f \leq R_g$ has another characterization:

2.31 Lemma g is totally linked to f if and only if R_f refines R_g.

And therefore

2.32 Corollary f and g are totally linked to each other iff $R_f = R_g$, i.e. $f \sim g$.

It is also immediate from the definition that

2.33 Lemma *g is totally unlinked to f if and only if every R_f-class intersects every R_g-class, and vice versa.*

The essence of a description of X by an observable f lies in the set of equivalence classes arising from that description, i.e. by the induced equivalence relation $R_f \in \mathbf{Q}X$. When there is an *alternate description* of X by another observable g, intuitively one expects to learn something more. The meet of two equivalence relations (Definition 2.15) when defined through their generators becomes

2.34 Lemma *Let f and g be two mappings with domain X. The meet $R_f \wedge R_g$ in $\mathbf{Q}X$ is*

$$(28) \qquad x\left(R_f \wedge R_g\right)y \quad \textit{iff} \quad f(x) = f(y) \textit{ and } g(x) = g(y).$$

One often abbreviates and denotes this meet as $R_{fg} = R_f \wedge R_g$. By Theorem 2.20, there exists an observable h of X such that $R_h = R_{fg}$.

Lemma 2.16 says that the equivalence classes of R_{fg} are obtained by forming the set-theoretic intersection of each R_f-equivalence class with each R_g-equivalence class. Some of them do not intersect, of course, and indeed, Definition 2.30 above classifies the possible intersections. In general (when g is partially linked or unlinked to f), alternate descriptions do give additional information. But in the particular case when g is totally linked to f, i.e. $R_f \leq R_g$, one has

$$(29) \qquad R_{fg} = R_f \wedge R_g = \inf\left\{R_f, R_g\right\} = R_f,$$

so here the additional observable g does not distinguish the elements of X any more then f already has.

Representation Theorems

Cayley's Theorem in group theory tells us that permutation groups are special, because every group is isomorphic to a group of permutations on a set. It turns out that lattices of equivalence relations (i.e. partition lattices) are analogously special: every lattice is isomorphic to a lattice of equivalence relations.

2.35 Definition If R_1 and R_2 are relations on X, the *relative product* $R_1 \circ R_2$ is the set of all ordered pairs $(x,y) \in X \times X$ for which there exists a $z \in X$ with $x R_1 z$ and $z R_2 y$. If R_1 and R_2 are equivalence relations, then because $x R_1 x$ one has $R_2 \subset R_1 \circ R_2$; similarly $R_1 \subset R_1 \circ R_2$. Thus

$$(30) \qquad R_1 \circ R_2 \subset R_1 \circ R_2 \circ R_1 \subset R_1 \circ R_2 \circ R_1 \circ R_2 \subset \cdots,$$

and it is easily seen that $R_1 \vee R_2$ is the union of this chain. It is possible, however, that $R_1 \vee R_2$ is actually equal to some term in the chain. For example, this is the case when X is a finite set. This, in fact, turns out to be true for any set X, in a precise sense as follows.

2.36 Definition Let L be a lattice. A *representation* of L is and ordered pair $\langle X, f \rangle$ where X is a set and $f : L \to \mathbb{Q}X$ is an injective (i.e. one-to-one) lattice homomorphism. The representation $\langle X, f \rangle$ is
(i)   *of type 1* if for all $x, y \in L$, $f(x) \vee f(y) = f(x) \circ f(y)$;
(ii) *of type 2* if for all $x, y \in L$, $f(x) \vee f(y) = f(x) \circ f(y) \circ f(x)$;
(iii) *of type 3* if for all $x, y \in L$, $f(x) \vee f(y) = f(x) \circ f(y) \circ f(x) \circ f(y)$.

In 1946, P. Whitman proved that every lattice had a representation:

2.37 Whitman's Theorem *Every lattice is isomorphic to a sublattice of the lattice of equivalence relations on some set X.*

Or more succinctly: *Every lattice is isomorphic to a partition lattice.*

In 1953, B. Jónsson found a simpler proof that gave a stronger result.

2.38 Theorem   *Every lattice has a type 3 representation.*

The proofs involved transfinite recursion, and produced (non-constructively) an infinite set X in the representation, even when the lattice L is a finite set.   For several decades, one of the outstanding questions of lattice theory was whether every *finite* lattice can be embedded into the lattice of equivalence relations on a *finite* set.   An affirmative answer was finally given in 1980 by P. Pudlák and J. Tůma:

2.39 Theorem   *Every finite lattice has a representation $\langle X, f \rangle$ with a finite set X.*

A representation of a lattice L induces an embedding of L into the lattice of subgroups of a group.   Given a representation $\langle X, f \rangle$ of L, let G be the group of all permutations on X that leave all but finitely many elements fixed, and let $\Sigma(G)$ denote the lattice of subgroups of G.   Define $h: L \to \Sigma(G)$ by

(31) $h(a) = \{\phi \in G : x\, f(a)\, \phi(x) \text{ for all } x \in X\}.$

[Note that $f(a) \in \mathbf{Q}X$, so $x\, f(a)\, \phi(x)$ in (31) is the statement ' x is $f(a)$-related to $\phi(x)$'; i.e. $(x, \phi(x)) \in f(a)$.]   One sees that h is an embedding (i.e. a one-to-one lattice homomorphism), thus

2.40 Theorem   *Every lattice can be embedded into the lattice of subgroups of a group.*

3

Continuatio:
Further Lattice Theory

Modularity

3.1 Definition Let L be a lattice, and let $x, y, z \in L$. The *modular identity* (which is self-dual) is

(*m*)   if $x \leq z$ then $x \vee (y \wedge z) = (x \vee y) \wedge z$.

Not all lattices satisfy property (*m*); but if a lattice does, it is said to be *modular*.

   Recall the *modular inequality* 2.5(*c*) [*if* $x \leq z$, then $x \vee (y \wedge z)$ $\leq (x \vee y) \wedge z$], which is satisfied by *all* lattices.

   Let G be a group and let $\Sigma(G)$ denote the lattice of subgroups of G. Let $\mathrm{N}(G)$ be the set of all *normal* subgroups of G. $\mathrm{N}(G)$ is a sublattice of $\Sigma(G)$, inheriting the same $\vee$ and $\wedge$. Recall (2.1) that for subgroups H and K of G, $H \wedge K = H \cap K$, and $H \vee K$ is the smallest subgroup of G containing H and K. For $H, K \in \mathrm{N}(G)$, the join becomes the simpler $H \vee K = HK$ in $\mathrm{N}(G)$. Note that this is not a 'different' $\vee$, but a consequent property because H and K are normal subgroups. $\mathrm{N}(G)$ is a modular lattice, while $\Sigma(G)$ in general is not.

62

3.2 Transposition Principle *In any modular lattice, the intervals* $[b, a \vee b]$ *and* $[a \wedge b, a]$ *are isomorphic, with the inverse pair of isomorphisms* $x \mapsto x \wedge a$ *and* $y \mapsto y \vee b$.

Two intervals of a lattice are called *transposes* when they can be written as $[b, a \vee b]$ and $[a \wedge b, a]$ for suitable a and b, hence the name of Theorem 3.2.

A natural question to ask after having Theorem 2.38, that every lattice has a type 3 representation, is whether all lattices have, in fact, representations of either type 1 or type 2 (*cf.* Definition 2.36). The answer is negative for general lattices, and is positive only for lattices with special properties, which serve as their characterizations.

3.3 Theorem *A lattice has a type 2 representation if and only if it is modular.*

The lattice $N(G)$ of normal subgroups of a group G is modular, whence by Theorem 3.3 it has a type 2 representation. It, indeed, has a natural representation $\langle X, f \rangle$ with $X = G$ (as the underlying set) and, for $H \in N(G)$, $f(H) = \{(x, y) \in G \times G : xy^{-1} \in H\}$. (This representation is in fact type 1.)

While type 2 representation is completely characterized by the single modular identity (m), the characterization of lattices with type 1 representations is considerably more complicated. The question of whether a set of properties exists that characterizes lattices with type 1 representations (i.e. such that a lattice has a type 1 representation if and only if it satisfies this set of properties) is an open question. It has been proven thus far that even if such a set exists, it must contain infinitely many properties.

Distributivity

3.4 Lemma *In any lattice L, the following three conditions are equivalent:*

(d1) *for all $x,y,z \in L$,* $x \wedge (y \vee z) = (x \wedge y) \vee (x \wedge z)$;
(d2) *for all $x,y,z \in L$,* $x \vee (y \wedge z) = (x \vee y) \wedge (x \vee z)$;
(m') *for all $x,y,z \in L$,* $(x \vee y) \wedge z \leq x \vee (y \wedge z)$.

3.5 Definition A lattice L is *distributive* if it satisfy one (hence all three) of the conditions *(d1)*, *(d2)*, and *(m')*.

Recall the *distributive inequalities* 2.5(b) [*(d1)* with $\geq$ in place of $=$ and *(d2)* with $\leq$ in place of $=$], which are satisfied by *all* lattices; but the conditions *(d1)*, *(d2)*, and *(m')* are not. Note also that the 'for all $x,y,z \in L$' quantifier is essential for their equivalence. In an arbitrary (non-distributive) lattice L, when one of *(d1)*, *(d2)*, and *(m')* is true for three *specific elements* $x,y,z \in L$, it does not necessarily imply that the other two are true for the same three elements.

Any chain (or totally ordered set) is distributive. The dual of a distributive lattice is distributive, and any sublattice of a distributive lattice is distributive. The power set lattice is distributive; it is in fact the canonical distributive lattice. Every distributive lattice has a representation in a power set lattice:

3.6 Theorem *A distributive lattice can be embedded into the power set lattice $\langle \mathbb{P}X, \subset \rangle$ of some set X.*

Combining condition *(m')* with the *modular inequality* 2.5(c), one has

3.7 Theorem *Every distributive lattice is modular.*

A distributive lattice also has the nice 'cancellation law':

3.8 Theorem   *For a lattice to be distributive, it is necessary and sufficient that*

(1)   *if* $x \wedge z = y \wedge z$ *and* $x \vee z = y \vee z$,   *then* $x = y$.

Complementarity

3.9 Definition   Let L be a lattice with least element 0 and greatest element 1 [whence $0 = \inf L = \sup\varnothing$ and $1 = \sup L = \inf\varnothing$]. A *complement* of an element $x \in L$ is an element $y \in L$ such that $x \vee y = 1$ and $x \wedge y = 0$.

The relation 'is a complement of' is clearly symmetric. Also, 0 and 1 are complements of each other.

3.10 Definition   A lattice L (with 0 and 1) is said to be *complemented* if all its elements have complements.

Let L be a lattice, $a, b \in L$, and $a \leq b$.   The interval $[a,b] \subset L$ is itself a lattice, with least element a and greatest element b.   A complement of $x \in [a,b]$ is thus a $y \in [a,b]$ such that $x \wedge y = a$ and $x \vee y = b$, in which case one also says x and y are *relative complements in the interval* $[a,b]$. The interval $[a,b]$ is *complemented* if all its elements have complements.

3.11 Definition   A lattice L is said to be *relatively complemented* if all its intervals are complemented.

Note that if L is a lattice with least element 0 and greatest element 1, then $[0,1] = L$ is an interval of L. So a relatively complemented lattice with 0 and 1 is complemented. We also know that

3.12 Theorem *Any complemented modular lattice is relatively complemented.*

The power set lattice PX is complemented. The complement of $S \subset X$ is the set-theoretic complement $S^c = X \sim S = \{x \in X : x \notin S\}$. PX is also relatively complemented. Let $A, B \in PX$ with $A \subset B$, and let $S \in [A, B]$, i.e. $A \subset S \subset B$. The complement of S in $[A, B]$ is the set $B \sim (S \sim A)$.

Recall (from the previous chapter) that QX denotes the collection of all equivalence relations on a set X. We saw (Theorem 2.18) that QX is a complete lattice. It is more:

3.13 Theorem QX *is a complemented lattice.*

PROOF We have already seen that the equality relation I is the least element, and the universal relation U is the greatest element in QX.

Let R be an equivalence relation on the set X, considered as its corresponding partition of X. We may assume that R is neither of the trivial partitions I and U. Let the blocks of R be denoted by A_i. I shall construct a partition R^c of X that is a complement of R. In each block A_i, choose a single representative $a_i \in A_i$, and denote the set $\{a_i\}$, which has exactly one element from each block, by S. Let R^c be the singular partition [Definition 1.17] consisting of the block S and the rest of the blocks singleton sets $\{x\}$ for each $x \in X \sim S$. Then

(2) $\qquad\qquad R \vee R^c = U \quad \text{and} \quad R \wedge R^c = I.$

Note that the existence of the set $\{a_i\}$ with exactly one element a_i from each block A_i, whence the existence of a singular partition, is equivalent to the Axiom of Choice (1.37). □

Since the choice of $a_i \in A_i$ is in general not unique, the above construction also shows that complements in $\mathbb{Q}X$ are not unique.

3.14 Theorem $\mathbb{Q}X$ *is a relatively complemented lattice.*

PROOF Let A, B, R be equivalence relations on the set X, with $R \in [A, B]$. Let the blocks of B be denoted by B_i. I shall construct a partition R^c of X that is a complement of R in the interval $[A, B]$.

Since $R \le B$, each block B_i is the disjoint union of a collection of blocks R_{ij} of R; and since $A \le R$, each block R_{ij} of R is itself the disjoint union of a collection of blocks A_{ijk} of A. In each block R_{ij} of R, choose a single block from its component blocks A_{ijk} of A. Merge all these chosen A_{ijk}s, after ranging through all the blocks R_{ij} of R, into one single subset of X denoted by S. Let R^c be the partition consisting of the block S, with the rest of the blocks all those A_{ijk}s of A *not* chosen in building S. In other words, other than S, the blocks of R^c coincide with those of A. Then one may verify that

(3) $R \vee R^c = B$ and $R \wedge R^c = A$.   □

Again, the choice of $A_{ijk} \subset R_{ij}$ is in general not unique, so the above construction also shows that relative complements in $\mathbb{Q}X$ are not unique.

An element may have more than one complement, or none at all. The cancellation law (Theorem 3.8) asserts that for a lattice to be distributive, it is necessary and sufficient that relative complements be unique (if they exist).

3.15 Theorem *In any interval of a distributive lattice, an element can have at most one complement. Conversely, a lattice with unique complements (whenever they exist) in every interval is distributive.*

Complementarity may also be used to characterize modular lattices:

3.16 Theorem *A lattice L is modular if and only if for each interval $[a,b] \subset L$, any two comparable elements of $[a,b]$ that have a common complement are equal; i.e. iff for all $[a,b] \subset L$ and $x_1, x_2, y \in [a,b]$, if*

(i) $x_1 \le x_2$ *or* $x_2 \le x_1$,
(ii) $x_1 \wedge y = x_2 \wedge y = a$, *and*
(iii) $x_1 \vee y = x_2 \vee y = b$,

then $x_1 = x_2$.

One may use these theorems to show that a particular lattice is *not* distributive by demonstrating an element with two distinct complements, or *not* modular by demonstrating an element with two distinct comparable relative complements. Thus, in view of the constructions in the proofs of Theorems 3.13 and 3.14, and Theorems 3.15 and 3.16, one may conclude that the full lattice $\mathbb{Q}X$ of *all* equivalence relations on a set X is *not* in general distributive, and *not* in general modular. But because of the representation theorems, it evidently contains distributive and modular sublattices.

3.17 Definition A *Boolean lattice* is a complemented distributive lattice.

In a complemented lattice, every element by definition has at least one complement. In a distributive lattice with 0 and 1, every element by Theorem 3.8 has at most one complement. Thus

68

3.18 Theorem *In any Boolean lattice L, each element x has one and only one complement x^*. Further, for all $x, y, z \in L$*

(i) $x \vee x^* = 1$, $x \wedge x^* = 0$;

(ii) $(x^*)^* = x$;

(iii) $(x \vee y)^* = x^* \wedge y^*$, $(x \wedge y)^* = x^* \vee y^*$.

A Boolean lattice is self-dual. Its structure may be considered as an algebra with two binary operations $\vee$, $\wedge$, and one unary operation $*$ (satisfying the requisite properties), whence it is called a *Boolean algebra*. Note that a Boolean algebra is required to be closed under the operations $\vee$, $\wedge$, and $*$. So a proper interval of a Boolean algebra may be a Boolean sublattice, but is not necessarily a Boolean subalgebra. A distributive lattice with 0 and 1, however, has a largest Boolean subalgebra formed by its complemented elements:

3.19 Theorem *The collection of all complemented elements of a distributive lattice with 0 and 1 is a Boolean algebra.*

The power set lattice PX is a Boolean algebra, called the *power set algebra* of X. A *field of sets* is a subalgebra of a power set algebra.

3.20 Stone Representation Theorem *Each Boolean algebra is isomorphic to a field of sets.*

Equivalence Relations and Products

3.21 Lemma *Let $X = X_1 \times X_2$ and let $R_1, R_2 \in QX$ be the equivalence relations on X induced by the natural projections $\pi_1 : X \to X_1$, $\pi_2 : X \to X_2$, i.e. $R_1 = R_{\pi_1}$, $R_2 = R_{\pi_2}$. Then*

(i) *Each R_1-class intersects every R_2-class; each R_2-class intersects every R_1-class;*

(ii)   *The intersection of an* R_1*-class with an* R_2*-class contains exactly one element of* X, *whence* $R_1 \wedge R_2 = I$ (*the equality relation*);

(iii) $R_1 \vee R_2 = U$ (*the universal relation*).

The conditions $R_1 \wedge R_2 = I$ and $R_1 \vee R_2 = U$, of course, say that R_1 and R_2 are complements in the lattice $\mathbb{Q}X$ (Definition 3.9 and Theorem 3.13). This lemma follows directly from the definitions and the observation that an R_1-class is of the form $\{(a,y): y \in X_2\}$ for some fixed $a \in X_1$, and an R_2-class is of the form $\{(x,b): x \in X_1\}$ for some fixed $b \in X_2$; in other words, each R_1-class $\pi_1^{-1}(a)$ is a copy of X_2, and each R_2-class $\pi_2^{-1}(b)$ is a copy of X_1.

The converse of Lemma 3.21 is also true:

3.22 Lemma   *Let* X *be a set and let* $R_1, R_2 \in \mathbb{Q}X$ *satisfy the three conditions* (i)–(iii) *in Lemma 3.21. Then* $X = X_1 \times X_2$, *where* $X_1 = X/R_1$ *and* $X_2 = X/R_2$.

PROOF By Lemma 2.16, the equivalence classes of $R_1 \wedge R_2$ are obtained by forming the set-theoretic intersection of each R_1-equivalence class with each R_2-equivalence class.   Given $R_1, R_2 \in \mathbb{Q}X$, a map

(4) $$\phi: X/(R_1 \wedge R_2) \to X/R_1 \times X/R_2$$

may therefore be defined, that sends a $R_1 \wedge R_2$-class to the uniquely determined ordered pair of R_1-class and R_2-class of which the $R_1 \wedge R_2$-class is the intersection. This map ϕ is one-to-one.

If condition 3.21(i) is satisfied, then ϕ is onto $X/R_1 \times X/R_2$, whence

(5) $$X/(R_1 \wedge R_2) \cong X/R_1 \times X/R_2 .$$

Condition 3.21(ii) then completes the proof to the requisite $X \cong X/R_1 \times X/R_2$. □

In terms of generating observables, one has

3.23 Lemma *Let X be a set equipped with two observables f, g. Then there is always an embedding (i.e. a one-to-one mapping)*

(6) $$\phi: X/R_{fg} \to X/R_f \times X/R_g .$$

This embedding is onto if and only if f and g are unlinked to each other.

Covers and Diagrams

The notion of 'immediate superior' in a hierarchy may be defined in any poset:

3.24 Definition Let X be a poset and $x, y \in X$. One says y *covers* x, or x *is covered by* y, if $x < y$ and there is no $z \in X$ for which $x < z < y$.

The covering relation in fact determines the partial order in a finite poset: the latter is the smallest reflexive and transitive relation that contains the former.

3.25 Definition Let X be poset with least element 0. An element $a \in X$ is called an *atom* if a covers 0.

In the poset $\langle PX, \subset \rangle$, for $A, B \subset X$, B covers A if and only if $A \subset B$ and $B \sim A$ contains exactly one element. Any singleton subset of X is an atom. In the poset $\langle QX, \leq \rangle$, for two partitions R_1 and R_2, R_2 covers R_1 if and only if one of the blocks of R_2 is obtained by the union of two blocks of R_1, while the rest of the blocks of R_2 are identical to those of R_1. In these two examples, note that we are considering the *full* posets PX and QX; with their subsets, the 'gaps' in the covers may of course be larger.

3.26 Hasse Diagram Using the covering relation, one may obtain a graphical representation of a *finite* poset X. Draw a point (or a small circle or a dot) for each element of X. Place y higher than x whenever $x < y$, and draw a straight line segment joining x and y whenever y covers x. The resulting graph is called a *(Hasse) diagram* of X.

Let us consider two simple examples. Let A be the three-element set $\{1,2,3\}$. Its power set is

$$PA = \{\varnothing, \{1\}, \{2\}, \{3\}, \{1,2\}, \{1,3\}, \{2,3\}, A\}.$$

The diagram of $\langle PA, \subset \rangle$ is

(7)

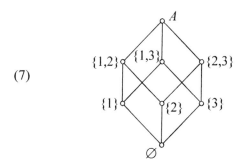

The partitions of A are $I = \{\{1\},\{2\},\{3\}\}$, $R_1 = \{\{1,2\},\{3\}\}$, $R_2 = \{\{1,3\}, \{2\}\}$, $R_3 = \{\{1\},\{2,3\}\}$, and $U = \{\{1,2,3\}\}$. The diagram of $\langle \mathbf{Q}A, \leq \rangle$ is

(8)

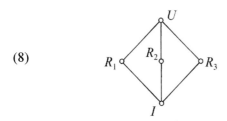

One sees that $x < y$ in X iff there is a path from y to x downward in the diagram of X. Thus any poset is defined (up to isomorphism) by its diagram. Also, the diagram of the dual poset $\tilde{X} = \langle X, \geq \rangle$ is obtained from that of $X = \langle X, \leq \rangle$ by turning the latter upside down.

Hesse diagrams are also useful in characterizing modular and distributive lattices. From Theorem 3.16, one sees that the property characterizing *non*modularity only involves five elements: viz. the endpoints of an interval, an element, and its two comparable complements. The lattice of these five elements may be represented in the following diagram, which is called (evidently) *the pentagon* as well as (obscurely) N_5:

(9)

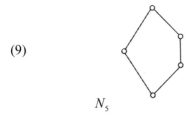

3.27 Theorem   *A lattice is modular if and only if it does not contain a sublattice isomorphic to the five-element lattice N_5. Equivalently, lattice is nonmodular if and only if it contains a sublattice isomorphic to the five-element lattice N_5.*

Every distributive lattice is modular (Theorem 3.7), but the converse is not true. The following five-element lattice, which is called (evidently) *the diamond* as well as (obscurely) M_3, is modular but not distributive:

(10)

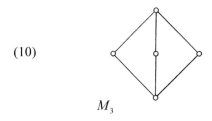

M_3

From Theorem 3.15, we see that the property characterizing *non*distributivity again involves five elements: viz. the endpoints of an interval, an element, and its two (not necessarily comparable) complements. The only two possible arrangements of these five elements are the pentagon N_5 and the diamond M_3.

3.28 Theorem   *A lattice is distributive if and only if it does not contain a sublattice isomorphic to the five-element lattice N_5 or M_3. Equivalently, lattice is nondistributive if and only if it contains a sublattice isomorphic to the five-element lattice N_5 or M_3.*

74

Semimodularity

3.29 Lemma *In any lattice, if $x \neq y$ and both x and y cover z, then $z = x \wedge y$. Dually, if $x \neq y$ and z covers both x and y, then $z = x \vee y$.*

3.30 Theorem *In a modular lattice,*

(i) *if $x \neq y$ and both x and y cover z (whence $z = x \wedge y$), then $x \vee y$ covers both x and y;*

(ii) *if $x \neq y$ and z covers both x and y (whence $z = x \vee y$), then both x and y cover $x \wedge y$.*

3.31 Corollary *In a modular lattice, x covers $x \wedge y$ if and only if $x \vee y$ covers y.*

3.32 Definition A lattice is (*upper*) *semimodular* if x covers $x \wedge y$ implies $x \vee y$ covers y. The dual property is called *lower semimodular*, for a lattice in which $x \vee y$ covers y implies x covers $x \wedge y$.

Corollary 3.31 says that a modular lattice is both (upper) semimodular and lower semimodular. Upper semimodularity is equivalent to the condition (i) in Theorem 3.30, and dually, lower semimodularity is equivalent to the condition (ii) in Theorem 3.30. Henceforth I shall follow the convention that 'semimodular' by itself means 'upper semimodular'.

The lattice of equivalence relations $\mathbf{Q}X$ is not modular if X contains four or more elements. However,

3.33 Theorem $\mathbf{Q}X$ *is a semimodular lattice.*

Chain Conditions

Most of the partially ordered sets and lattices we encounter are infinite, but many of them satisfy certain 'finiteness conditions'.

3.34 Lemma *In any poset $\langle X, \leq \rangle$ the following conditions are equivalent:*

(a) *[ascending chain condition, ACC] every ascending chain becomes stationary: if*

(11) $\qquad x_1 \leq x_2 \leq x_3 \leq \cdots,$

then there exists $n \in \mathbb{N}$ such that $x_k = x_n$ for all $k \geq n$;

(b) *every strictly ascending chain terminates: if*

(12) $\qquad x_1 < x_2 < x_3 < \cdots,$

then the chain has only finitely many terms;

(c) *[maximum condition] every nonempty subset of X has a maximal element.*

PROOF $(a) \Rightarrow (b)$ is trivial, because the chain in (b) can become stationary only by terminating.

$(b) \Rightarrow (c)$ follows, because for a nonempty subset $Y \subset X$, one may pick $x_1 \in Y$. If x_1 is not maximal, one may choose $x_2 \in Y$ such that $x_1 < x_2$. Generally, for each $x_k \in Y$, either x_k is maximal, or there exists $x_{k+1} \in Y$ such that $x_k < x_{k+1}$. Thus one obtains a strictly ascending chain of the form in (b), which must then terminate. The last element in the chain is then maximal in Y.

$(c) \Rightarrow (a)$: given an ascending chain of the form in (a), let x_n be maximal in the set $\{x_1, x_2, x_3, \ldots\}$. Then $x_k \leq x_n$ for all $k \in \mathbb{N}$, whence with the ascending chain condition $x_n \leq x_{n+1} \leq x_{n+2} \leq \cdots$, one must have $x_n = x_{n+1} = x_{n+2} = \cdots$; i.e. the chain becomes stationary. $\square$

Dually, one has

3.35 Lemma *In any poset $\langle X, \leq \rangle$ the following conditions are equivalent:*

(a)   [*descending chain condition, DCC*] *every descending chain becomes stationary: if*

(13) $x_1 \geq x_2 \geq x_3 \geq \cdots,$

   then there exists $n \in \mathbb{N}$ such that $x_k = x_n$ for all $k \geq n$;

(b)   *every strictly descending chain terminates: if*

(14) $x_1 > x_2 > x_3 > \cdots,$

   then the chain has only finitely many terms;

(c)   [*minimum condition*] *every nonempty subset of X has a minimal element.*

Recall Theorem 1.30 that any nonempty *finite* subset of *any* poset has minimal and maximal elements. The maximum and minimum conditions 3.34(c) and 3.35(c) — for *every* nonempty subset, finite or infinite — are *not* satisfied by *all* posets. The two lemmata say that when a poset satisfies condition (c), then it also equivalently satisfies the corresponding conditions (a) and (b). Note that the proof of the implication (b)$\Rightarrow$(c) requires the Axiom of Choice (1.37), and it may be shown that this is indispensable. Indeed, the implication 3.34(a)$\Rightarrow$(c) is Zorn's Lemma (1.36). Stated otherwise, without the Axiom of Choice (whence its equivalent Zorn's Lemma), the maximum condition is stronger than the ascending chain condition; but with the Axiom of Choice, both are equivalent.

The poset of natural numbers $\langle \mathbb{N}, \leq \rangle$ satisfies the *DCC*. Condition 3.35(b) says that an *infinite* strictly descending chain cannot exist. This fact is the basis of an invention by Pierre de Fermat:

3.36 The Method of Infinite Descent *Suppose that the assumption that a given natural number has a given property implies that there is a smaller natural number with the same property. Then no natural number can have this property.*

Note that the method of infinite descent actually uses the fact that is the 'opposite' of its name: there *cannot* be infinite descent in natural numbers. Stated otherwise, using the method, one may prove that certain properties are impossible for natural numbers by proving that if they hold for any numbers, they would hold for some smaller numbers; then by the same argument, these properties would hold for some still-smaller numbers, and so on *ad infinitum*, which is impossible because a sequence of natural numbers cannot strictly decrease indefinitely. It may even be argued that Fermat used this method in (almost) all of his proofs in number theory. (He might have, perhaps, even used it in the one proof that a margin was too narrow to contain!)

The next two lemmata say that induction principles hold for posets with chain conditions.

3.37 Lemma *Let $\langle X, \leq \rangle$ be a poset satisfying the ACC. If $P(x)$ is a statement such that*

(i) $P(x)$ *holds for all maximal elements x of X;*
(ii)   *whenever $P(x)$ holds for all $x > y$ then $P(y)$ also holds;*

then $P(x)$ is true for every element x of X.

PROOF Let $Y = \{x \in X : \neg P(x)\}$ (i.e., Y is the collection of all $x \in X$ for which $P(x)$ is false). I shall show that Y has no maximal element. For if $y \in Y$ is maximal, then consider elements $x \in X$ such that $x > y$. Either no such elements exist, or $P(x)$ has to be true, because y is maximal. But then condition (ii) implies that $P(y)$ is true, contradicting $y \in Y$. (When there are no elements

78

$x \in X$ with $x > y$, the antecedent of condition (ii) is vacuously satisfied.) Since $\langle X, \leq \rangle$ satisfies the *ACC*, whence by Lemma 3.34 also the maximum condition, the only subset of X that has no maximal element is empty. Thus $Y = \varnothing$, and so $P(x)$ is true for every element x of X. □

Dually, one has

3.38 Lemma *Let $\langle X, \leq \rangle$ be a poset satisfying the DCC. If $P(x)$ is a statement such that*

(i) *$P(x)$ holds for all minimal elements x of X;*
(ii) *whenever $P(y)$ holds for all $y < x$ then $P(x)$ also holds;*

then $P(x)$ is true for every element x of X.

Note that in both Lemmata 3.37 and 3.38, condition (i) is in fact a special case of (ii). If x is a minimal element of X, then there are no elements $y \in X$ with $y < x$. The antecedent of condition 3.38(ii) is vacuously satisfied, whence $P(x)$ is true; i.e. (ii)⇒(i). Condition (i) is included in the statements of the lemmata because maximal and minimal elements usually require separate arguments. Compare Lemma 3.38 with ordinary mathematical induction; we see that (i) is analogous to ordinary induction's 'initial step', and (ii) is analogous to the 'induction step'. Indeed, Lemmata 3.37 and 3.38 are known as Principles of *Transfinite Induction*. Lemma 3.38 is used more often in practice than Lemma 3.37, because it is usually more convenient to use the *DCC* and minimum condition than their dual counterparts.

3.39 Definition A poset $\langle X, \leq \rangle$ is *well-ordered* if every nonempty subset of X has a minimal element.

This is, of course, simply the minimum condition of Lemma 3.35(*c*). The concept of 'well-ordered set' has a separate set-theoretic history, and is intimately tied to that of ordinal number (*cf.* Theorem 1.34 and 1.35). The fact that $\langle \mathbb{N}, \leq \rangle$ is a well-ordered set is the basis for ordinary mathematical induction. The following results are immediate.

3.40 Lemma   *A well-ordered set is a chain.*

3.41 Lemma   *Any finite chain is well-ordered.*

3.42 Lemma   *Any subset of a well-ordered set is well-ordered.*

3.43 Definition An element x of a lattice L is *join-irreducible* if $x = \sup M = \bigvee_{y \in M} y$ for some finite subset M of L implies $x \in M$. Dually, an element x of a lattice L is *meet-irreducible* if $x = \inf M = \bigwedge_{y \in M} y$ for some finite subset M of L implies $x \in M$.

Note that by definition, (since $\varnothing$ is a finite subset of M) the least element 0 of L (if it exists) is *not* join-irreducible, because $0 = \sup \varnothing$, and the greatest element 1 of L (if it exists) is *not* meet-irreducible, because $1 = \inf \varnothing$. For a join-irreducible element x, if $x = y \vee z$, then $x = y$ or $x = z$. Dually, for a meet-irreducible element x, if $x = y \wedge z$, then $x = y$ or $x = z$.

The following important theorems follow from the transfinite induction lemmata 3.37 and 3.38:

3.44 Theorem   *If a lattice satisfies the ascending chain condition, then every element can be expressed as a meet of a finite number of meet-irreducible elements.*

3.45 Theorem   *If a lattice satisfies the descending chain condition, then every element can be expressed as a join of a finite number of join-irreducible elements.*

Recall (Definition 3.25) that in a poset X with least element 0, an element $a \in X$ is called an *atom* if a covers 0.

3.46 Theorem *An atom is join-irreducible.*

PROOF Let a be an atom (whence $0 < a$), and let $a = b \vee c$. Then $0 \leq b \leq a$ and $0 \leq c \leq a$. Since there are no other elements between 0 and a, b and c must be either 0 or a. But $0 \vee 0 = 0$, so either $b = a$ or $c = a$. □

PART II

Systems, Models, and Entailment

If, then, it is true that the axiomatic basis of theoretical physics cannot be extracted from experience but must be freely invented, can we ever hope to find the right way? Nay, more, has this right way any existence outside our illusions? Can we hope to be guided safely by experience at all when there exist theories (such as classical mechanics) which to a large extent do justice to experience, without getting to the root of the matter? I answer without hesitation that there is, in my opinion, a right way, and that we are capable of finding it. Our experience hitherto justifies us in believing that nature is the realisation of the simplest conceivable mathematical ideas. I am convinced that we can discover by means of purely mathematical constructions the concepts and the laws connecting them with each other, which furnish the key to the understanding of natural phenomena. Experience may suggest the appropriate mathematical concepts, but they most certainly cannot be deduced from it. Experience remains, of course, the sole criterion of the physical utility of a mathematical construction. But the creative principle resides in mathematics. In a certain sense, therefore, I hold it true that pure thought can grasp reality, as the ancients dreamed.

— Albert Einstein (10 June 1933)
On the Methods of Theoretical Physics
Herbert Spencer Lecture, University of Oxford

In this second movement, the timbre of my composition changes. I move from abstract algebra into the domains of ontology and epistemology.

System is a basic undefined term, a primitive. It takes on the intuitive meaning of 'a collection of material or immaterial things that comprises one's object of study'.

The crux in the formulation of a theory of living systems is the conception of *model*. It is the nature of the *relation* between the *entailment* patterns of two systems that allows one to serve as a model of the other. The purpose of modelling is that one may learn something new about a system of interest by studying a different system that is its model.

4

The Modelling Relation

The essence of a modelling relation consists of specifying an *encoding* and a corresponding *decoding* of particular system characteristics into corresponding characteristics of another system, in such a way that *implication* in the model corresponds to *causality* in the system. (I shall presently explain these italicized terms in detail below.) Thus in a precise mathematical sense a theorem about the model becomes a prediction about the system. A general theory of the modelling relation results when these remarks are given a rigorous setting. This theory has many important implications: to more general situations of metaphor, to the way in which distinct models of a given system are related to each other, and to the manner in which distinct systems with a common model may be compared.

The modelling relation is the point of departure in Rosen's science. It was explored in detail in Chapters 2 and 3 of *AS*, and also in Chapter 3 of *LI*. The present chapter contains a précis of the theme of, as well as my variations on, the subject.

Dualism

4.1 Self   Any organism — whether observer, perceiver, or cognizer — automatically creates a dualism between *self* and *non-self*.

The concept of 'self' is a universal primitive, indeed, *the* universal primitive, from which everything in the universe unfolds. If I represent 'self' as a *set* I, then the recognition of self is the identification of the property 'belonging to' I, which is itself a primitive in set theory. The non-self is, therefore, the complementary set I^c in a suitable universe. Stated otherwise, if one considers the 'membership relation' $\in$, self is $\in$, and non-self is $\notin$.

4.2 Ambience   The 'non-self' may also be called one's *ambience*. The ambience comprises all that inhabits the external or outer world, the world of events and phenomena (including other observers). An organism draws the sharpest possible distinction between oneself and one's ambience, and proceeds on the basis that there is a real, fundamental distinction between them.

The dualism between internal and external is one of the most ancient in a sentient being's perception of the universe. This dualism intrudes itself at the most basic levels. In particular, for human beings, it complicates our 'science'. Science is supposed to deal with the objective phenomena in the external world, but these need, however, to be perceived by the senses that are of the subjective internal or inner world of the cognizer. The understanding of these phenomena means a translation into a realm of language and symbol which does not belong to the external world.

The world was, of course, here before we were. Without any hearer around, however, while a tree falling in the forest may still make a sound, there will not be a *science* of the sound. The word 'science', after all, extends its original meaning of *knowledge*, which implies a cognizant observer. (Note the answer to any question, existential or otherwise, depends on the definition of the terms involved. If by the word 'sound' one means, say, 'the sensation caused in the ear, or the mental image created in the brain, by vibrating molecules', then of course *by definition* sound and the hearing of it are coexistent, thence Berkeley's falling-tree question becomes rhetorical, posed to simply affirm a tautology. But if 'sound' means 'a longitudinal pressure wave in an elastic medium', then the concepts of sound and hearing are uncoupled, whence 'unheard sound' is not an oxymoron.) The requirement of understanding the objective by symbolic means is almost a definition of cognition. In the deepest sense, the claim of a surrogacy between phenomena and their description is the essence of modelling between external world and the parallel internal one. Without a modeller, there is no modelling.

The establishment of relationships between the internal world of ideas and language and the external world of sensory phenomena is also the hallmark of the *theory of systems*. The necessity of treating external and internal phenomena together is one of the crucial characteristics of *system theory*, which has introduced a new element into the philosophy of science over the past few decades. While there had been a few preliminary works in the field, the subject of 'general system theory' was considered to be founded in 1954 by Ludwig von Bertalanffy, Kenneth Boulding, Anatol Rapoport, and Ralph Gerard. Note that in the name 'general system theory', the adjective 'general' modifies the noun 'theory', whence the topic is the generalities of 'system theory'; 'general' is *not* attributed to 'systems', so the topic is *not* the theory of 'general systems'. The definitive introduction to the subject was written by a founder, the still-precious *General System Theory* by von Bertalanffy [1968].

4.3 "Systems [*sic*] Theory" Consider the terms 'theory of systems' and 'system theory' in the previous paragraph; in particular, note the singular form *system* in the latter: *not* "systems theory". This last usage is a solecism that became accepted when it had been repeated often enough, a very example of 'accumulated wrongs become right'. Recall that von Bertalanffy's masterwork is called *General System Theory*. (In some of his later writings, the term "systems theory" did occasionally appear. I have in my collection some copies of his original typescripts, in which he had written "system theory", but in the published versions they mysteriously mutated to "systems theory" — evidence of the handiwork of an over-zealous copy editor, perhaps...)

Just think of 'set theory', 'group theory', 'number theory', 'category theory', etc. Of course one studies more than one object in each subject! Indeed, one would say in the possessive 'theory of sets', 'theory of groups', 'theory of numbers', 'theory of categories', ...; one says 'theory of systems' for that matter. But the point is that when the noun of a mathematical object (or indeed any noun) is used as adjective, one does not use the plural form.

4.4 Natural System Natural science is one attempt to come to grips with what goes on in the external world. It has taught one to isolate from one's ambience conspicuous parts, which one may call *natural systems*. The extraction of a natural system from one's ambience then creates a new dualism, between the *system* and its *environment*. A specification of what the system is like at a particular time is its *state*. As science has developed since the time of Newton, we have learned to characterize systems in terms of states, and to cast the basic problems of natural science in terms of temporal sequences of state *transitions* in systems. These sequences are determined in turn by the character of the system itself, and by the way it interacts with the environment. Thus one has the

Primitive A *natural system* is

(*a*)   a part, whence a subset, of the external world; and

(*b*)   a collection of qualities, to which definite relations can be imputed.

If 'self' is represented by the set I, then a natural system N may be represented by a subset $N \subset I^c$. Note that I have used the symbol N to denote both a natural system *and* a set that represents it. Indeed, I also have I as self and a set representing the same. This equivalence is the essence of the modelling relation that I shall explicate presently. Here, let us simply note in passing that it is not too great an exercise of faith to believe that *everything is a set*: 'a set of apples', 'a set of celestial bodies', 'a set of cells of an organism', 'a set of metabolic and repair components', 'a set of mechanistic parts', a set containing infinitely many members, a set consisting of a single item, an empty set,...

4.5 Quid est veritas?

> 'Reality' is one of the few words which mean nothing
> without quotes.
>
> — Vladimir Nabokov (1956)
> *On a Book Entitled «Lolita»*

One learns about systems, their states, and their state-transition sequences through observation, through measurement. This, of course, is what observers do. But a *mere* observer is not a scientist. Indeed, basic features of the observer's internal world enter, in an essential way, in turning an observer into a scientist. Often, these features are *imputed* to the ambience of the observer, and treated as if they too were the results of observation. Models and the modeller's behaviour shape each other. The models realized in the anticipatory systems that are ourselves are *relative truths*, and are in fact the 'constitutive parameters' of our individuality, or as Rosen put it, "subjective notions of good and ill".

One may speak of *absolute truths* concerning formal systems, in the universe of mathematics. But there is no such luxury for natural systems, in the external world outside the realm of formalism. In the natural world, 'reality' is subjective, 'truth' is relative. We can indeed agree about life, the universe, and everything, *if* (and what a big *if* this is!) we can agree on our answers to *the question*, in Pontius Pilate's immortal words: "What is truth?" (*John* 18:38).

4.6 Formal System A *formalism* is a 'sublanguage' specified entirely through its syntax. The importance of making it a sublanguage resides in (*a*) its capacity, through the larger language in which it sits, for semantic function, and (*b*) one may explore a formalism through purely syntactic means, independent of any such semantic function, if one wishes to do so. There is a close analogy between extracting a formalism from a language and extracting a natural system from an observer's ambience; one may therefore call a formalism a *formal system*. Note that the concept includes, but is not limited

88

and therefore not equivocated to, Hilbert's *formalization*. In the broadest sense, *mathematics is the study of such formal systems*, whence one has the next

Primitive A *formal system* is an object in the universe of mathematics.

In the formal world, the axioms of a formal system define its objective reality, and logic predicates its absolute truths.

In Chapter 7, I shall give a *definition* of formal system that encompasses this primitive without loss of generality. I shall be concerned with the internal syntactic structures of formal systems, and the ways in which semantic content can be attached to formal systems. For now, let us concentrate on the close relations that exist between natural systems in the external world, and formal systems in the internal one.

Natural Law

It can be commonly agreed that no one, whether experimenter, observer, or theorist, does science at all without believing that nature obeys laws or rules, and that these natural regularities can be at least partly grasped by the mind. That nature obeys laws is often subsumed under the notion of *causality*. The articulation of these causal laws or relationships means, in brief, that one can establish a correspondence between events in the world and propositions in some appropriate language, such that the causal relations between events are exactly reflected in implication relations between corresponding propositions.

4.7 Causality and Perception 'Law of Nature', or *Natural Law*, consists of two independent parts. The first of these comprises a belief, or faith, that what goes on in the external world is not entirely arbitrary or whimsical. Stated in positive terms, this is a belief that successions of events in that world are governed by definite relations, usually called *causal*. Without such a belief, there could be no such thing as science. Causality, and ideas of entailment in general, guarantee a kind of regularity that one expects in nature and in science, in the sense that the same causes imply the same effects. In short, causality is 'objective'. I shall explicate the topic of causation in more philosophical and scientific details in the next chapter.

The second constituent of Natural Law is a belief that the causal relations between events can be grasped by the mind, articulated and expressed in language. Therefore, one sees in the causal world the operation of laws in terms of which the events themselves may be understood. 'Perceived causality' then becomes subjective. This 'perception' aspect of Natural Law posits a relation between the syntactic structure of a language and the semantic character of its external referents. This relation is different in kind from entailment within language or formalisms (i.e., implication or inference, which relate purely linguistic entities), and from entailment between events (i.e., causal relations between things in the external world). *Natural Law, therefore, posits the existence of entailments between events in the external world and linguistic expressions (propositions) about those events.* Stated otherwise, it posits a kind of *congruence* between implication (a purely syntactic feature of languages or formalisms) and causality (a purely semantic, extra-linguistic constituent of Natural Law).

One may summarize thus:

Natural Law makes two separate assertions about the self and its ambience:

I.   The succession of events or phenomena that one perceives in the ambience is not arbitrary: there are *relations* (e.g. causal relations) manifest in the world of phenomena.

II. The posited relations between phenomena are, at least in part, capable of being *perceived* and grasped by the human mind; i.e. by the cognitive self.

Science depends in equal parts on these two separate axioms of Natural Law. In short, Axiom I, that causal order exists, is what permits *science* to exist in the abstract, and Axiom II, that this causal order can be imaged by implicative order, is what allows *scientists* to exist. Both are required.

4.8 Wigner   The theorist's job is essentially to bring causal order and implicative order into congruence.   There appears no *a priori* reason, however, to expect that purely syntactic operations (i.e., inferences on propositions about events) should in fact correspond to causal entailments between events in the external world.   Pure mathematicians like to boast that for the objects of their studies, they do not.   Surprisingly often, however, even pure mathematics of the most abstract origins turns out to be useful in explaining natural phenomena.   If one chooses one's language carefully, and expresses external events in it in just the right way, the requisite homology appears between implication in the language and causality in the world described by the language.   The physicist Eugene Wigner once delivered a lecture [Wigner 1960] on "the unreasonable effectiveness of mathematics in the natural sciences".   Wigner would not have written his now-famous article if he felt that mathematics was only 'reasonably effective', or even 'reasonably ineffective', in science — the reasonable is not the stuff of miracles, and gives one no *reason* to reason about it further.   Wigner obviously felt, however, that the role played by mathematics in the sciences was in some sense excessive, and it was this excess which he regarded as counterintuitive.

There are two prongs to Wigner's disquiet about the role of mathematics in science. The first is that mathematics, taken in itself as an abstract entity, should have such success in dealing with extra-mathematical referents. The second, which builds upon the first, notes that the criteria which have guided the historical development of mathematics have apparently been unrelated to any such extra-mathematical referents; they have been, rather, selections of subjective mathematical interest, arena of the exercise of cleverness, and most of all, pageants of abstract beauty. Why, Wigner asks, should formalisms developed according to such criteria allow extra-mathematical referents at all, let alone with such fidelity? His essay provides evidence to bolster his impression, but he does not attempt to account for the excess which he perceives.

A relation between a language or formalism and an extra-linguistic referent, which manifests such a congruence between syntactic implication within language and causality in its external referent, will be called a *modelling relation*. I shall next describe such relations more precisely, before investigating what they themselves entail, and in so doing provide a possible explanation to Wigner's miracle.

Model versus Simulation

4.9 Arrow Diagram

(1)

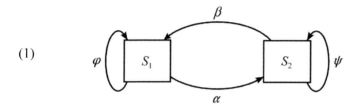

Figure (1) contains the components I need to describe what a *modelling relation* is between a system S_1 and a system S_2. Often, S_1 is a natural system and S_2 is a formal system; but I shall begin with the most general case where each of S_1 and S_2 can be either natural or formal. Later, I shall specialize on the prototypical situation, as well as other natural/formal system combinations for S_1 and S_2.

The crux of the matter lies in the arrows of the diagram, which I have labelled φ, ψ, α, and β. The arrows φ and ψ represent entailment in the systems S_1 and S_2, respectively. The arrow α is called the *encoding* arrow. It serves to associate features of S_1 with their counterparts in S_2. The arrow β denotes the inverse activity to encoding; namely, the *decoding* of features of S_2 into those of S_1.

The arrows α and β taken together thus establish a kind of *dictionary*, which allows effective passage from one system to the other and back again. However, I may remark here on the peculiar status of the arrows α and β. Namely, they are not a part of either systems S_1 or S_2, nor are they entailed by anything either in S_1 or in S_2.

4.10 Simulation   A modelling relation exists between systems S_1 and S_2 when there is a *congruence* between their entailment structures. The vehicle for establishing a relation of any kind between S_1 and S_2 resides, of course, in the choice of encoding and decoding arrows, the arrows α and β. A *necessary condition* for congruence involves all four arrows, and may be stated as 'whether one follows *path* φ or *paths* α, ψ, β *in sequence*, one reaches the same destination'. Expressed as composition in mathematical terms, this is

(2) $\varphi = \beta \circ \psi \circ \alpha.$

If this relation is satisfied, one says that S_2 is a *simulation* of S_1.

Let $f : X \to Y$ be a mapping representing a process in the entailment structure of the arrow φ in S_1. Consider a mapping $g : \alpha(X) \to \alpha(Y)$ (which is a process in the entailment structure of the arrow ψ in S_2) that makes the diagram

(3)

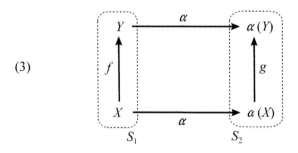

commute (which means for *every* element x in X, whether it traces through the mappings f followed by α, or through α followed by g, one gets the same result in $\alpha(Y)$; i.e. the equality

(4) $\alpha(f(x)) = g(\alpha(x))$

holds *for all* $x \in X$). Note that this commutativity condition for simulation places no further restrictions on the mapping g itself, other than that it needs to reach the correct final destination. Such emphasis on the results *regardless of the manner in which they are generated* (i.e. with no particular concern on underlying principles) is the case when S_2 is a *simulation* of S_1.

4.11 Model   If, however, the mapping g is *itself* entailed by the encoding α, i.e. if $g = \alpha(f)$, whence the mapping in S_2 is $\alpha(f): \alpha(X) \to \alpha(Y)$, then one has the commutative diagram

(5)

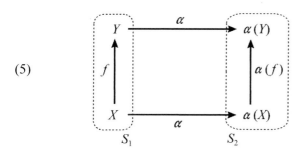

and the equality corresponding to (4), for every element x in X, is

(6) $\alpha(f(x)) = \alpha(f)(\alpha(x))$.

When this more stringent condition (6) is satisfied, the simulation is called a *model*. If this *modelling relation* is satisfied between the systems S_1 and S_2, one then says that there is a *congruence* between their entailment structures, and that S_2 is a *model* of S_1. This kind of congruence between entailment structures is defined by the mathematical entity called *functor* (consult the Appendix for definitions and examples) in category theory, which I shall explain briefly later (*cf.* 4.17 below).

A simulation of a process provides an alternate description of the entailed effects, whereas a model is a special kind of simulation that additionally also provides an alternate description of the entailment structure of the mapping representing the process itself. It is, in particular, easier to obtain a simulation than a model of a process.

4.12 Remarks   Examples are in order. For instance, Claudius Ptolemy's *Almagest* (*c.* AD 150) contained an account for the apparent motion of many heavenly bodies. The Ptolemaic system of epicycles and deferents, later with adjustments in terms of eccentricities and equant points, provided good geometric simulations, in the sense that there were enough parameters in defining the circles so that any planetary or stellar trajectory could be represented reasonably accurately by these circular traces in the sky. Despite the fact that Ptolemy did not give any physical reasons why the planets should turn about circles attached to circles in arbitrary positions in the sky, his simulations remained the standard cosmological view for 1400 years. Celestial mechanics has since, of course, been progressively updated with better theories of Copernicus, Kepler, Newton, and Einstein.   Each improvement explains more of the underlying principles of motion, and not just the trajectories of motion. The universality of the Ptolemaic epicycles is nowadays regarded as an extraneous mathematical artefact irrelevant to the underlying physical situation, and it is for this reason that a representation of trajectories in terms of them can only be regarded as simulation, and not as model.

As another example, a lot of the so-called 'models' in the social sciences are really just sophisticated kinds of curve-fitting, i.e. simulations. These activities are akin to the assertion that since a given curve can be approximated by a polynomial, it must be a polynomial. Stated otherwise, curve-fitting without a theory of the shape of the curve is simulation; model requires understanding of how and why a curve takes its shape.

In short: simulation describes; model explains.

'Simulation' is based on the Latin word *similis*, 'like, similar'. A *simulacrum* is 'something having merely the form or appearance of a certain thing, without possessing its substance or proper qualities'. 'Model' in Latin is *modulus*, which means 'measure', herein lies a fine nuance that implies a subtle increase in precision. (It is interesting to note that in *FM — Fundamentals of Measurement and Representation of Natural Systems*, the first book of the Rosen trilogy — measurement and similarity are two main topics.) In common usage, however, the two words 'simulation' and 'model' are often synonyms, meaning:

○ a simplified description of a system put forward as a basis for theoretical understanding
○ a conceptual or mental representation of a thing
○ an analogue of different structure from the system of interest but sharing an important set of functional properties.

Some, alternatively, use 'model' to mean mathematical theory, and 'simulation' to mean numerical computation. What I have presented above, however, are *Robert Rosen's definitions* of these two words.

The Prototypical Modelling Relation

I now specialize to the prototypical modelling relation when S_1 is a natural system and S_2 is a formal system.

4.13 Interpretation of the Arrows When S_1 is a natural system, φ is *causal entailment*. It may be thought of as the entailment of subsequent states by present or past states. It is what an observer sees diachronically when looking at a system. The arrow φ thus makes no reference to anything pertaining to language, or indeed to any internal activity of the observer, beyond the basic act of isolating the system and observing the causal entailment in the first place. In short, the *existence* of causal entailment is *ontological*, but its *representation* as the arrow φ is, however, *epistemological*. The fact that the natural system S_1 with the arrow φ can be represented at all is due to Axiom I of Natural Law.

The arrow ψ schematically represents the entailment apparatus of the formalism S_2, its inferential structure, implications. This *inferential entailment* is entirely syntactic. It makes no reference to semantics, meaning, or any external referents whatever. In short, inferential entailment ψ is strictly *epistemological*.

The *encoding* arrow α serves to associate features of S_1 with formal tokens in S_2. The simplest and perhaps the most familiar kind of encoding is the expression of results of *measurement* in numerical terms. (This topic was investigated in detail in *FM*.) Numbers, of course, are formal objects; the association of numbers with meter readings is the most elementary kind of encoding of a natural system in a formal one. In short, encoding α is our *description* of the ontology.

The *decoding* arrow β denotes the complementary activity to encoding; namely, the association of elements of the formalism S_2 into specific external referents, observable properties of the natural system S_1. In short, decoding β is our *interpretation* of our epistemology.

Thus encoding and decoding let one pass effectively from the natural world to the formal one and back again. As I mentioned above, they cannot be meaningfully said to be *caused* by S_1 or anything in it; nor can they be said to be *implied* by anything in S_2. The formal system S_2 with its inferential entailment arrow ψ, together with the encoding and decoding arrows α and β, are Axiom II of Natural Law.

4.14 Summary The situation may be represented in the following canonical diagram, with a change-of-names of the symbols:

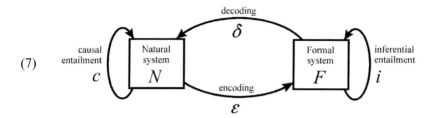

(7)

A *modelling relation* exists between the natural system N and the formal system F when

(8) $\qquad i = \varepsilon(c)$ and $c = \delta \circ i \circ \varepsilon.$

If these conditions are satisfied, F is a *model* of N, and N is a *realization* of F.

Let me explain alternatively what the above congruence conditions (8) mean. One thinks of the causal entailment structure c as embodied in state-transition sequences in N; it is what an observer sees when simply watching events in N unfold. The encoding arrow α pulls features of N into the formal system F. More precisely, it endows these features with formal images in F, images on which the inferential entailment structure i of F may operate.

One may think of these 'observed' images as 'hypotheses' or 'premises' in F. The inferential structure of F then specifies what these 'hypotheses' entail within the formal system F; this process of entailment in F is precisely the arrow i. The results of applying inferential rules to hypotheses generates 'theorems' in F. The particular 'theorems' in which one is now interested are those arising from hypotheses coming from N via the encoding ε.

It is evident that such 'theorems', when decoded from F to N via the arrow δ, become assertions ('predictions') about N. The commutativity requirement in the modelling condition then requires that one always gets the same answer, whether (*a*) one simply watches the operation of causal entailment c in the natural system N itself, or (*b*) one encodes N into F via the arrow ε, apply the inferential processes i of F to what is encoded, and then decode the resulting theorems, via the decoding arrow δ, into predictions about N.

4.15 Natural Law Revisited The deceptively simple diagram of the prototypical modelling relation above allows the reformulation of the concept of Natural Law in a mathematically rigorous way. Tersely, Natural Law asserts that any natural system N possesses a formal model F, or conversely, is a realization of a formalism F. Stated otherwise, Natural Law says that any process of causal entailment in the external world may be faithfully represented by homologous inferential structure in some formal system F with the appropriate encodings and decodings. It must be stressed that *Natural Law alone does not tell us how to accomplish any of this; it merely says that it can be done.*

This equivalence of causality in the natural domain and inference in the formal domain is an epistemological principle, the axiom

Every process is a mapping.

Just like the axiom "Everything is a set." leads to the identification of a natural system N and its representation as a set (*cf.* 4.4), mathematical equations representing causal patterns of natural processes are results of the identification of entailment arrows and their representations as mappings.

As a cautionary note, it must be emphasized that this equivalence is a consequence of the *model*, the accessibility of which is predicated by Natural

Law. *Simulation* is promiscuous; the less stringent requirement in the encoding means that a causal process may very well be manipulated so that its *function* is lost (*cf.* 4.10 and 4.11), in which case a natural process may not be represented by a formal mapping. I shall revisit simulation in the context of simulability in Chapter 8.

Structure is the order of parts, represented by sets; function is the order of processes, represented by mappings. The very fact that the right-hand side of the modelling relation diagram (7) is an object in the universe of mathematics thus implies, in a sense, that *the concept of Natural Law already entails the efficacy of mathematics*, which Wigner was astonished to find so unreasonable. Mathematics combines generality of concepts with depth of details, and is the language of nature. Perhaps what is truly surprising is not the 'can be done' part, but that we should have been so good at the 'how'. After all, modelling itself, the choice of appropriate sets and mappings $\{F, \varepsilon, \delta\}$ of formal system, encoding, and decoding given a natural system N, is more an art than a science. But then again, mathematics is both high art and supreme science.

Mathematics is *Regina scientiarum*; it adds lucidity and clarity to science. The tree of science has many branches, but the trunk is mathematics. A caveat, however, is that a danger of mathematical modelling is in abstracting too much away. One must always remember the semantics, not just the syntax. And one must learn the importance of alternate descriptions. Generality and depth must be part of the modelling endeavour itself, manifested in the *plurality* of models from diverse branches of mathematics. Wigner's miracle is not the all-encompassing "mathematics is effective in explaining *everything*", only that "mathematics is unreasonably effective in the natural sciences", and that what it can do it can usually do exceptionally well. Mathematical modelling, therefore, is not the reduction of science to mathematics. The error of Reductionism (i.e., to physics) is not the claim that physics can explain other sciences, but that it *exhausts* 'reality', that *all* sciences should have its format.

The General Modelling Relation

In the previous discussion on the prototypical modelling relation, I have been concerned with the case $S_1 = N$ and $S_2 = F$, making manifest some of the parallels that exist between the external world of events or phenomena and the internal world of language and mathematics. Indeed, the modelling relation, and the concept of Natural Law on which it rests, are merely direct expressions of these parallels. Next, I consider other natural/formal system combinations for S_1 and S_2.

4.16 Homology   When both S_1 and S_2 are formal systems, one has a modelling relation *within mathematics itself.*   By 'modelling within mathematics', I mean the establishment of homologies between different kinds of inferential structures, arising from different parts of mathematics. In effect, one part of mathematics is treated like the external world; its inferential properties treated like causal entailment. Such 'internal modelling' within mathematics allows one to bring one part of mathematics to bear on another part, often to the most profound effect.

Examples of such 'internal modelling' abound. Consider, for instance, Cartesian Analytic Geometry, which created an arithmetic model of Euclid's *Elements*, and thereby brought algebraic reasoning to bear on the corpus of geometry. Later, the consistency of 'non-Euclidean' geometries was proved by establishing Euclidean models of non-Euclidean objects. Whole theories in mathematics, such as the theory of Group Representations, rest entirely on such notions. Henri Poincaré ushered a new era into mathematics by showing how to build other kinds of algebraic models of geometric objects. His idea of homotopy, and later, of homology, showed how to create group-theoretic images of topological spaces, and to deduce properties of the latter from those of the former.

4.17 Category Theory   In 1945, a whole new branch of mathematics was developed, by Samuel Eilenberg and Saunders Mac Lane, initially to formalize these methodologies initiated by Poincaré. This came to be called *category theory*, and its subject matter was precisely the relations between different inferential structures within mathematics itself. In fact, it can be regarded as a *general theory of modelling relations* within mathematics. The Appendix in this monograph is a terse introduction to the theory.

The active agents of comparison between categories (*i.e.*, between different kinds of formalisms or inferential structures) are called *functors*. The formal counterpart of Natural Law in this purely abstract setting is the existence of nontrivial functors α between categories S_1 and S_2:

(9)

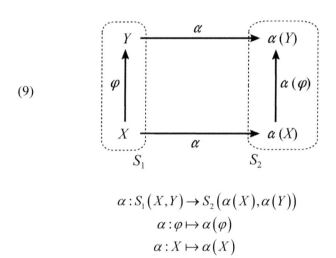

$$\alpha : S_1(X,Y) \rightarrow S_2(\alpha(X), \alpha(Y))$$
$$\alpha : \varphi \mapsto \alpha(\varphi)$$
$$\alpha : X \mapsto \alpha(X)$$
$$\alpha : Y \mapsto \alpha(Y)$$

In mathematics, there is also a subject in axiomatics and foundations called *model theory*. A *model* for an axiomatic theory is simply a system of objects satisfying the axioms, chosen from some other theory. The topic is intimately related to consistency and completeness, and Hilbert's axiomatization and proof theory. In this monograph, I shall not stray into this chapter on foundational matters of mathematics, the exploration of which may begin with Kleene's timeless *Introduction to Metamathematics* [1952]. I shall have occasions to refer to Kleene again.

4.18 Analogues

(10)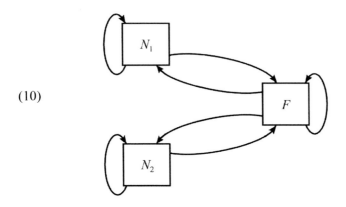

In figure (10), there are two different natural systems N_1, N_2 which possess the same formal model F (or alternatively, which constitute distinct realizations of F). It is not hard to show that one can then 'encode' the features of N_1 into corresponding features of N_2 and conversely, in such a way that the two causal structures, in the two *natural systems* N_1 and N_2, are brought into congruence. That is, one can construct from the above figure a commutative diagram of the form shown in figure (11). This is a modelling relation *between two natural systems*, instead of a natural system and a formal one.

(11)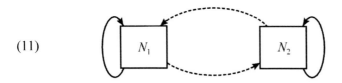

Under these circumstances depicted in the two previous figures, the proper term to use is that the natural systems N_1 and N_2 are *analogues*. Analogous systems allow us to learn about one by observing the other. Relations of analogy underlie the efficacy of 'scale models' in engineering, as well as all of the various 'principles of equivalence' in physics. But the relation of analogy cuts much deeper than this. Natural systems of the most diverse kinds (e.g. organisms and societies, economic systems and metabolisms) may be analogous; analogy is a relation between natural systems which arises through the models of their causal entailments, and not directly from their material structures. As such, analogy and its cognates offer a most powerful and physically sound alternative to reductionism (*viz.* 'share a common model' and therefore 'analogous', as opposed to 'one encompasses the other').

4.19 Alternate Models

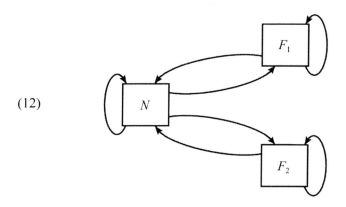

(12)

A complementary diagram to that of figure (10) is shown in figure (12). Here, a single natural system N is modelled in two distinct formalisms F_1, F_2. The question here is: What, if any, is the relation between the formalisms F_1 and F_2?

The answer here is not in general as straightforward as before; it depends entirely on the extent of the 'overlap' between the two encodings of N in F_1 and F_2, respectively. In some cases, one can effectively build at least some encoding and decoding arrows between the two formalisms. For a couple of examples, consider Dirac's transformation theory formulation of quantum mechanics which unifies Heisenberg's matrix mechanics and Schrödinger's wave mechanics, and the relation between the thermodynamic and statistical-mechanical models of fluids. In other cases, there exists no formal relation between F_1 and F_2. One then has the situation in which N *simultaneously* realizes two distinct and independent formalisms; the various Bohr's complementarities for microphysical phenomena are examples.

4.20 Largest Model   Many practical and theoretical questions are raised in situations of this last type; some of them bear crucially on the limits of reductionism. It is often asserted, and still more widely believed, that physics *implies* reductionism; that the only way to relate natural systems is by analyzing them down to a common set of constituents: molecules, atoms, or elementary particles. In the reductionistic view, a scientific theory that is not firmly grounded on physicochemical principles is by definition wrong. The end result of such an analysis is an encoding of any natural system into a formalism which serves to express any system property in terms of these ultimate constituents. In some sense, this is the largest formalism, the largest model, which can exist; any other model is, in formal terms, some kind of quotient model or submodel of this biggest one.

In this case, the independence of two formalisms F_1 and F_2, that N simultaneously realizes, is only apparent. Reductionism holds that one can always embed F_1 and F_2 in some larger formalism F, which is again a model, and from which F_1 and F_2 can be recaptured by purely formal means. An all-encompassing largest model is the metaphorical all-explaining 'theory of everything'.

The existence of such a largest formalism, which itself models a given natural system N, and from which all others can be formally generated, would constitute a new postulate about the nature of the material world itself. Some kinds of natural systems admit such a largest model, but others do not. Indeed, if one pursues this matter further, it appears that the distinction, between those that do admit a largest model and those that do not, has many of the properties of the distinction between inanimate and animate, or of simple and complex. I shall pursue these matters later on in this monograph. Rosen's previous works [*AS, LI, EL*] initiated these investigations.

5

Causation

Felix qui potuit rerum cognoscere causas

[Happy is one who comes to know the causes of things]

> — Virgil (29 BC)
> *Georgics*
> Book II, line 490

Aristotelian Science

Aristotle's *categories of causation* made their first appearance, albeit only in passing, in Rosen's publications in Chapter 7 of *AS*. The topic then received detail treatment in *LI* (notably Sections 3E, 3G, and 5I). The Philosopher's ancient text on causality, Chapter 3 of Book II of *Physics*, presented some of the most influential concepts in human thought. The four causes dominated philosophical and scientific thinking in the Western world for millennia, until the Newtonian revolution that is 'the mechanization of the world picture'.

5.1 Wisdom and Knowledge

O Sapientia,
quae ex ore Altissimi prodiisti,
attingens a fine usque ad finem,
fortiter suaviterque disponens omnia:
veni ad docendum nos viam prudentiae.

[O Wisdom,
coming forth from the mouth of the Most High,
reaching out from one end to another,
mightily and sweetly guiding all things:
Come to teach us the way of knowledge.]

— Advent Antiphon for 17 December
attributed to Benedictine monks
(*c.* sixth century AD)

Σοφία (*sophia*) is the Greek word for (and also the Greek goddess of) 'wisdom'. *Philosophy* is therefore literally 'the liking of wisdom', and has come to mean 'the use of reason and argument in seeking truth and knowledge'.

Sapientia is the Latin word for 'wisdom', hence *Homo sapiens* is Latin for 'wise man'.

Γνῶσις (*gnosis*) is the Greek word for 'knowledge'. But in English it has mutated to mean 'esoteric knowledge of spiritual mysteries'.

Scientia is the Latin word for 'knowledge'. Hence *Arbor scientia* is the 'tree of knowledge' in the Garden of Eden. But the word 'science' has been specialized (indeed, *mechanized*) to mean a branch of knowledge conducted on prescribed principles involving the systematized observation of and experiments with phenomena, especially concerned with the material and functions of the physical universe. This ingrained notion of science is an artefact of the age of analysis.

Note that the full title of *Principia*, Isaac Newton's 1687 masterwork, is *Philosophiæ naturalis Principia mathematica* (Mathematical principles of natural philosophy). 'Natural philosophy' had then been the term used to describe the subject that was the study of nature, while the word 'science' had been more specialized and referred to the Aristotelian concept of knowledge, that which was secure enough to be used as *a sure prescription for exactly how to do something.* John Locke, in *An Essay Concerning Humane Understanding* (1690) wrote that "natural philosophy is not capable of being made a science", in the sense that a prescriptive scientific method was too restrictive too encompass the study of nature — an early statement of "not all processes are algorithmic"!

I shall continue the exploration on science versus natural philosophy, in terms of analysis versus synthesis, in Chapter 7.

5.2 Αἴτιον Aristotle was concerned with γνῶσις, i.e. knowledge in its original general sense. He contended that one did not really know a 'thing' (which to Aristotle meant a *natural system*) until one had answered its 'why?' with its αἴτιον (primary or original 'cause'). In other words, Aristotle's *science* is precisely the subjects for which one knows the answers to the interrogative 'why?'.

Aristotle's original Greek term αἴτιον (*aition*) was translated into the Latin *causa*, a word which might have been appropriate initially, but which had unfortunately diverged into our contemporary notion of 'cause', as 'that which produces an effect'. The possible semantic equivocation may be avoided if one understands that the original idea had more to do with 'grounds or forms of explanation', so a more appropriate Latin rendering, in hindsight, would probably have been *explanatio*.

5.3 Whys and Wherefores The interrogative "why?" has a synonym in English in the archaic "wherefore?". One of Shakespeare's most quoted lines is often misunderstood. When Juliet asked, "O Romeo, Romeo, wherefore art thou Romeo?", she was not checking his whereabouts, but asking why he had to be, of all things, a member of the hated rival Montague clan and inherited such an unfortunate family name. 'Wherefore' means 'why' — for what purpose, reason, or end — not 'where'. Indeed, Juliet's "wherefore" line leads in to her famous "What's in a name?" speech.

While 'wherefore' has disappeared from modern English usage (other than the not-infrequent misuse of "Wherefore art ...?" as a pretentious substitution of "Where is/are ...?"), the pleonasm 'whys and wherefores' has survived. The expression is at least as old as Shakespeare (*Comedy of Errors*, 1590):

> "Was there ever any man thus beaten out of season,
> When in the why and the wherefore
>   is neither rhyme nor reason?"

Note the singular, which was once a common form: that is the way Captain Corcoran, Sir Joseph, and Josephine sing it in Gilbert and Sullivan's *HMS Pinafore* (1878):

> "Never mind the why and wherefore,
> Love can level ranks, and therefore, ..."

The usual meaning is perhaps a bit more than just that of the individual words; the redundancy is used as a way to emphasize that what is needed is not just 'a reason', but 'the *whole* reason', or '*all* the causes'.

The lyrics quoted above also provide a hint on the subtle differences between 'why' and 'wherefore'. While the words themselves are synonymous, their corresponding answers take different (but equivalent) forms. Often, an answer to a question "why?" is "because"; i.e. an answer to "Why q ?" is "q because p.", which is the conditional statement in the form "q, if p":

(1) $q \leftarrow p$.

An answer to a question "wherefore?" can also be "because", but is more congenially phrased as "therefore"; i.e. an answer to "Wherefore q?" is "p therefore q.", which is the conditional statement in the form "p, only if q":

(2) $p \rightarrow q$.

The Prolegomenon contains further musings of conditional statements, and Louie [2007] interprets their implications in the context of the etymology of the Rosen lexicon.

Aristotle's Four Causes

5.4 Relational Diagram   *Relational diagrams* in *graph-theoretic form* made their first appearance in Chapter 9 of *LI*. A simple mapping $f:A \rightarrow B$ has the relational diagram

(3)

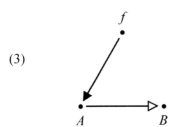

where a hollow-headed arrow denotes the *flow* from input in A to output in B, and a solid-headed arrow denotes the induction of or constraint upon this flow by the *processor* f. An unnecessarily degenerate interpretation of diagram (3) in completely mechanistic terms characterizes the flow as the *software*, and the processor as the *hardware*. The solid/hollow-headed arrow symbolism was first introduced in Section 9B of *LI*. Its form evolved a few times, and settled on this depiction in arrow diagram (3) (which is [9E.4] and [10C.1] in *LI*).

When the mapping is represented in the element-chasing version $f : a \mapsto b$ (*cf.* Remark 1.5), the relational diagram may be drawn as

(4)

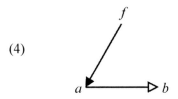

(where I have also eliminated the dots that represent the vertices of the graph).

5.5 Entailment Symbol The processor and output relationship may be characterized 'f *entails* b' (Sections 5H and 9D in *LI*). I denote this entailment as

(5) $f \vdash b$

where $\vdash$ is called the *entailment symbol*.

The graph-theoretic and entailment forms (3), (4), and (5) are *models* of the mapping, very examples of 'modelling within mathematics' as explained in Chapter 4.

5.6 Examples in the Natural and Formal Worlds A marble sculpture of Aristotle and a mapping $f : a \mapsto b$ (alternatively $f : A \to B$ and $f \in H(A, B)$) both provide excellent illustrations of Aristotle's four causes. The former is a physical object in the natural world, and the latter is a mathematical object in the formal world. We therefore seek answers to the questions "Why marble sculpture of Aristotle?" and "Why mapping?".

Recall (5.2) that Aristotle's original idea of causation had more to do with 'grounds or forms of explanation' for a natural system. It is with this sense of 'cause' that I identify components of the two examples as their four Aristotelian causes. There is no philosophical problem with this exercise for the *natural system* that is the marble sculpture. But for the *formal system* that is a mapping, it requires further justification. As I explained in the previous chapter, through the modelling relation, mappings are the formal-system embodiment, in terms of their inferential entailment, of the causal entailment in natural systems. It is through the axiom *"Every process is a mapping."* (*cf.* 4.15) that components of mappings represent the four causes.

5.7 Materia The *material cause* (of a thing) is "that out of which a thing comes into being and that which remains present in it".

Thus for the marble sculpture, the material cause is the marble, while that out of which the mapping comes to be is its *input* $a \in A$. One may choose to identify the material cause as either the input element a or the input set, the domain A.

5.8 Forma The *formal cause* is "the account of the essence and the genera to which the essence belongs".

The formal cause of the sculpture is its specifying features. The mapping's form, or its statement of essence, is the *structure* of the mapping itself as a morphism. Note that the Greek term for 'form' is $\mu o \rho \varphi \acute{\eta}$ (*morphé*), the etymological root of 'morphism'. The forms $f \in H(A, B)$ and $f : a \mapsto b$ (i.e., the entailment patterns of the morphism f that maps a general element $a \in A$ to its corresponding image $b \in B$) imply the relational diagrams (3) and (4) above; the formal cause of the mapping is thus the *ordered pair of arrows*

(6)　　　　

112

The arrows implicitly define the processor *and* the flow from input to output. The compositions of these arrows also need to follow the category rules. Alternatively, when the material cause, the exact nature of the input, is immaterial (which is the essence of relational biology), the formal cause may just be identified with the *entailment symbol*

(7)   ⊢

which implicitly defines the processor and the output. The identification of a morphism with its formal essence (6) or (7) is an interpretation of the category axioms in 'arrows-only', *i.e.*, graph-theoretic, terms.

5.9 Efficientia   The *efficient cause* is "that which brings the thing into being, the source of change, that which makes what is made, the 'production rule'".

   Thus the efficient cause of the sculpture is the sculptor, and for the mapping it is the *function* of the mapping as a processor. The difference between the formal cause and the efficient cause of a mapping is that the former is what f *is* (*i.e.*, $f \in H(A, B)$), and the latter is what f *does* (*i.e.*, $f : a \mapsto b$). One may simply identify the efficient cause as the processor itself, whence also the solid-headed arrow that originates from the processor

(8) $f \longrightarrow$

5.10 Finis   The *final cause* is "an end, the purpose of the thing, the 'for the sake of which'".

   The final cause of a sculpture of Aristotle is to commemorate him. The purpose of the mapping, why it does what it does, is its *output* $b \in B$. One may choose to *either* identify the final cause as the output element b, *or* consider b to be the entailed effect and the output set, the codomain B, to be the final cause. The Greek term τέλος (*télos*, translated into *finis* in Latin), meaning 'end' or 'purpose', covers two meanings: the end considered as the object entailed (*i.e.*, *b itself*), or the end considered as the entailment of the object (*i.e.*, the *production* of *b*). In both cases, the final cause may be identified as *b*, whence also the hollow-headed arrow that terminates on the output

(9) $$\longrightarrow b$$

One might, indeed, consider final cause to be ambiguous. It is either or both (*i.e.* the end considered as the object entailed or considered as the entailment of the object) depending on how one looks at it. In fact, an inherent ambiguity in final cause may be the underlying reason that it is an indispensable defining property of organisms. As a rational alternative to the claim that to speak of final cause is to 'preach religion', this inherent ambiguity may serve as a means to readmitting teleology back into science. I shall have more to say on the topics of ambiguity and impredicativity, and recast these in algebraic-topological terms, later on in this monograph.

5.11 Diagrams Material and formal causes are what Aristotle used to explain static things, i.e., things as they are, their *being*. Efficient and final causes are what he used to explain dynamic things, i.e. how things change and come into being, their *becoming*.

Here is a succinct summary of the four causes as components in the relational diagram of a mapping:

(10)

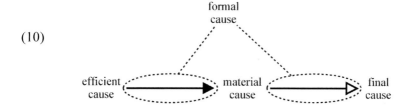

Without the material cause, the three causes are in the entailment diagram:

(11)

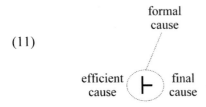

Connections in Diagrams

5.12 Ουροβόρος   The *ouroboros*, the 'tail-devouring snake', is an ancient symbol depicting a serpent (or dragon) swallowing its own tail and forming a cycle. It often represents *self-referencing* in its many guises. I now consider the possible and impossible ouroboros for a mapping.

The relational diagram

(12)

represents the *self-referencing processor*

(13) $a \longrightarrow a$

An interpretation of the arrow diagrams (12) and (13) is in order. The 'self-referencing' symbolism does not mean that one has '$a(a) = b$'. The situation represented is where a mapping $f : A \rightarrow B$ is uniquely determined by a specific element $a \in A$ in its domain. As a simple example, for a *fixed* $a_0 \in A$, consider the mapping $f : A \rightarrow \{0,1\}$ defined by $f(a_0) = 1$, and $f(a) = 0$ for $a \neq a_0$; such f is, indeed, the *characteristic mapping* $\chi_{\{a_0\}}$ (*cf.* A.3). *Each* $a_0 \in A$ determines its corresponding characteristic mapping $\chi_{\{a_0\}}$ uniquely; the identification $a \leftrightarrow \chi_{\{a\}}$ establishes a correspondence (i.e., an isomorphism) between A and a set $H(A, \{0,1\})$ of morphisms from A to $\{0,1\}$. Isomorphic objects are considered categorically the same (see the Appendix for more details). Thus arrow diagrams (12) and (13), in this example, are abstract representations of '$a \cong \chi_{\{a\}}$'. We shall encounter more examples of such self-referencing in Chapter 12, when I examine alternate realizations of (M,R)-systems.

When the loop is at the other end, one has the relational diagram

(14)

which represents the *self-inference*

(15) $\qquad a \longrightarrow\!\!\!\!\!\triangleright a$

With the same consideration for isomorphic objects as above, arrow diagrams (14) and (15) only need to represent a mapping $f : A \rightarrow A$ for which a and $f(a)$ are isomorphic (in the category concerned); in other words, since here the domain and codomain are the same object, the mapping $a \mapsto f(a)$ is an *automorphism*. This may, depending on the emphasis, be on occasion interpreted as $f : a \mapsto a$, which may in turn represent either the *identity mapping* $1_A \in H(A, A)$ or the *fixed point* a of the mapping f.

The self-entailed mapping

(16)

has no [non-self] predecessor in efficient entailment, and as such may be referred to (albeit somewhat erroneously in theological terms) as a 'Garden of Eden' object. St. Thomas Aquinas (we shall encounter him again below in 5.19) wrote in his masterwork *Summa Theologica* that "There is no case known (neither is it, indeed, possible) in which a thing is found to be the efficient cause of itself; for so it would be prior to itself, which is impossible." To Aquinas, a Garden of Eden object is necessarily entailed by a "first efficient cause" that is, of course, God. But I digress...

The self-entailed mapping (16) is, in any case, an impossibility in the category **Set**, except trivially when its domain A is either empty or a singleton set, since the existence of $f \vdash f$ would involve an infinite hierarchy of hom-sets:

(17) $$f \in H\left(A, H\left(A, H\left(A, H\left(A, \cdots\right)\right)\right)\right).$$

Vacuously, for an empty domain, since $H(\varnothing, Y) = \{\varnothing\}$ for any set Y (*cf.* A.4), the hierarchy of hom-sets in (17) collapses to $\{\varnothing\}$. Thus f is the empty mapping $\varnothing$, whence the tautology $\varnothing \vdash \varnothing$ ("Nothing comes from nothing.", as it were). If A is a singleton set, then f is clearly determined by its *only* functional value.

Note that *given* a mapping f, of course one has f itself. But this is the statement of the entailment of existence ' $f \vdash \exists f$ ' (see 5.18 below on immanent causation). The ouroboros ' $f \vdash f$ ' is a causation different in kind (see 5.15 on functional entailment). Note also that the impossibility of the existence of the nontrivial ouroboros $f \vdash f$ is a statement in naive set theory (and categories of sets with structure, which form the universe with which we are concerned). In hyperset theory [Azcel 1988], $f \vdash f$ does exist, and is precisely analogous to the prototypical hyperset equation $\Omega = \{\Omega\}$, which has a unique solution.

5.13 Sequential Composition   Relational and entailment diagrams of mappings may be composed. For example, consider the two mappings $f \in H(A, B)$ and $g \in H(X, A)$: *the codomain of g is the domain of f.* Thus

(18) $\qquad X \xrightarrow{\ g\ } A \xrightarrow{\ f\ } B$.

Let the element chases be $f : a \mapsto b$ (whence $f \vdash b$) and $g : x \mapsto a$ (whence $g \vdash a$): *the final cause of g is the material cause of f.* The relational diagrams of the two mappings connect at the common node a as

(19)

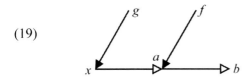

This *sequential composition* of relational diagrams represents the composite mapping $f \circ g \in H(X, B)$ with $f \circ g : x \mapsto b$, and has the abbreviated relational diagram

118

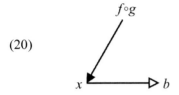

(20)

whence the corresponding entailment diagram is

(21) $f \circ g \vdash b$

Note that in these diagrams (20) and (21) for the single efficient cause $f \circ g$, both efficient causes f and g, as well as the (final) final cause b, are accounted for.

5.14 Hierarchical Composition   Now consider two mappings $f \in H(A,B)$ and $g \in H(X,H(A,B))$: *the codomain of g contains f*. Because of this 'containment', the mapping g may be considered to occupy a higher 'hierarchical level' than the mapping f. Let the element chases be $f : a \mapsto b$ (whence $f \vdash b$) and $g : x \mapsto f$ (whence $g \vdash f$): *the final cause of g is the efficient cause of f*. Then one has the *hierarchical composition* of relational diagrams

(22)

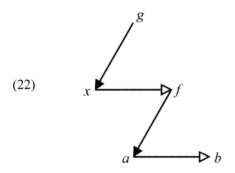

with the corresponding composition of entailment diagrams

(23) $g \vdash f \vdash b$.

A comparison of (21) and (23) shows that sequential composition and hierarchical composition are different in kind: they are *formally* different.

While the diagrams (22) and (23) *may* contract into something similar in form to (20) and (21), namely

(24)

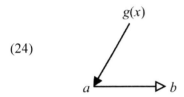

and

(25) $g(x) \vdash b$,

in these abbreviated forms the entailed efficient cause f becomes 'hidden'. Since the accounting (and tracking) of *all* efficient causes in an entailment system is crucial in our synthesis in relational biology (more on this in later chapters), one needs to preserve every solid-headed arrow and every entailment symbol $\vdash$. So there will not be any abbreviation of hierarchical compositions.

5.15 Functional Entailment $g \vdash f$ is a 'different' mode of entailment, in the sense that it entails a mapping: *the final cause of one morphism is the efficient cause of another morphism.* It is given the name of *functional entailment* (Section 5I of *LI*). When one is concerned not with *what entails*, but only *what is entailed*, one may simply use the notation

120

(26) $\vdash f$.

Note that there is nothing in category theory that mandates an absolute distinction between sets and mappings. Indeed, in the cartesian closed category **Set** (*cf.* A.53 and Example A.19(iii)), one has

(27) $H\left(X,H(A,B)\right) \cong H\left(X \times A, B\right);$

thus $g \in H\left(X,H(A,B)\right)$ that entails a mapping and has a hom-set as codomain may be considered equivalently as the isomorphic $g \in H\left(X \times A, B\right)$ that has a simple set as codomain. Functional entailment is therefore not *categorically* different; it is, however, *formally* different (as concluded previously). It warrants a new name because it plays an important role in the 'closure to efficient causation' characterization of life (which, incidentally, is the *raison d'être* of this monograph: much more on this later).

5.16 Other Modes of Connection Two mappings, with the appropriate domains and codomains, may be connected at different common nodes. We have already seen two:

(28)

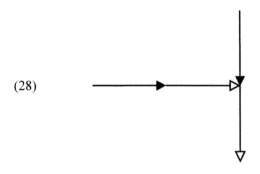

is the sequential composition (19), and

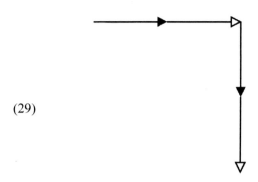

(29)

is the hierarchical composition (22). These two connections are the only *compositions* of two mappings. For a connection to be a composition, the hollow-headed arrow of one mapping must terminate on a node of the other mapping: the first mapping must *entail* something in the second. So, after (28) and (29), the only remaining possibility of composition is the connection

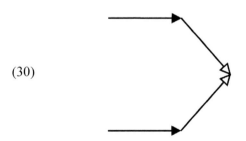

(30)

But this configuration simply shows two mappings with a common codomain, and the mappings do not compose.

The connection

(31)

is degenerate, because when the efficient causes of two mappings coincide, so must their domains and codomains (since a mapping uniquely determines its domain and codomain; *cf.* 1.8). Thus the geometry of (31), with two solid-headed arrows originating from the same vertex, is not allowed as an entailment pattern.

The connection

(32)

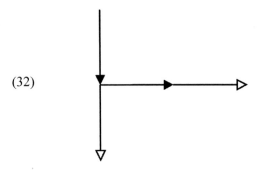

shows that the *domain* of one mapping consists of mappings; i.e., the material cause of one is the efficient cause of the other. The two mappings have common features, but this entailment geometry is not a composition.

The final possibility, the 'crossed-path' connection

(33)
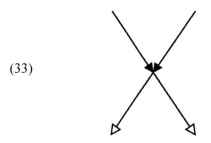

is bad notation, since it is unclear which solid-headed arrow is paired with which hollow-headed arrow. So to avoid confusion it should be resolved into two disjoint diagrams thus

(34)
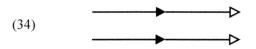

Note that the patterns (30) and (32) may also be resolved without loss of entailment structure into two disjoint diagrams (34).

5.17 Multiple Connections and Resolution It is possible that two mappings are connected at more than one common node. The relational diagram, however, may be resolved into single connections for analysis. For example, the relational diagram

124

(35)

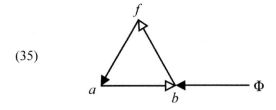

may be resolved into the hierarchical composition

(36)

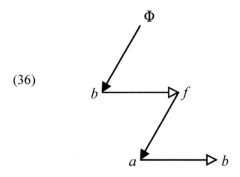

while preserving the entailment

(37) $\Phi \vdash f \vdash b$.

Note that the phrase *while preserving the entailment* is important here. This is because diagram (35) my also be resolved into the sequential composition

(38)

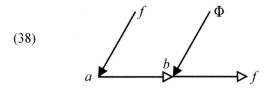

which (*cf.* sequential composition 5.13 above) abbreviates to the relational diagram

(39)

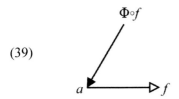

whence the corresponding entailment diagram is

(40) $\Phi \circ f \vdash f$.

Comparing (37) with (40), one sees that the latter loses one entailment in the process. Thus one must be careful in a resolution analysis to preserve hierarchical compositions.

Similarly, the relational diagram

(41)

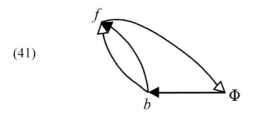

may be resolved into the hierarchical composition

126

(42)

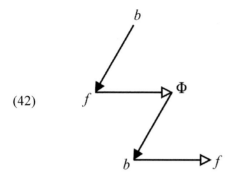

while preserving the entailment

(43) $b \vdash \Phi \vdash f$.

Thus the union of these two examples, the relational diagram

(44)

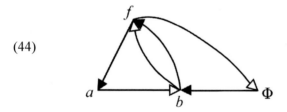

may be resolved into the *hierarchical cycle* (i.e. cycle with hierarchical compositions)

(45)

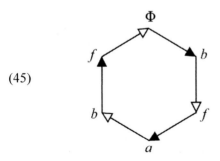

with the cyclic entailment

(46)

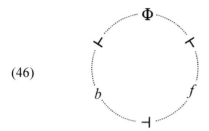

I shall explain entailment cycles in the next chapter, and I shall have a lot more to say on this particular entailment system (44)–(46) in Chapter 11.

In beata spe

5.18 Immanent Causation Now let us consider the 'inverse problem' of entailment. If an object b is entailed, then *there exists* a morphism f such that $f \vdash b$ (which implicitly implies the existence of a set A, the domain of f, whence $f \in H(A,B)$, and the existence of an element $a \in A$ such that $f : a \mapsto b$). In other words, *entailment itself entails the existence of an efficient cause.* In particular, if a morphism $f \in H(A,B)$ is functionally entailed, then *there exists* a morphism $g \in H(X, H(A,B))$ (which implicitly implies the existence of a set X and an element $x \in X$) such that $g : x \mapsto f$. Symbolically, this situation may be summarized

(47) $\quad (\vdash f) \vdash (\exists g : g \vdash f).$

The entailment of the *existence* of something (often on a higher hierarchical level) is termed *immanent causation* (Section 9F of *LI*) in philosophy. There are many different nuances in the various definitions of

128

immanent causation in the philosophical literature, but they all involve 'an external agent causing something to exist', hence *ontological* in addition to *epistemological* considerations.

5.19 St. Thomas Aquinas Ontological considerations necessitate an escape from the Newtonian trap of mechanistic simplification, in which epistemology entails and hence swallows ontology. In the pre-Newtonian science that is *natural philosophy*, a natural system is studied in terms of its *existence* and *essence*. See Chapter 17 of *EL* for a succinct discussion. The equation therein

CONCRETE SYSTEM = EXISTENCE + ESSENCE

is something that could have come directly from St. Thomas Aquinas (1225–1274). Aquinas's writings include *De Principiis Naturae* (The Principles of Nature) and *De Ente et Essentia* (On Being and Essence), which explain Aristotelian (and post-Aristotelian) physics and metaphysics. Apart from his commentaries on Aristotle, Aquinas did not write anything else of a strict philosophical nature. But his theological works are full of philosophical insights that would qualify him as one of the greatest natural philosophers.

Before Aquinas, theologians like St. Augustine placed their activities within a Platonic context. Aquinas absorbed large portions of Aristotelian doctrine into Christianity. It is, of course, not my purpose here to digress into a comparison between Plato and Aristotle. With gross simplification, one may say that Plato took his stand on idealistic principles, so that the general implies the particular, while Aristotle based his investigations on the physical world, so that the particular also predicts the general. Plato's method is essentially deductive, while Aristotle's is both inductive and deductive. Stated otherwise, for Plato the world takes its shape from ideas, whereas for Aristotle ideas take their shape from the world (*cf.* Natural Law discussed in Chapter 4).

Aristotle's teleological view of nature may be summarized as "Nature does nothing in vain." Using this regulative principle, Aristotle realized that the understanding of function and purpose is crucial to the understanding of nature. Aquinas elaborated on Aristotle's science of *ens qua ens* (beings in their capacities of being), and developed his own metaphysical insight in so doing. To Aquinas, the key factor of any 'reality as a reality' was its existence, but existence was not just being present. A being is not a being by virtue of its matter, but a being of what it is, i.e. its essence. This constitutive principle is called *esse*, or 'the act of existing'. Aquinas frequently used the Aristotelian dictum *"vita viventibus est esse"* ("for living things, to be is to live").

One can see in these Aristotelian and Thomastic principles the germ of relational biology: a natural system is alive not because of its matter, but because of the constitutive organization of its phenomenological entailment. The *esse* of an organism is this special entailment that shall be my subject of investigation later.

5.20 Exemplary Causation   With the distinction between the concepts of essence and existence, Aquinas added a fifth cause, called *exemplary cause*. It is defined as "the causal influence exercised by a model or an exemplar on the operation of an agent", i.e., 'that which entails'. In terms of our first example, the marble sculpture of Aristotle, before the sculpture is realized, the *model* of the sculpture must already be in the mind of the efficient cause, the sculptor. The *bauplan* in the mind of the agent is the exemplary cause. In terms of our second example, the mapping $f : a \mapsto b$, when it is functionally entailed, say when $\exists g : g \vdash f$, the entailing mapping g is the exemplary cause.

5.21 Michelangelo

The Artist

Nothing the greatest can conceive
That every marble block doth not confine
Within itself: and only its design
The hand that follows intellect can achieve.

The ill I flee, the good that I believe,
In thee, fair lady, lofty and divine,
Thus hidden lie; and so that death be mine,
Art, of desired success, doth me bereave.

Love is not guilty, then, nor thy fair face,
Nor fortune, cruelty, nor great disdain,
Of my disgrace, nor chance nor destiny,
If in they heart both death and love find place
At the same time, and if my humble brain,
Burning, can nothing draw but death from thee.

— Michelangelo Buonarroti
Sonnet 151 (composed *c*.1538–1544)
Translated by Henry Wadsworth Longfellow

As expounded in his sonnet, Michelangelo contended that the sculpture already existed in a block of marble. 'To sculpt' meant 'to take away', not 'to add'. His philosophy is that the efficient cause, realized as the sculptor's hand, "follows intellect" and takes out the superfluous surroundings to liberate the idea that is already extant. So the exemplary cause, instead of being the *bauplan* in the mind of the agent, is according to Michelangelo the hidden sculpture imprisoned in matter. Michelangelo's alternate description, however, still fits the requirement of 'that which entails'.

6

Topology

Network Topology

For a collection of mappings in a formal system, their compositions may give rise to a very complicated pattern of inferential entailment in a network. Here is an example of what a relatively simple one may look like:

(1)

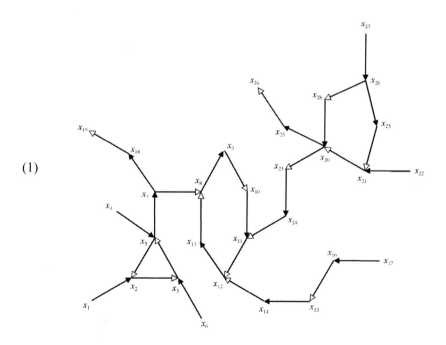

Recall (5.13 and 5.14) that two mappings compose sequentially when the final cause of one is the material cause of the other, while two mappings compose hierarchically when the final cause of one is the efficient cause of the other. The isomorphism between an efficient cause and its representation as a solid-headed arrow (5.9) provides an important link between a formal system and its relation diagram in graph-theoretic form:

6.1 Theorem *A network G of inferential entailment in a formal system contains a particular efficient cause f if and only if the path of G in the relational diagram contains the solid-headed arrow that corresponds to f.*

Because of the isomorphism, I shall use the same symbol G to denote both the network of inferential entailment and its relational diagram, and both are referred to as an *entailment network*.

As we discussed in 5.6, the axiom "*Every process is a mapping.*" allows us to identify components of mappings with the Aristotelian causes. In what follows, the 'isomorphism' between an efficient cause of a natural process and the corresponding efficient cause of its formal mapping that is the solid-headed arrow is invoked implicitly. Thus through the modelling relation, a description of a property of functional entailment either causally in a natural system or inferentially in its formal-system model is extended dually to the other domain.

A collection of interconnecting edges is called a *graph*, and called a *directed graph* (*digraph* for short) when every edge has an associated direction. Thus the relational diagram in graph-theoretic form of a formal system is a digraph. The digraph topology of relational diagrams is the subject of this chapter.

6.2 Analysis situs Topology is a nonmetric and nonquantitative mathematical discipline sometimes called 'rubber-sheet geometry'. Its propositions hold as well for objects made of rubber, under deformations, as for the rigid figures from common metric geometry. It deals with fundamental geometric properties that are unaffected when one stretches, shrinks, twists, bends, or otherwise distorts an object's size and shape (but without gluing or tearing). Another name for topology is *analysis situs*: analysis of position. Topology deals with different problems and ideas in several different branches, including general (point-set) topology, differential topology, and algebraic topology. Note that algebraic topology is the inspiration of category theory, which is the mathematical language of Robert Rosen's modeling relation (*cf.* Chapter 4).

Topology began with a paper on the puzzle of the Königsberg bridges by Leonhard Euler (1707–1783), entitled *Solutio problematis ad geometriam situs pertinentis* ("The solution of a problem relating to the geometry of position"). The title indicates that Euler was aware that he was dealing with a different type of geometry where distance was not relevant. The paper was presented to the Academy of Sciences at St. Petersburg in 1735. It appeared in the 1736 edition of *Commentant Academiae Scientiarum Imperialis Petropolitanae*, although the volume was not actually published until 1741. An English translation of the paper is reprinted in Euler [1736].

Euler described the problem thus:

"The problem, which I understand is quite well known, is stated as follows: In the town of Königsberg in Prussia there is an island A, called 'Kneiphof', with the two branches of the river (Pregel) flowing around it, as shown in Figure 1.

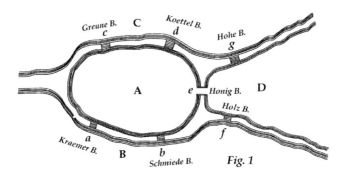

Figure 1. The seven Königsberg bridges.

134

There are seven bridges, a, b, c, d, e, f and g, crossing the two branches. The question is whether a person can plan a walk in such a way that he will cross each of these bridges once but not more than once. I was told that while some denied the possibility of doing this and others were in doubt, there were none who maintained that it was actually possible. On the basis of the above I formulated the following very general problem for myself: Given any configuration of the river and the branches into which it may divide, as well as any number of bridges, to determine whether or not it is possible to cross each bridge exactly once."

6.3 Graph Theory The puzzle of the Königsberg bridges is a classic exercise in topology, a 'network problem'. Network topology is more commonly known as *graph theory*. (Two good references on graph theory are Trudeau [1993] and Gross & Yellen [1999], to which the reader may refer for further exploration on the subject. Note, however, that some terminology has not been standardized, so the definitions that I present in what follows may differ from another author's usage.) Euler's method of solution (recast in modern terminology here) was to replace the land areas by *vertices*, and the bridges by *edges* connecting these vertices:

(2)

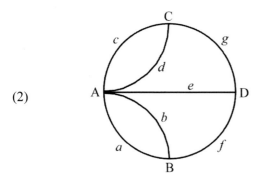

The resulting topological object is called a *graph*, in which only the configuration of the vertices and edges in terms of their relative ordering and connections is important, but not the distances. Graph (2) is, indeed, Euler's formal-system *model* of the natural system of the Königsberg bridges. The problem of crossing the bridges is then *encoded* into that of traversing the graph with a pencil without lifting it from the paper, in one continuous trace of the edges, passing along each edge exactly once. A graph for which this is possible is called *traversable*, and the continuous trace is now known as an *Eulerian path*. Stated otherwise, the geometric problem of crossing the Königsberg bridges now becomes a graph-theoretic one: to determine whether graph (2) is traversable.

A (*graph*) *edge* may be considered as an unordered pair of vertices that are its end points. For example, in (2) the edge f is the unordered pair of vertices $\{B, D\}$. When the two end points are identical, *i.e.* when an edge joins a vertex to itself, the edge is called a *self-loop*. Graph (2) has no self-loops. Note that the presence of self-loops does not affect the continuity of a trace of the edges — a graph with self-loops is traversable if and only if the graph reduced from eliminating all the self-loops is traversable.

A *path* in a graph is a continuous trace of edges. In other words, a path from vertex A to vertex B in a graph G is a consecutive sequence of edges $\{v_0, v_1\}, \{v_1, v_2\}, \{v_2, v_3\}, ..., \{v_{n-1}, v_n\}$ (where each edge $\{v_{i-1}, v_i\}$ is in G) with $v_0 = A$ and $v_n = B$. What we have in (2) is more properly called a *connected* graph, a graph in which there is a path from any vertex to any other vertex. But since we are only concerned with the topic of traversability here, we need only deal with connected graphs for now: a disconnected graph is clearly not traversable.

Multiple edges are two or more edges joining the same two vertices in a graph. In (2), a and b are multiple edges, since they are both $\{A, B\}$. A *simple graph* is a graph that contains no self-loops and no multiple edges. A *multigraph* is a graph in which multiple edges, but no self-loops, are permitted. Euler's graph of the Königsberg bridges in (2) is a multigraph. A *pseudograph* is a graph in which both self-loops and multiple edges are permitted.

136

The number of edges meeting at a vertex is called its *degree*. Note that a self-loop contributes 2 to the degree of its (only) vertex. A vertex is called *odd* or *even* according to its degree. Since an edge connects two vertices, it follows that the sum of the degrees over all vertices in a graph is even, whence a graph must have an even number of odd vertices.

Euler reasoned that, with the possible exception of the initial vertex and the final vertex, each vertex of a traversable graph had to have even degree. This was because in the middle of a journey, when passing through a land area, one had to enter on one bridge and exit on a different bridge; so each visit to a land area added two to the degree of the corresponding vertex. In the beginning of the journey, the traveler required only one bridge to exit; and at the end, only one bridge to enter — so these two vertices might be odd. If, however, the point of departure coincided with the point of arrival, then this vertex would also have even degree. A path is *closed* when final vertex = initial vertex. A closed Eulerian path is called an *Eulerian circuit*.

Thus Euler discovered that if a graph has only even vertices, then it is traversable; also, the journey may begin at any vertex, and after the trace the journey ends at the same initial vertex. If the graph has exactly two odd vertices, then it is still traversable, but it is not possible to return to the starting point: the journey must begin at one odd vertex and end at the other. If the graph has more than two odd vertices, then it is not traversable. The general principle is that, for a positive integer n, if the graph contains $2n$ odd vertices, then it will require exactly n distinct journeys to traverse it.

In the graph (2) of the Königsberg bridges, all four vertices are odd; the graph is therefore not traversable. In other words, Euler provided a mathematical proof, as some of the Königsbergers had empirically verified, that a walk crossing each of the seven bridges exactly once was impossible.

In sum, Euler proved the following

6.4 Theorem

(*a*) *A graph possesses an Eulerian circuit if and only if its vertices are all of even degree.*

(*b*) *A graph possesses an Eulerian path if and only if it has either zero or two vertices of odd degree.*

6.5 Digraph A graph in which every edge has an associated direction (*i.e.*, each edge has an initiating vertex and a terminating vertex) is called a *directed graph*, or *digraph* for short. In a digraph, a (*directed*) *edge* may be considered as an *ordered* pair of vertices that are its end points. For example, in the relational diagram

(3)

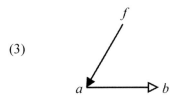

representing the mapping $f: a \mapsto b$, the solid-headed arrow is a directed edge represented by the ordered pair of vertices (f, a), and the hollow-headed arrow is a directed edge represented by the ordered pair of vertices (a, b). In a directed graph, the degree of a vertex has to be split into two entities. The number of edges terminating at a vertex v (*i.e.*, inwardly directed edges on v, or directed edges of the form $(\bullet, v)$) is the *indegree* of v. The number of edges initiating from a vertex v (*i.e.*, outwardly directed edges on v, or directed edges of the form $(v, \bullet)$) is the *outdegree* of v.

Traversability for a digraph has an additional requirement: the underlying (undirected) graph itself has to be traversable first, but the Eulerian path also has to follow the directions of the edges. Explicitly, one has the

6.6 Theorem

(a) *A directed graph possesses an Eulerian circuit if and only if the indegree of every vertex is equal to its outdegree.*

(b) *A directed graph possesses an Eulerian path if and only if the indegree of every vertex, with the possible exception of two vertices, is equal to its outdegree. For these two possibly exceptional vertices, the indegree of one is one smaller than its outdegree, and the indegree of the other is one larger than its outdegree.*

Traversability of Relational Diagrams

6.7 Ordered-Pairwise Construction While an entailment network is a digraph, the reverse is not true: a general digraph is not necessarily the entailment network of a formal system. The partitioning of directed edges into solid-headed and hollow-headed arrows in a relational diagram comes with stringent requirements on the topology of an entailment network. In particular, the ordered-pairwise construction of solid-headed and hollow-headed arrows in the formal cause diagram

(4)

predicates that in an entailment network G of a formal system, a solid-headed arrow must be followed by a hollow-headed arrow. This also implies that the number of solid-headed arrows and hollow-headed arrows in G must be equal (therefore the total number of edges must be even).

6.8 Four Degrees of a Vertex In an entailment network, the degree of a vertex v has to be split into four entities: the number of inwardly directed solid-headed arrows, the number of inwardly directed hollow-headed arrows, the number of outwardly directed solid-headed arrows, and the number of outwardly directed hollow-headed arrows. I shall denote these four numbers $\varepsilon_i(v)$, $\tau_i(v)$, $\varepsilon_o(v)$, and $\tau_o(v)$, respectively. (The ε is for the efficient cause that is the solid-headed arrow, and the τ is for the telos, final cause, that is the hollow-headed arrow; the i and o are for 'in' and 'out'.) The indegree of v is therefore $\varepsilon_i(v) + \tau_i(v)$, and the outdegree $\varepsilon_o(v) + \tau_o(v)$.

The requirement that a solid-headed arrow must be followed by a corresponding hollow-headed arrow says

(5) $\qquad \varepsilon_i(v) = \tau_o(v) \quad$ for all $v \in G$.

There are some other relations among the four degrees. One must have

(6) $\qquad \sum_v \varepsilon_i(v) = \sum_v \varepsilon_o(v)$

(where the sum is over all vertices of the graph; i.e. $\sum_{v \in G}$); this sum is simply the total number of solid-headed arrows. Similarly, the sum

(7) $\qquad \sum_v \tau_i(v) = \sum_v \tau_o(v)$

is the total number of hollow-headed arrows. Since the entailment network G of a formal system must contain the same number of solid-headed and hollow-headed arrows (it also follows from the equality(5)), the four sums appearing in (6) and (7) are in fact all equal. If I call the common value of this four sums n, then the total number of edges (arrows) in the graph G is $2n$, and the sum of the degrees over all vertices in G is $4n$.

6.9 Example To fix ideas, consider the relational diagram

(8)

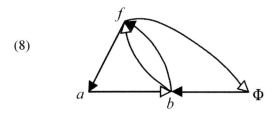

140

which we have met in the previous chapter (diagram (44) of Chapter 5). It has four vertices and six edges — three each of solid-headed and hollow-headed arrows. The sum of the degrees over all vertices is twice the number of edges, hence 12. Vertices a and Φ have indegree 1 and outdegree 1, while vertices b and f have indegree 2 and outdegree 2. Thus by Theorem 6.6(a), as a digraph, (8) is traversable and has an Eulerian circuit.

As a relational diagram, (8) may have the degrees of its vertices enumerated thus:

(9)
$$\begin{cases} \left(\varepsilon_i(a),\tau_i(a),\varepsilon_o(a),\tau_o(a)\right)=(1,0,0,1) \\ \left(\varepsilon_i(b),\tau_i(b),\varepsilon_o(b),\tau_o(b)\right)=(1,1,1,1) \\ \left(\varepsilon_i(f),\tau_i(f),\varepsilon_o(f),\tau_o(f)\right)=(1,1,1,1) \\ \left(\varepsilon_i(\Phi),\tau_i(\Phi),\varepsilon_o(\Phi),\tau_o(\Phi)\right)=(0,1,1,0) \end{cases},$$

with

(10) $$n=\sum_v \varepsilon_i(v)=\sum_v \tau_i(v)=\sum_v \varepsilon_o(v)=\sum_v \tau_o(v)=3.$$

6.10 Further Constraints A relational diagram has more constraints on its topology than the equal number of solid-headed and hollow-headed arrows. In 5.16, I explained why the bifurcation

(11)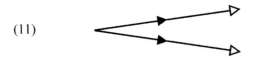

is a forbidden degenerate pattern. This means a vertex in a relational diagram G may have at most one solid-headed arrow initiated from it; i.e. for each $v \in G$,

(12) $$\varepsilon_o(v)=0 \text{ or } 1.$$

Likewise, the 'crossed-path' connection

(13)

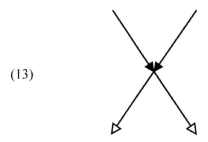

is disallowed, whence there cannot be more than one solid-headed arrow terminating at a vertex. Thus for each $v \in G$,

(14) $\varepsilon_i(v) = 0$ or 1.

6.11 Alternating Arrows   When tracing a path in a relational diagram G, one, of course, must follow the direction of the arrows. In addition, when tracing *functional entailment paths* in the network, a proper path must consist of an alternating sequence of solid-headed and hollow-headed arrows. So, for traversability *as a digraph*, Theorem 6.6 says that (*a*) G has an Eulerian circuit if and only if

(15) $\varepsilon_i(v) + \tau_i(v) = \varepsilon_o(v) + \tau_o(v)$ for all $v \in G$,

and (*b*) G has an Eulerian circuit if and only if the equality (15) of indegree and outdegree holds with one possibly pair of exceptional vertices v_1 and v_2, for with

(16) $$\begin{cases} \left[\varepsilon_o(v_1) + \tau_o(v_1)\right] - \left[\varepsilon_i(v_1) + \tau_i(v_1)\right] = 1 \\ \left[\varepsilon_i(v_2) + \tau_i(v_2)\right] - \left[\varepsilon_o(v_2) + \tau_o(v_2)\right] = 1 \end{cases}.$$

142

Since the condition $\varepsilon_i(v) = \tau_o(v)$ for all $v \in G$ must be satisfied by any relational diagram, traversable or not (equation (5) above), one has the corresponding, more specific, theorem for traversability *as a relational diagram*:

6.12 Theorem

(*a*) *A relational diagram (of the entailment pattern of a formal system) possesses an Eulerian circuit if and only if*

(17) $\qquad \varepsilon_i(v) = \tau_o(v)$ *and* $\tau_i(v) = \varepsilon_o(v)$ *for all* $v \in G$.

(*b*) *A relational diagram possesses an Eulerian path if and only if the equalities in* (17) *holds with the possible exception of two vertices* v_1 *and* v_2. *For these two possibly exceptional vertices,*

(18) $\qquad \begin{cases} \varepsilon_o(v_1) - \tau_i(v_1) = 1 \\ \tau_i(v_2) - \varepsilon_o(v_2) = 1 \end{cases}.$

The Topology of Functional Entailment Paths

6.13 Tree   The mappings in an entailment network may compose in such a way that no paths are closed, so that the arrows connect in branches of a tree; for example

(19)

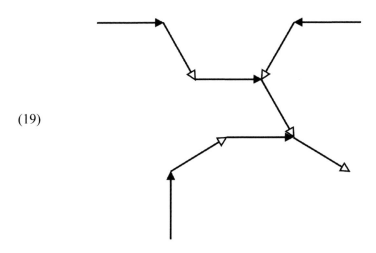

Note that 'cycles' may form in the non-directed graph sense, for example

(20)

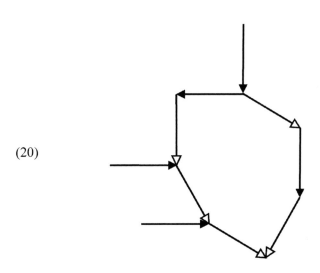

144

But since one must follow the direction of the arrows when tracing a path, a 'cycle' with some reversed arrows is *not* a cycle, *i.e.* not a closed path in the digraph sense of a relational diagram.

6.14 Closed Path of Material Causation   A path in a relation diagram *is* closed, *i.e.* forms cycles, however, if the arrows involved have a consistent direction. When the compositions involved in the cycle are all sequential, one has a *closed path of material causation*. For example, when three mappings have a cyclic permutation of domains and codomains,

(21) $f \in H(A,B), \quad g \in H(B,C), \quad h \in H(C,A),$

their sequential compositions result in a cycle consisting of *hollow-headed arrows entirely* (with solid-headed arrows peripheral to the cycle):

(22)

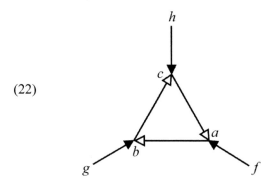

The three mappings compose to

(23) $h \circ g \circ f : A \to A,$

which, as we saw in 5.12, may, depending on the emphasis, be interpreted as the automorphism

(24) $a \cong h \circ g \circ f(a),$

the *identity mapping*

(25) $h \circ g \circ f = 1_A \in H(A, A),$

or the *fixed point* a of the mapping $h \circ g \circ f$,

(26) $h \circ g \circ f(a) = a.$

Cyclic permutation of the three mappings also gives

(27) $f \circ h \circ g : B \to B$

and

(28) $g \circ f \circ h : C \to C,$

with the corresponding automorphism, identity mapping, and fixed point interpretations in their appropriate domains.

It is easy to see that the number of mappings involved in a closed path of material causation may be any finite number (instead of three in the example), and the above discussion may be extended accordingly. Thus a closed path of material causation is formally analogous to the simple relation diagram with a self-loop

(29)

146

6.15 Closed Path with Exactly One Efficient Cause When *all but one* of the compositions involved in a cycle are sequential, with the exception a hierarchical composition, one has the following situation:

(30)

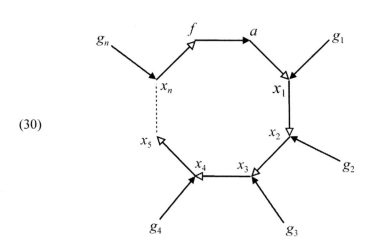

The mappings

(31)
$$f(a) = x_1 \text{ with } g_1(x_1) = x_2, \ g_2(x_2) = x_3, \ ...,$$
$$g_{n-1}(x_{n-1}) = x_n, \text{ and } g_n(x_n) = f$$

compose to

(32) $g_n \circ g_{n-1} \circ \cdots \circ g_1 \circ f(a) = f,$

or

(33) $\Phi \circ f(a) = f \text{ where } \Phi = g_n \circ g_{n-1} \circ \cdots \circ g_1.$

Thus the cycle (30) may be abbreviated as

(34)

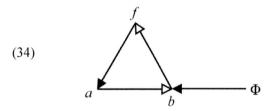

which is one of the multiple connections we encountered in 5.17. Note that *only one* mapping (namely f) is functionally entailed in this topology. Stated otherwise, in this cycle there is *exactly one solid-headed arrow.*

6.16 Closed Path of Efficient Causation   When *two* *or* *more* compositions involved in the cycle are hierarchical, one has a *closed path of efficient causation.* In other words, a closed path of efficient causation is an entailment cycle that contains two or more efficient causes.

For example, consider three mappings from a hierarchy of hom-sets,

$$\begin{aligned} f &\in H(A,B), \\ g &\in H(C,H(A,B)), \\ h &\in H(D,H(C,H(A,B))) \end{aligned}$$
(35)

with entailments

$$\begin{aligned} f &\vdash b, \\ g &\vdash f, \\ h &\vdash g. \end{aligned}$$
(36)

148

Their hierarchical compositions form the relational diagram

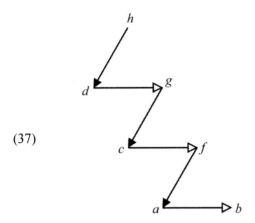

(37)

Now suppose there is a correspondence between the sets B and $H\big(D, H\big(C, H(A, B)\big)\big)$ — I shall explain one of the many ways to achieve this correspondence in the next section, and some alternate ways in later chapters. Then an isomorphic identification between b and h may be made, whence $f \vdash b$ may be replaced by

(38) $f \vdash h,$

and a cycle of hierarchical compositions results

(39)

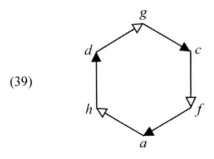

with the corresponding cyclic entailment pattern

(40)

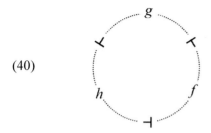

Formally, one has the

6.17 Definition A *hierarchical cycle* is the relational diagram in graph-theoretic form of a closed path of efficient causation.

Note that in a hierarchical cycle (for example, arrow diagram (39)), there are *two or more solid-headed arrows* (since a closed path of efficient causation is defined as a cycle containing *two or more* hierarchical compositions). Because of Definition 6.17, that a hierarchical cycle is the formal-system representation (i.e. encoding) of a closed path of efficient causation in a natural system, trivially one has the following

6.18 Lemma *A natural system has no closed path of efficient causation if and only if none of its models has hierarchical cycles.*

Stated contrapositively, the statement is

6.19 Corollary *A natural system has a model containing a hierarchical cycle if and only if it has a closed path of efficient causation.*

Because of this equivalence of a closed path of efficient causation in a natural system and a hierarchical cycle in its model, the term *hierarchical cycle*, although defined for formal systems, sometimes gets decoded back as an alternate description of the closed path of efficient causation itself. In other words, one may speak of a hierarchical cycle of inferential entailments as well as a hierarchical cycle of causal entailments. Thus 'hierarchical cycle' joins the ranks of 'set', 'system', etc., as words that inhabit both the realms of natural systems and formal systems.

Algebraic Topology

6.20 Homology   A hierarchical cycle may be constructed in terms of a sequence of algebraic-topological hom-sets $\{H_n\}$. Define

(41) $H_0 = B$,

(42) $H_1 = H(A, B)$,

and

(43) $H_n = H\left(H_{n-2}, H_{n-1}\right)$ for $n \geq 2$.

Analogous to modular arithmetic $\mathbb{Z}/\!\equiv\, = \mathbb{Z}_m$ (*cf.* 1.15), the infinite sequence $\{H_n\}$ reduces to m members $\{H_0, H_1, ..., H_{m-1}\}$ if one has

(44) $H_n \cong H_j$ if $n \equiv j \pmod{m}$, for $n \geq m$ and $j = 0, 1, ..., m-1$;

or, equivalently,

(45) $H_{mk} \cong H_0$, $H_{mk+1} \cong H_1$, ..., $H_{mk+m-1} \cong H_{m-1}$, for $k = 0, 1, 2, ...$

or

(46) $H_n \cong H_{n-m}$ for $n \geq m$.

This semantic correspondence is an 'infinity-to-m hierarchical projection' that closes the hierarchical cycle.

The isomorphism $H_n \cong H_{n-m}$ is something that cannot be derived from *syntax* alone. One needs to know something *about* the maps involved, *i.e.* the *semantics*, to reach this identification. For example, suppose $m = 3$ (as in the three-mapping example in the previous section). One way to establish $H_n \cong H_{n-3}$ is as follows. An $x \in H_{n-3}$ defines an *evaluation map* $\hat{x} \in H(H_{n-1}, H_{n-2})$ by

(47) $\hat{x}(z) = z(x) \in H_{n-2}$ for $z \in H_{n-1}$.

If one imposes the *semantic* requirement that $\hat{x}$ be *monomorphic*, then the existence of the inverse map

(48) $\hat{x}^{-1} \in H(H_{n-2}, H_{n-1}) = H_n$

is entailed, whence

(49) $x \mapsto \hat{x}^{-1}$

is the embedding that allows $x \in H_{n-3}$ to be interpreted as a map $x \cong \hat{x}^{-1} \in H_n$. Again, the identification $x \cong \hat{x}^{-1}$ is something that can only be reached through semantics and not syntax alone.

152

With the hom-sets and mappings constructed thus, one has, given $x \in H_{n-3}$, $y \in H_{n-2}$, and $z \in H_{n-1}$, the simple cyclic entailment pattern

(50)

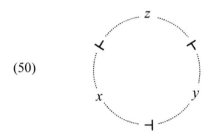

and the relational diagram

(51)

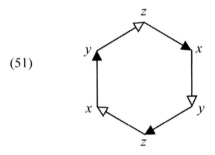

which one may also present in a 'dual' circular element-chasing version

(52)

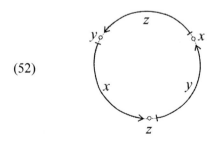

6.21 Helical Hierarchy The infinity-to-three hierarchical projection is summarized succinctly in the following graph of helical hierarchy:

(53)

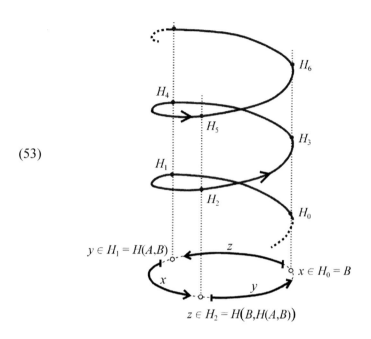

The helix has three (or m for the general case) hierarchical levels per turn in an apparent ever-increasing infinitely sequence. But the isomorphism of hom-sets means that

(54) $H_{3k} \cong H_0, \quad H_{3k+1} \cong H_1, \quad H_{3k+2} \cong H_2, \quad \text{for} \quad k = 0,1,2,...$

so there are in fact only *three* (m) distinct maps:

(55) $\begin{cases} x \in H_0 = B \\ y \in H_1 = H(A,B) \\ z \in H_2 = H(B, H(A,B)) \end{cases}$

154

with their entailment pattern in cyclic permutation, shown in diagram (53) as the bottom circle that is the vertical projection of the helix. The bottom circle is, of course, simply the element-chasing digraph (52).

From diagrams (51) and (52), one sees that for $x \in H_0 = B$, $y \in H_1 = H(A,B)$, and $z \in H_2 = H(B,H(A,B))$

$$
\begin{aligned}
x \circ z \circ y &\in H(H_2, H_2), \\
(56) \quad z \circ y \circ x &\in H(H_1, H_1), \quad \text{and} \\
y \circ x \circ z &\in H(H_0, H_0)
\end{aligned}
$$

are automorphisms, which may also, depending on the context, be interpreted as identity morphisms or fixed points in the appropriate objects. Note, in particular, that for this closed path of efficient causation one may have the identity morphism

$$
(57) \qquad x \circ z \circ y = 1_{H_2} = 1_{H(B,H(A,B))};
$$

compare this with $h \circ g \circ f = 1_A \in H(A,A)$ in (25) for three mappings in a closed path of material causation — note in particular the different hierarchical levels to which the morphisms belong.

I note in passing that the algebraic 'infinity-to-m hierarchical projection' and the geometric 'helical hierarchy' just introduced have a topological analogue. In complex analysis, there is a general method for turning a many-valued 'mapping' of a complex variable into a single-valued mapping of a point on a complex manifold, a *Riemann surface*. The standard geometric illustration of the piecing together of a Riemann surface from 'sheets with slits' resembles our graph (53) of the hierarchical helix and its projection.

6.22 Hypersets We have already encountered, in 5.12, the prototypical hyperset $\Omega = \{\Omega\}$ as an analogue of the ouroboros $f \vdash f$, which is not a **Set**-object.

The **Set**-theoretic hierarchical cycle inhabits both worlds: it also has its analogue in hyperset theory. For example, a two-mapping hierarchical cycle

(58)

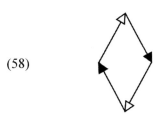

is isomorphic to the (solution of the) hyperset (equation) $\Omega = \{\{\Omega\}\}$, while a three-mapping hierarchical cycle

(59)

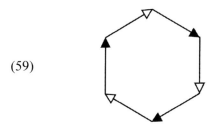

is isomorphic to the hyperset $\Omega = \{\{\{\Omega\}\}\}$. In general, an n-mapping hierarchical cycle is isomorphic to the hyperset $\Omega = \underbrace{\{\{\cdots\{}_{n}\Omega\underbrace{\}\cdots\}\}}_{n}$. The interested reader is referred to Azcel [1988] for all the details on hyperset theory.

Closure to Efficient Causation

6.23 Definition A natural system is *closed to efficient causation* if its every efficient cause is entailed within the system, i.e., if every efficient cause is functionally entailed within the system.

It is important to note that 'closure to efficient causation' is a condition on efficient causes, *not* on material causes. Thus a system that is closed to efficient causation is not necessarily a 'closed system' in the thermodynamic sense. (In thermodynamics, a *closed system* is one that is *closed to material causation*, i.e., a system that allows energy but not matter to be exchanged across its boundary.)

Let N be a natural system and let $\kappa(N)$ be all efficient causes in N. If N is closed to efficient causation, one may symbolically write

(60) $\qquad \forall f \in \kappa(N) \; \exists \Phi \in \kappa(N) : \Phi \vdash f.$

6.24 Eulerian Circuit In terms of relation diagrams G, 'every efficient cause functionally entailed' means that if a vertex v initiates a solid-headed arrow, it must terminate at least one hollow-headed arrow. Due to $\varepsilon_o(v) = 0$ or 1 (restriction (12)), this simply means that if $\varepsilon_o(v) = 1$ one must have $\tau_i(v) \geq 1$. That is,

(61) $\qquad \tau_i(v) \geq \varepsilon_o(v) \quad \text{for all } v \in G.$

Note that as a consequence of this inequality, the Eulerian path condition (Theorem 6.12(*b*))

(62) $\qquad \varepsilon_o(v_1) - \tau_i(v_1) = 1$

for an exceptional vertex v_1 cannot occur.

The equality

$$(63) \qquad \sum_v \tau_i(v) = \sum_v \varepsilon_o(v)$$

(*cf.* the argument leading to (6)=(7) in 6.8) in fact turns the inequality (61) into an equality

$$(64) \qquad \tau_i(v) = \varepsilon_o(v) \quad \text{for all} \quad v \in G.$$

This is because if

$$(65) \qquad \tau_i(v_1) > \varepsilon_o(v_1) \quad \text{for some} \quad v_1 \in G,$$

it would force

$$(65) \qquad \tau_i(v_2) < \varepsilon_o(v_2) \quad \text{for some other} \quad v_2 \in G$$

in compensation, in order to keep the sums in (63) equal; but (65) contradicts (61). Thus, with the equality (64), and the equality (5) which is satisfied by all relational diagrams, one has the requisite conditions of Theorem 6.12(*a*) for Eulerian circuits:

6.25 Theorem *Closure to efficient causation for a natural system means it has a formal system model in which all of the efficient causes in its causal entailment structure are contained in closed paths; i.e., all efficient causes are components of hierarchical cycles.*

6.26 More Than Hierarchical Cycles Note that 'closed to efficient causation' is more stringent than simply 'containing a hierarchical cycle in its entailment pattern'. The latter property only requires the *some*, but not necessarily all, efficient causes to be part of a hierarchical cycle; on the other hand, the former property requires *all* efficient causes to be in hierarchical cycles.

158

As an example, consider the following entailment diagram

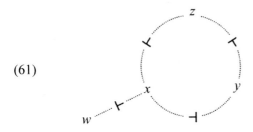

(61)

While the three maps $\{x, y, z\}$ forms a hierarchical cycle in its entailment structure, the map w is not entailed, whence (the system represented by) this entailment pattern is *not* closed to efficient causation..

Herein lies a cause of the confusion on the term 'closure to efficient causation'. Some people use it to mean 'a closed path containing *some* efficient causes exists', instead of Theorem 6.25 '*all* of the efficient causes are contained in closed paths' that is a consequence of Definition 6.23. The discrepancy is, however, simply due to their different usage of the word 'closure' (or 'closed'), rather than an outright error on their part. (Humpty Dumpty is never far away!) It still remains that systems satisfying the more stringent *universal* ('for all') condition form a *proper subset* of systems satisfying the *existential* ('for some') condition. Note that a 'universal characterization' is consistent with other mathematical usage of the term 'closure'. For example, in topology, a subset of a metric space is *closed* if it contains *all* (not just some) of its cluster points; in algebra, a set is *closed* under a binary operation if the result of combining *every* pair (not just some pairs) of elements of the set is also included in the set.

6.27 Connected Components One must also note that 'closed to efficient causation' only means that every efficient cause is part of a hierarchical cycle, but it is not necessary to have *one* single hierarchical cycle that contains all efficient causes. The causal entailment patterns (and therefore the inferential entailment networks) need not be connected: but each network is a collection of connected components. So the requirement for 'closed to efficient causation' is that *in each connected component* all of the efficient causes are contained in a single close path.

By Theorem 6.1, one has

6.28 Theorem   *A natural system is closed to efficient causation if and only if each connected component in its relational diagram has a closed path that contains all the solid-headed arrows.*

This brings us back to the topological topic of traversability we discussed in the beginning of this chapter. In (a connected component that is) a *multigraph*, a cycle that contains all the solid-headed arrows necessarily, because of the pairwise construction of the solid-headed and hollow-headed arrows, contains all the hollow-headed arrows as well. Indeed, the cycle must contain all the solid-headed arrows and hollow-headed arrows in an alternating sequence. A cycle containing *all* the arrows (recall 6.3) corresponds to the graph-theoretic concept of Eulerian circuit. In *pseudographs*, since a single arrow may form a self-loop, a cycle that contains all the solid-headed arrows may or may not be an Eulerian circuit. But this cycle will still be part of an Eulerian path.

I shall revisit *traversability* when I explicate (M,R)-systems and their realizations in Chapters 11 and 12.

PART III

Simplex and Complex

To find the simple in the complex, the finite in the infinite
— that is not a bad description of the aim and essence of
mathematics.

> — Jacob T. Schwartz (1986)
> *Discrete Thoughts: Essays on*
> *Mathematics, Science and Philosophy*
> Chapter 7

With lattice theory from Part I and modelling theory from Part II (along with category theory from the Appendix), we are now equipped to make our approach to the subject of Part III, the dichotomy of simplexity versus complexity.

7

The Category of Formal Systems

Categorical System Theory

In Chapter 4, I considered *formal system* as a primitive in our epistemology, and described it as an object in the universe of mathematics. 'An object in the universe of mathematics' may, of course, be interpreted as an 'object' in an appropriate category. Now I formalize the term, without loss of generality, in the

7.1 Definition A *formal system* is a pair $\langle S, F \rangle$, where S is a set, and F is a collection of observables of S, *i.e.* $F \subset \bullet^S$, such that $0 \in F$, where 0 is (the equivalence class of) the constant mapping on S.

Recall (Definition 2.23) that an observable of S is a mapping f with domain S. Because of the $0 \in F$ requirement, the collection F of observables of S is always nonempty.

Quite frequently, we are more interested in the equivalence relation R_f induced on S by f rather than f itself. So we may pass on to equivalences classes in $\bullet^S$, and consider $F \subset \bullet^S/\sim = \mathbb{Q}S$ (*cf.* 2.24). This, incidentally, explains the 'equivalence class of' in the definition of the constant mapping $0 \in F$. 0 is not necessarily the 'zero mapping' (one that sends every element of S to the number zero), since the codomain is not required to contain the number zero. The important function of 0 is that $R_0 = U$, the universal relation on S, which simply serves to identify the set S itself. The universal relation U, indeed, recognizes the property of 'belonging to S', which is a primitive concept in set theory.

As in any formal object that is a 'set with structure', when the 'specifying structure' F is understood, one may sometimes *refer* to a formal system $\langle S, F \rangle$ by its underlying 'set of states' S (where a *state* is simply defined as a 'member of S', i.e., the formal-system analogue of its natural-system counterpart; *cf.* 4.4). On the other hand, since $0 \in F$ implicitly entails S, a formal system may (analogous to the 'arrows-only' interpretation of the category axioms; *cf.* A.1) also be considered as *defined* by F itself. In other words, a formal system is characterized by its set of observables, i.e., by an *operational definition*.

That F is a collection of observables of S, $F \subset \bullet^S$, means $F \in \mathsf{P} \bullet^S$. But because of the base point $0 \in F$, F cannot be an *arbitrary* element of $\mathsf{P} \bullet^S$: one actually has $F \in \mathsf{P}_0 \bullet^S$ [see 2.6 for a discussion of the pointed power set $\mathsf{P}_* A$ of a set A]. But since both $\mathsf{P} A$ and $\mathsf{P}_0 A$ are complete lattices [see 2.12] (which will be the important fact invoked later), for simplicity of notation I shall continue with P instead of P_0 (unless the latter is explicitly required for clarity).

7.2 Resolution Associated with a formal system $\langle S, F \rangle$ there is an equivalence relation $R_F \in \mathsf{Q} S$ defined by $R_F = \bigwedge_{f \in F} R_f$ (*cf.* Definition 2.15 and Lemmata 2.16 and 2.34). In this notation, $R_{\{0, f\}} = R_f$. One may say that the formal system $\langle S, F \rangle$ is characterized by R_F, or has *resolution* R_F.

Note that the correspondence $F \mapsto R_F$ is a *projection*, whence some information is lost in the process: there is in general no way to recover the collection F of observables, or $\{ R_f : f \in F \}$, from the single equivalence relation $R_F = \bigwedge_{f \in F} R_f$. Also note that there may not be an observable $h \in F$

that generates the equivalence relation R_F, i.e., although mathematically there exists $h \in \bullet^S$ such that $R_F = R_h$ (*cf.* Theorem 2.20), h (and all of its ~-equivalent observables) may not be in F.

7.3 The Category S An observable f of S is only required to have domain S; its codomain may be any arbitrary set. It is conventional to take $\mathrm{cod}(f) = \mathbb{R}$, the set of real numbers (whence $f \in \mathbb{R}^S$). The evaluation of a *real-valued mapping* on a set S is a formal metaphor of the measurement process. For most of our purposes $\mathrm{cod}(f) = \mathbb{R}$ is sufficient, but Definition 7.1 allows further generalizations when required (*cf.* the discussion on qualitative and quantitative in 2.25). With restriction to the real codomain, a formal system in the more general Definition 7.1 is identical to that defined in our previous theses [*FM, CS*]. In *Categorical System Theory* [*CS*], I studied the category S of all formal systems, in which the objects are pairs $\langle S, F \rangle$ where S is an arbitrary set and $F \subset \mathbb{R}^S$. Now I generalize the category S to have objects $\langle S, F \rangle$ with $F \subset \bullet^S$.

7.4 S-Morphism An S-morphism $\phi \in S((S_1, F_1), (S_2, F_2))$ is a pair of mappings $\phi \in \mathrm{Set}(S_1, S_2)$ and $\phi \in \mathrm{Set}(F_1, F_2)$ such that for all $f \in F_1$ for all $s, s' \in S_1$,

(1) $\qquad f(s) = f(s') \Rightarrow (\phi f)(\phi s) = (\phi f)(\phi s'),$

i.e., $sR_f s'$ implies $(\phi s) R_{\phi f} (\phi s')$.

Note that this *compatibility condition* (1) is equivalent to saying for all $G \subset F_1$ for all $s, s' \in S_1$, $sR_G s'$ implies $(\phi s) R_{\phi G} (\phi s')$, where $\phi G = \{\phi f : f \in G\} \subset F_2$. This means that for all $G \subset F_1$, ϕ can be considered as a mapping from S_1/R_G to $S_2/R_{\phi G}$.

One always defines $\phi 0 = 0$. This is compatible because $0s = 0s'$ implies $0(\phi s) = 0(\phi s')$. Note also that for any observable f, the assignment $\phi f = 0$ is acceptable.

7.5 Identity Define $1_{(S,F)} \in \mathbf{S}\big((S,F),(S,F)\big)$ by for all $s \in S$ $s \mapsto s$ and for all $f \in F$ $f \mapsto f$. Thus for all $G \subset F$ $G \mapsto G$. Then $1_{(S,F)}$ satisfies the compatibility condition (1).

7.6 Composition in S Define composition of morphisms in **S** as simultaneously the compositions on the states and on the observables; i.e., if $\phi : (S_1, F_1) \to (S_2, F_2)$ and $\psi : (S_2, F_2) \to (S_3, F_3)$, define $\psi \circ \phi : (S_1, F_1) \to (S_3, F_3)$ by for every $s \in S_1$ $\psi \circ \phi(s) = \psi\big(\phi(s)\big)$ and for every $f \in F_1$ $\psi \circ \phi(f) = \psi\big(\phi(f)\big)$. Note for $f \in F_1$ and $s, s' \in S_1$, $sR_f s'$ implies $(\phi s) R_{\phi f} (\phi s')$, which in turn implies $\psi(\phi s) R_{\psi(\phi f)} \psi(\phi s')$; so $\psi \circ \phi$ satisfies the compatibility condition (1).

One easily verifies that composition so defined is associative, and for $\phi : (S_1, F_1) \to (S_2, F_2)$, $1_{(S_2, F_2)} \circ \phi = \phi = \phi \circ 1_{(S_1, F_1)}$

7.7 Isomorphism If $\phi : (S_1, F_1) \to (S_2, F_2)$ and $\psi : (S_2, F_2) \to (S_1, F_1)$ are such that $\psi \circ \phi = 1_{(S_1, F_1)}$ and $\phi \circ \psi = 1_{(S_2, F_2)}$, then it is easy to see that $\phi : S_1 \to S_2$ and $\phi : F_1 \to F_2$ must be bijections (**Set**-isomorphisms) and that for $f \in F_1$ and $s, s' \in S_1$, $f(s) = f(s')$ if and only if $(\phi f)(\phi s) = (\phi f)(\phi s')$, i.e., for every $G \subset F_1$ $S_1 / R_G = S_2 / R_{\phi G}$.

Thus isomorphic systems are abstractly the same in the sense that there is a 'dictionary' (one-to-one correspondence) between the states and between the observables inducing the 'same' equivalence relations on the states. In particular, if F and G are two sets of observables on S and there is a bijection $\phi : F \to G$ such that for all $f \in F$ $f \sim \phi f$, then the two systems (S,F) and (S,G) are isomorphic with the **S**-isomorphism $1_S : S \to S$,

$\phi : F \to G$. Since categorical constructions are only unique up to isomorphism, in the category **S** all constructions (S,F) are only 'unique up to $\sim$-equivalent observables' (i.e., one can always replace F by an $\sim$-equivalent set of observables G in the above sense) even when the set of states S is held fixed. This last comment is particularly important for all constructions in **S**.

Constructions in S

I now briefly explore several category-theoretic constructions in **S** that will be of use later. The reader may consult *CS* for further detailed examples and proofs.

7.8 Product Products in the category **S** exist. For a family $\{(S_i,F_i):i\in I\}$, the product is $(S,F)=\prod_{j\in I}(S_j,F_j)$ with an I-tuple of **S**-morphisms of the form $\pi_i:(S,F)\to(S_i,F_i)$. S is defined as the cartesian product $\prod S_j$ of the sets of states. F is defined as the 'cartesian product' $\prod F_j$ of the sets of observables interpreted as follows: $f=(f_j:j\in I)\in F$ is an observable of S defined by

(2) $\qquad (f_j:j\in I)(s_j:j\in I)=(f_j(s_j):j\in I).$

Note that the codomain of f is the cartesian product set of the codomains of the f_js.

The projections are obviously defined by $\pi_i((s_j:j\in I))=s_i$ and $\pi_i((f_j:j\in I))=f_i$. It is easily checked that the π_is are indeed **S**-morphisms.

The terminal object in **S** is $(1,\{0\})$ where 1 is the singleton set, the terminal **Set**-object. The unique **S**-morphism from any system to $(1,\{0\})$ is the one that sends all states to 1 and all observables to 0.

7.9 Meet as Product Let f and g be observables on S. Recall (Lemma 2.34) that the meet $R_{fg} = R_f \wedge R_g$ of their equivalence relations R_f and R_g on S is defined by

(3) $\qquad sR_{fg}s'$ if and only if $f(s) = f(s')$ and $g(s) = g(s')$.

Note that there may not be an observable of S that generates the equivalence relation R_{fg}, i.e., although mathematically there exists $h \in \bullet^S$ such that $R_{fg} = R_h$, the set of all possible observables of S, as a representation of a natural system, may not contain (the $\sim$-equivalence class of) this h.

There is always an embedding $\phi : S/R_{fg} \to S/R_f \times S/R_g$ that maps $(s)_{fg} \mapsto \left((s)_f , (s)_g \right)$. Via this embedding, a state $s \in S$ is represented by the pair of numbers $(f(s), g(s))$. This embedding ϕ is in general one to one, but it is onto if and only if f and g are totally unlinked (to each other; *cf.* Lemma 2.33).

This **Set**-product representation can be constructed neatly as an **S**-product. Consider the two systems $(S,\{f,0\})$ and $(S,\{g,0\})$. The **S**-product of these two systems is $(S \times S, F)$, where $F = \{0,(f,0),(0,g),(f,g)\}$, with the natural projections. Now consider further the system $(S,\{f,g\})$. There exist **S**-morphisms

(4) $\qquad \phi_1 : (S,\{f,g\}) \to (S,\{f,0\})$ and $\phi_2 : (S,\{f,g\}) \to (S,\{0,g\})$

defined by, for every $s \in S$,

(5) $\qquad \phi_1(s)=s; \quad \phi_1 f=f, \quad \phi_1 g=0$

and

(6) $\qquad \phi_2(s)=s; \quad \phi_2 f=0, \quad \phi_2 g=g.$

Hence by the universal property of the product, there exists a unique $\phi:\big(S,\{f,g\}\big)\to\big(S\times S,F\big)$ that makes the diagram commute. Namely, ϕ is defined by sending $s\in S$ to $\phi(s)=(s,s)$ — the diagonal map — and by $\phi f=(f,0)$, $\phi g=(0,g)$. So one has the following diagram:

(7)

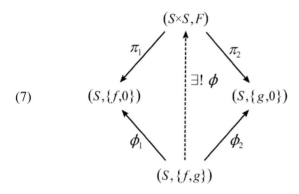

In particular, ϕ being an **S**-morphism implies that $\phi:S/R_{\{f,g\}}$ $\to S\times S/R_{\{(f,0),(0,g)\}}$. ϕ is a one-to-one mapping (on S) and $R_{\{f,g\}}=R_{fg}$ hence $S/R_{\{f,g\}}=S/R_{fg}$. Also, $S\times S/R_{\{(f,0),(0,g)\}}\cong S/R_f\times S/R_g$. Thus ϕ is indeed the one-to-one map from S/R_{fg} to $S/R_f\times S/R_g$, and that the degree of onto-ness of ϕ is an indication of the lack of linkage between f and g. The onto-ness of a morphism is discussed in the Appendix in A.44.

7.10 Equalizer For **S**-morphisms $\phi, \psi : (S_1, F_1) \rightarrow (S_2, F_2)$, $\mathrm{eq}(\phi, \psi)$ $= (E, H)$ may not exist. The equalizer would have to be given by $E = \{s \in S : \phi s = \psi s\}$, $H = \{f|_E : f \in F_1, \phi f = \psi f\}$ and $\iota : (E, H) \rightarrow (S_1, F_1)$ would be the inclusion morphism. But $\iota(f|_E) = f$ may not be uniquely defined because there may be another $g \in F_1$ such that $g|_E = f|_E$ and $\phi g = \psi g$. Thus an **S**-equalizer only exists when the inclusion map from H to F_1 is single-valued.

Note when $(E, H) = \mathrm{eq}(\phi, \psi)$ does exist, $\iota : (E, H) \rightarrow (S_1, F_1)$ has the property that for all $s, s' \in E$ and for all $g \in H$, $g(s) = g(s')$ if and only if $(\iota g)(s) = (\iota g)(s')$, i.e., $E/R_g \cong \iota(E)/R_{\iota g}$. Further, any **S**-morphism $\chi : (X_1, G_1) \rightarrow (X_2, G_2)$ that is one-to-one on the states and on the observables, and that has this property (that $X_1/R_g \cong \chi(X_1)/R_{\chi g}$ for all $g \in G_1$) is an equalizer. It is easy to construct a pair of **S**-morphisms ϕ_1, ϕ_2 with domain (X_2, G_2) such that $(X_1, G_1) = \mathrm{eq}(\phi_1, \phi_2)$. Thus although **S** does not have equalizers for every pair of **S**-morphisms, given an **S**-morphism ϕ with the correct properties one can always find a pair of **S**-morphisms for which ϕ is the equalizer.

7.11 Coproduct The category **S** has coproducts. The coproduct is $(S, F) = \coprod_{j \in I} (S_j, F_j)$ where $S = \coprod S_j$ is the coproduct of the S_js in **Set** (i.e., the disjoint union $S = \bigcup \{j\} \times S_j$) and $F = \{0\} \cup \{(j, f) : j \in I, f \in F_j, f \neq 0\}$ defined as follows. For $f \in F_j$, $f \neq 0$, the observable (j, f) of S is defined by

$$(8) \qquad (j, f)(k, s) = \begin{cases} f(s) & \text{if } j = k \\ (k, s) & \text{if } j \neq k \end{cases}.$$

The natural injections are $\iota_j : (S_j, F_j) \to (S, F)$ with $\iota_j(s) = (j, s)$ for $s \in S_j$, and $\iota_j(f) = (j, f)$ for $f \in F_j$ with $f \neq 0$ and $\iota_j(0) = 0$.

The initial object in **Set** is the empty set $\varnothing$, thence the initial object in **S** is $(\varnothing, \{0\})$. For any system (S, F), the unique **S**-morphism from $(\varnothing, \{0\})$ to (S, F) is the empty mapping on $\varnothing$ with $0 \mapsto 0 \in F$.

7.12 Coequalizer The category **S** also has coequalizers, constructed as follows. Let $\phi, \psi : (S_1, F_1) \to (S_2, F_2)$. Let $Q = S_2/R$ where R is the intersection of all equivalence relations on S_2 containing $\{(\phi(s), \psi(s)) \in S_2 \times S_2 : s \in S_1\}$ and of all R_{F_2}. So in particular for $t, t' \in S_2$, tRt' implies for all $g \in F_2$ $g(t) = g(t')$. Let $\chi : S_2 \to Q$ be the canonical projection $\chi(t) = (t)_R$. This takes care of the map on the states. As for the observables, let R on F_2 be the intersection of all equivalence relations containing $\{(\phi f, \psi f) \in F_2 \times F_2 : f \in F_1\}$, and let $\chi : F_2 \to H = F_2/R$ be, naturally, $\chi g = (g)_R$, such that $R_{(g)_R}$ is the equivalence relation on S_2 generated by $\{R_{g'} : g' \in (g)_R\}$, i.e., $R_{(g)_R}$ is the finest equivalence relation on S_2 such that it is refined by each of the $R_{g'}$, $g' \in (g)_R$. Putting it another way, $R_{(g)_R}$ is defined to be the supremum of the family $\{R_{g'} : g' \in (g)_R\}$ in the lattice of all equivalence relations on S_2. One sees, then, that $R_{(g)_R}$ is refined by R on S_2 and hence $(g)_R$ is well defined on $Q = S_2/R$, so one can consider $\mathrm{dom}(g)_R = Q$. Finally, to check $\chi : (S_2, F_2) \to (Q, H)$ so defined is indeed an **S**-morphism, let $g \in F_2$ and $t, t' \in S_2$; then $g(t) = g(t')$ implies $(g)_R(t) = (g)_R(t')$ hence $(g)_R(t)_R = (g)_R(t')_R$. So $tR_g t'$ does imply $\chi(t) R_{\chi g} \chi(t')$. Further, $\chi \circ \phi = \chi \circ \psi$.

Now if $\chi' : (S_2, F_2) \to (Q', H')$ is such that $\chi' \circ \phi = \chi' \circ \psi$, then $\{(t, t') \in S_2 \times S_2 : \chi'(t) = \chi'(t')\}$ is an equivalence relation on S_2 containing

172

R. Thus $\pi(t)_R = \chi'(t)$ is well defined on $Q = S_2/R$. Similarly, $\pi(g)_R = \chi'g$ is well defined on H. $\chi' = \pi \circ \chi$ and it is unique.

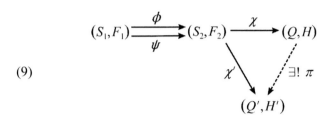

(9)

Finally, we have to check that π is an **S**-morphism. Note that for every $g' \in (g)_R$ (i.e., $g'Rg$), $\chi'g' = \chi'g$ because $\{(g,g') \in F_2 \times F_2 : \chi'g = \chi'g'\}$ is an equivalence relation on F_2 and since for every $f \in F_1$ $\chi'(\phi f) = \chi'(\psi f)$, this equivalence relation contains all $(\phi f, \psi f)$ and hence contains R. Also since χ' is an **S**-morphism, for each $g' \in (g)_R$ we have $g'(t) = g'(t')$ implying $(\chi'g')(\chi't) = (\chi'g')(\chi't')$, i.e., $(\chi'g')(\chi't) = (\chi'g)(\chi't')$. Thus $R_{\chi'g}$ is 'refined' by each of $R_{g'}$ (on F_2). Since $R_{(g)_R}$ is the supremum of $\{R_{g'} : g' \in (g)_R\}$, we have $R_{(g)_R} \subset R_{\chi'g}$. Therefore $(g)_R(t)_R = (g)_R(t')_R$ in Q implies $(g)_R(t)_R = (g)_R(t')_R$ in S_2, which in turn implies that $(\chi'g)(\chi't) = (\chi'g)(\chi't')$ in Q', i.e., $\pi(g)_R[\pi(t)_R] = \pi(g)_R[\pi(t')_R]$ in Q', whence $\pi : (Q,H) \to (Q',H')$ is indeed an **S**-morphism.

It is apparent that whereas products and equalizers are easy to define in **S**, their dual concepts are a lot more complicated. This is indeed observed in many familiar categories (*cf.* A.36). A difficult problem in the study of a specific category is in fact to explicitly describe its coproducts and coequalizers ('colimits').

Hierarchy of S-Morphisms and Image Factorization

7.13 S-Monomorphisms A mono in the category **S** is an **S**-morphism that is injective as set mappings on the set of states and on the set of observables. For suppose $\phi:(S_1,F_1)\rightarrow(S_2,F_2)$ is a mono and there are distinct states s and s' in S for which $\phi(s)=\phi(s')$, then consider $\psi_1,\psi_2:(S_1,F_1)\rightarrow(S_1,F_1)$ with ψ_1 mapping all states in S to s, ψ_2 mapping all states in S to s', and both ψ_1 and ψ_2 acting as identity on F_1. It is easy to check that in this case the **S**-morphisms ψ_1 and ψ_2 are such that $\phi\circ\psi_1=\phi\circ\psi_2$ but $\psi_1\neq\psi_2$, a contradiction. So $\phi:S_1\rightarrow S_2$ must be injective. Also, suppose distinct observables f and f' in F_1 are such that $\phi f=\phi f'$. Then consider $\psi_1,\psi_2:(\{s\},\{f,f'\})\rightarrow(S_1,F_1)$ where $s\in S_1$, ψ_1 is the inclusion, and $\psi_2(s)=s$, $\psi_2 f=f'$, $\psi_2 f'=f$. Again ψ_1, ψ_2 are **S**-morphisms with $\phi\circ\psi_1=\phi\circ\psi_2$ but $\psi_1\neq\psi_2$, a contradiction. So $\phi:F_1\rightarrow F_2$ is also injective. Conversely, if an **S**-morphism $\phi:(S_1,F_1)\rightarrow(S_2,F_2)$ is injective on both S_1 and F_1, it is mono.

Now suppose $\phi:(S_1,F_1)\rightarrow(S_2,F_2)$ is an equalizer and that S_1 is nonempty. (F_1 is already nonempty because $0\in F_1$.) Say $\phi=\text{eq}(\psi_1,\psi_2)$ for $\psi_1,\psi_2:(S_2,F_2)\rightarrow(X,H)$. Then, as an equalizer, $\phi:(S_1,F_1)\rightarrow(S_2,F_2)$ is isomorphic to an inclusion (see 7.10). So in particular for $f\in F_1$ and $s,s'\in S_1$, $f(s)=f(s')$ if and only if $(\phi f)(\phi s)=(\phi f)(\phi s')$, i.e., $S_1/R_f\cong\phi(S_1)/R_{\phi f}$. Thus ϕ^{-1} is well defined on $\phi(S_1)$ and $\phi(F_1)$ and can be extended to an **S**- morphism on (S_2,F_2). (We need a nonempty S_1 for the same reason as in **Set**.) So in **S**, an equalizer with nonempty domain is split mono.

174

In the examples in *CS*, I have shown that an **S**-mono is not necessarily an **S**-equalizer, so the hierarchy for monomorphisms in **S** is (for $\phi:(S_1,F_1)\to(S_2,F_2)$ with nonempty S_1)

(10) split mono $\Leftrightarrow$ equalizer $\Rightarrow$ mono $\Leftrightarrow$ injection (on both S_1 and F_1).

7.14 S-Epimorphisms In **S**, an epi is the same as an **S**-morphism that is surjective on both the set of states and the set of observables. For suppose $\phi:(S_1,F_1)\to(S_2,F_2)$ is an epi and there is an $s\in S_2\sim\phi(S_1)$, then $\psi_1,\psi_2:(S_2,F_2)\to(\{0,1\},\{0\})$, where $\psi_1=\chi_{\phi(S_1)}$ on S_2, $\psi_1 f=0$ for all $f\in F_2$, $\psi_2=\chi_{S_2}$ on S_2, and $\psi_2 f=0$ for all $f\in F_2$, provide a pair of **S**-morphisms such that $\psi_1\circ\phi=\psi_2\circ\phi$ but $\psi_1\neq\psi_2$, a contradiction. So $\phi(S_1)=S_2$. Now suppose there is an $f\in F_2\sim\phi(F_1)$, then $\psi_1,\psi_2:(S_2,F_2)\to(S_2,F_2)$ where $\psi_1=1_{(S_2,F_2)}$, $\psi_2=1_{S_2}$ on S_2 and $\psi_2 f=0$ for all $f\in F_2$, is an example in which $\psi_1\circ\phi=\psi_2\circ\phi$ but $\psi_1\neq\psi_2$, again a contradiction. Thus $\phi(F_1)=F_2$. Conversely, an **S**-morphism $\phi:(S_1,F_1)\to(S_2,F_2)$ that is onto both S_2 and F_2 is epi. Thus in **S**, one has

(11) split epi $\Rightarrow$ coequalizer $\Rightarrow$ epi $\Leftrightarrow$ surjection (onto both S_2 and F_2).

In *CS* I have shown that the two preceding one-way implications are indeed irreversible; so the preceding is the hierarchy for epimorphisms in **S**.

Note that although the two hierarchies in **S** for the dual concepts of monomorphisms and epimorphisms are not the same, this is *not* a counterexample to the principle of categorical duality (see A.30). The principle only states that if is a statement about a category **C**, then Σ^{op} is *universally* true if Σ is. For a *particular* category, it may very well happen that Σ is true but Σ^{op} is not.

7.15 Image Factorization   The category **S**, also, has epi-equalizer and coequalizer-mono factorizations. The diagram

(12)

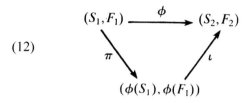

with $\pi = i$ on (S_1, F_1) and ι = inclusion is an epi-equalizer factorization $\phi = \iota \circ \pi$ of ϕ.

Consider the equivalence relation $R = \{(s, s') \in S_1 \times S_1 : \phi(s) = \phi(s')\}$ on S_1 and $R = \{(f, f') \in F_1 \times F_1 : \phi f = \phi f'\}$ on F_1; the diagram

(13)

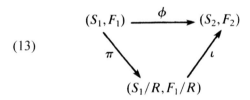

with π = natural projection (where $F_1/R \subset \mathbb{R}^{S_1/R}$ is to be interpreted as in the construction of coequalizers in 7.12) and ι defined by $\iota(s)_R = \phi(s)$, $\iota(f)_R = \phi f$ (since sRs' iff $\phi s = \phi s'$, fRf' iff $\phi f = \phi f'$, ι well defined) is then a coequalizer-mono factorization of ϕ.

Note that although both the epi-equalizer and coequalizer-mono factorizations are unique up to isomorphism, the two factorizations are not necessarily isomorphic (an example is the case of **Top**, A.45).

7.16 Subobjects In **S**, as we saw, there are two distinct types of monomorphisms — namely, that of an equalizer (= split mono) and that of a mono (= injective morphism). I shall say that $\phi : (S_1, F_1) \to (S_2, F_2)$ is an **S**-*subsystem* (or simply (S_1, F_1) is a subsystem of (S_2, F_2)) if ϕ is an equalizer, and it is an **S**-*monosubobject* (or simply (S_1, F_1) is a monosubobject of (S_2, F_2)) if ϕ is mono. So a subsystem is a monosubobject but not vice versa.

Note that *subsystem* implies that for each $f \in F_1$ $S_1/R_f \cong \phi(S_1)/R_{\phi f}$ ($\phi : S_1/R_f \to S_2/R_{\phi f}$ is one-to-one), i.e., $f(s) = f(s')$ if and only if $(\phi f)(\phi s) = (\phi f)(\phi s')$; whereas *monosubobject* does not have this 'backward implication' ($\phi : S_1/R_f \to S_2/R_{\phi f}$ is not necessarily one-to-one). A subsystem, therefore, is the appropriate subobject of a system that preserves most of its structures. On the other hand, a monosubobject may be used to define a partial order on **S**, with $(S_1, F_1) \leq (S_2, F_2)$ if and only if (S_1, F_1) is a monosubobject of (S_2, F_2). Biological implications of this partial order may be found in *CS*. In this monograph, I shall proceed slightly differently, and specialize on the partial order for various collections of observables on the same set of states (*cf.* 7.23 below).

The Lattice of Component Models

Let N be a natural system.

7.17 Definition A *model* of N is a finite collection of formal systems $\{\langle S_i, F_i \rangle : i = 1, ..., n\}$ such that the collection of mappings $\{F_i : i = 1, ..., n\}$ satisfy the entailment requirements of the modelling relation. Each formal system $\langle S_i, F_i \rangle$ is called a *component* of the model.

I shall consider next, in detail, the meaning of the phrase 'satisfy the entailment requirements of the modelling relation'.

7.18 Nuances of Dualism   Recall in 4.4 that the primitive *natural system* is thus attributed that it is (*a*) a part, whence a subset, of the external world; and (*b*) a collection of qualities, to which definite relations can be imputed.

Rosen continued the explication on the concept of a natural system [*AS*, Section 2.1] with the following:

> ...a natural system from the outset embodies a mental construct (i.e., a relation established by the mind between percepts) which comprises a hypothesis or model pertaining to the organization of the external world.
>
> In what follows, we shall refer to a perceptible quality of a natural system as an *observable*. We shall call a relation obtaining between two or more observables belonging to a natural system a *linkage* between them. We take the viewpoint that the study of natural systems is precisely the specification of the observables belonging to such a system, and a characterization of the manner in which they are linked. Indeed, for us *observables are the fundamental units of natural systems, just as percepts are the fundamental units of experience.*

Note the nuance here, that of the subtle difference between a *material system* (or a physical system) and a *natural system*. A material system is ontological, it being simply any physical object in the world. A natural system, on the other hand, is epistemological, since the partitioning of the external world and the formation of percepts and their relations are all mental constructs (and are therefore entailed by the bounds of mental constructs). In short, a natural system is a subjectively-defined representation of a material system. Recall, as we discussed in 4.13, that the existence of causal entailment in a natural system is ontological, but the representation of causality, by an arrow (i.e., as mappings), is epistemological.

Likewise, note the nuance between a *formal system* (Definition 7.1) and a *model* (Definition 7.17). For a general formal system $\langle S, F \rangle$, the only requirement for the collection of mappings F is $0 \in F \subset \bullet^S$, with no size limits. A model is a functorial image of a natural system. Recall (4.15) the Natural Law axiom "Every process is a mapping." My formal definition (Definition 2.23) of *observable of a set X* (a mapping with domain X) categorically models an *observable of a natural system* (a perceptible quality). Thus the mappings in a model are observables in both senses. In particular, the number of percepts are finite (it may be a very large number, but finite nonetheless), therefore *the number of observables of a model is finite*.

7.19 Finitude St. Thomas Aquinas in his *Summa Theologica* wrote that "in efficient causes it is not possible to go on to infinity". There is a philosophical debate as to whether Aquinas intended to say that an infinitely long causal chain (i.e., in our terminology an infinite sequence of hierarchical compositions) would be impossible, or that there are only finitely many efficient causes in the universe. For our purpose, a natural system (being a mental construct) can have only finitely many efficient causes, and a model has only finitely many mappings.

A model, an abstraction by the modeller, is by definition an *incomplete description*. Thus, if $\{\langle S_i, F_i \rangle : i = 1, ..., n\}$ is a model (that there are *finitely many model components* $\langle S_i, F_i \rangle$ is already part of Definition 7.17), then each F_i must be a *finite subset* of $\bullet^{S_i}$.

The requirement that the F_is (hence the totality of observables $\bigcup_{i=1}^{n} F_i$ of N) are to be *finite* sets looks like a very severe mathematical restriction. But in mathematical modelling of natural systems, a finiteness restriction is not unrealistic: all one requires is that the sets are finite, and there is no restriction on how small the sets have to be. So the sets could be singletons, have 10^{10} elements, or have 10^{100} elements and still be finite. After all, Sir James Jeans, in *The Astronomical Horizon* [1945], defined the universe as a gigantic machine the future of which is inexorably fixed by its state at any given moment, that it is "a self-solving system of $6N$ simultaneous differential equations, where N is Eddington's number". Sir Arthur Eddington, in *The*

Philosophy of Physical Science [1939], asserted (evidently poetically) that $N = 2 \times 136 \times 2^{256}$ ($\sim 10^{79}$) is the total number of particles of matter in the universe. The point is that it is a *finite* number. Thus the set of states of a natural system is certainly finite at one time (this is not to be confused with the set of all *possible* states a system can have), and the set of observables on a natural system at one time is also clearly finite.

A graph with finitely many edges (and finitely many vertices) is called a *finite graph*. While one may study *infinite* graphs, the subject of graph theory (*cf.* Chapter 6) is almost always finite graphs. In view of the isomorphism given in Theorem 6.1, I summarize the epistemological finitude as the

7.20 Axiom of Finitude
(a) *a natural system has finitely many efficient causes*;
(b) *a model has finitely many mappings*;
(c) *the relational diagram in graph-theoretic form (of the entailment patterns of a natural system) is a finite graph.*

7.21 Further Entailment Requirements   Let $\langle S, F \rangle$ be a component of a model. Since $I \leq R_f$ for each $f \in F$ (where I is the equality relation on S), one has $I \leq R_F$. But one almost always has $I < R_F$: to have $I = R_F$ is to say that one has a *complete description* of a component set S of the natural system N (since the resolution is down to every single element of S), which does not usually happen in a model component $\langle S, F \rangle$ unless S is exceedingly simple.

It is important to note the epistemological difference between the equivalence relations U and I. The universal relation $U = R_0$ induced by $0 \in F$ allows us to identify the *whole* natural system S, to distinguish elements that belong to S from those that do not. This differentiation of self from non-self is a requirement of Natural Law. Note that if $\langle S, F \rangle$ is a model component of N then so trivially is $\langle S, \{0\} \rangle$. The equality relation I, on the other hand, identifies all the *individual elements* of S, and this is a description that is rarely available to us. Another way to summarize the situation succinctly is that the equality relation I and the universal relation U characterize, respectively, the left-hand side and the right-hand side of the membership relation $\in$.

The modelling relation imposes restrictions on mappings that qualify to be members of F, since the mappings are functorial images of processes. The available observables of S, which can belong to a family F so that $\langle S,F \rangle$ is a model component, therefore form a *proper subset* $H(S, \bullet)$ of $\bullet^S$ (see item A.3 on the category **Set**). In particular, $\{R_f : f \in F\} \neq \mathbf{Q}S$. Further restrictions apply to F: since linkages of mappings model relations of percepts, F cannot be an *arbitrary* collection of observables of S.

7.22 Definition Let S be a set such that $\langle S, \{0\} \rangle$ is a model component of a natural system N. The collection of *all* model components of the form $\langle S,F \rangle$ with $F \in \mathbf{P} \bullet^S$ is denoted $\mathbf{C}(S)$.

Note that while by Theorem 2.20 there exists an observable h of S such that $R_h = R_F$, there is no requirement that $h \in F$. But evidently $\langle S, \{0,h\} \rangle$ and $\langle S,F \rangle$ may be considered *equivalent* model components (in the sense of ~-equivalent observables in the isomorphism $\bullet^S/\!\!\sim \, \cong \mathbf{Q}S$; *cf.* 2.24); in other words, if $\langle S,F \rangle \in \mathbf{C}(S)$, then also $\langle S, \{0,h\} \rangle \in \mathbf{C}(S)$.

I now proceed to construct $\mathbf{C}(S)$ into a lattice. For simplicity I shall use the term 'model of S' to abbreviate the verbose but more proper term 'model component of the form $\langle S,F \rangle$ of the natural system N', *i.e.* an element $\langle S,F \rangle \in \mathbf{C}(S)$.

7.23 Joining Models Given $\langle S,F \rangle, \langle S,G \rangle \in \mathbf{C}(S)$, define the *join* of these two models of S as

(14) $\qquad \langle S,F \rangle \vee \langle S,G \rangle = \langle S, F \cup G \rangle$.

Note that the join operator $\vee$ of $\mathbf{C}(S)$ is defined *covariantly* through the join operator $\cup$ of the power set $\mathbf{P} \bullet^S$. One easily verifies that

(15) $\qquad R_{F \cup G} = R_F \wedge R_G$;

thus the characterizing equivalence relation of a join in $\mathbf{C}(S)$ corresponds on the other hand *contravariantly* to the meet operator $\wedge$ of $\mathbf{Q}S$.

If $F \subset G$, then $R_F \supset R_G$ as subsets of $S \times S$, whence G *refines* F, in the obvious sense that $R_G \leq R_F$ in the lattice $\mathbf{Q}S$. The inclusion $F \subset G$ also means $F \cup G = G$, whence $\langle S, F \rangle \vee \langle S, G \rangle = \langle S, F \cup G \rangle = \langle S, G \rangle$, and therefore $\langle S, F \rangle \leq \langle S, G \rangle$ [with the natural definition, that $x \leq y$ if and only if $x \vee y = y$]. So note the covariant implication:

(16) $\qquad F \subset G \ \Rightarrow \ \langle S, F \rangle \leq \langle S, G \rangle.$

The converse is not true: $\langle S, F \rangle \leq \langle S, G \rangle$ does not imply $F \subset G$. I leave it as an easy exercise for the reader to demonstrate a counterexample.

Consider the trivial model $\langle S, \{0\} \rangle \in \mathbf{C}(S)$. Since $0 \in F$ for any model $\langle S, F \rangle \in \mathbf{C}(S)$, one has $\{0\} \cup F = F$, whence $\langle S, \{0\} \rangle \vee \langle S, F \rangle = \langle S, F \rangle$. This says $\langle S, \{0\} \rangle$ is the *least element* of $\mathbf{C}(S)$. Note the contravariance in this correspondence: while the universal relation U corresponding to the constant mapping is the *greatest* element in the lattice $\mathbf{Q}S$, the trivial model $\langle S, \{0\} \rangle$ is the *least* element of $\mathbf{C}(S)$.

The dual operator is obviously defined thus:

7.24 Meeting Models Given $\langle S, F \rangle, \langle S, G \rangle \in \mathbf{C}(S)$, define the *meet* of these two models of S as

(17) $\qquad \langle S, F \rangle \wedge \langle S, G \rangle = \langle S, F \cap G \rangle.$

Note that the meet operator $\wedge$ of $\mathbf{C}(S)$ is again defined covariantly, through the meet operator $\cap$ of the power set $\mathbf{P} \bullet^S$. While the join of two models is a useful construction in combining models — the more observables, *i.e.* more alternate descriptions, a model has, the more information one gains on the system — the meet of two models has no practical purpose other than the mathematical structure requires it. Indeed, there is no simple relationship dual to $R_{F \cup G} = R_F \wedge R_G$: in general, R_F and R_G does not have to combine in any way to give $R_{F \cap G}$.

The greatest element (if it exists) of $\mathbf{C}(S)$ would have to be a model $\langle S, G \rangle$ such that for every $\langle S, F \rangle \in \mathbf{C}(S)$, $\langle S, F \rangle \wedge \langle S, G \rangle = \langle S, F \cap G \rangle$ $= \langle S, F \rangle$. [Recall that $x \leq y$ if and only if $x \wedge y = x$.] This would require $F \cap G = F$ for every set F of observables, whence G must contain *all* the observables of S. Such *Godlike perspective* on a system — having access to the collection G of all observables — is, however, usually not available to us. We must conclude, therefore, that for a *general* natural system S (or more properly, a set S representing a component of a general natural system N), either the complete collection G cannot be determined, or even if it can be, we must have $\langle S, G \rangle \notin \mathbf{C}(S)$; stated otherwise, *generically*, $\mathbf{C}(S)$ does *not* have a greatest element. Those natural systems S for which $\mathbf{C}(S)$ does have a greatest element are, therefore, very specialized, highly *nongeneric*. I shall explore these specialized systems in the next chapter.

The definitions of join and meet in $\mathbf{C}(S)$ establish a (covariant) embedding of $\langle \mathbf{C}(S), \vee, \wedge \rangle$ into $\langle \mathbf{P} \bullet^S, \cup, \cap \rangle$ and a (contravariant) isomorphism between $\langle \mathbf{C}(S), \vee, \wedge \rangle$ and $\langle \mathbf{Q}S, \vee, \wedge \rangle$ in the category of lattices, whence the collection of all model components has a representation as a sublattice (and hence inheriting properties) of the two canonical lattices (*cf.* Lemma 2.8). I state this important fact as the

7.25 Theorem   *The collection of model components* $\mathbf{C}(S)$ *is a lattice.*

The Category of Models

7.26 Model Network The collection of mappings in a model $\{\langle S_i, F_i \rangle : i = 1, ..., n\}$, when represented as a relational diagram in graph-theoretic form, is a network of blocks and arrows. Each component $\langle S_i, F_i \rangle$ may be represented by a block, and an arrow is drawn from $\langle S_i, F_i \rangle$ to $\langle S_j, F_j \rangle$ if there is a mapping $f \in F_i$ such that $\mathrm{cod}(f) = S_j$ or $\mathrm{cod}(f) \cap F_j \neq \varnothing$. (Note that this is different from the existence of an **S**-morphism from $\langle S_i, F_i \rangle$ to $\langle S_j, F_j \rangle$.) Here is an example:

(18)

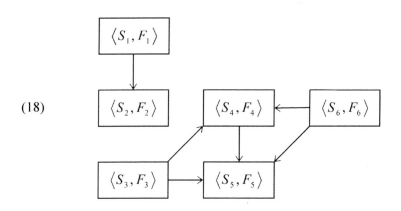

The main purpose of a model network diagram is to show how the various model components are interconnected. A mapping $f \in F_i$ may have its codomain $\mathrm{cod}(f)$ not related to any other components $\langle S_j, F_j \rangle$. These images may be considered the 'environmental outputs' of the component; they are understood to be implicitly present, and usually not explicitly shown; on the occasions when they are shown for emphasis, they appear as arrows initiating from the component and terminating in the ambience. Similarly,

184

'environmental inputs' are not usually represented; when they are, they appear as arrows initiating from the ambience and terminating in a component.

The solid-headed and hollow-headed arrow distinction used in connection with the relational diagram of a mapping (*cf.* 5.4) may be extended analogously to a *model network*. A mapping $f \in F_i$ such that $\text{cod}(f) = S_j$ entails a material cause, and may be represented by a hollow-headed arrow. A mapping $f \in F_i$ such that $\text{cod}(f) \cap F_j \neq \varnothing$ entails an efficient cause, and may be represented by a solid-headed arrow. Note, however, the usage of the two kinds of arrows are for the distinction of their causal differences, but the arrows do not represent the same entities in an entailment network of mappings and in a model network of components. In particular, in an entailment network, solid-headed and hollow-headed arrows come in formal-cause pairs, but there is no such relational requirement in an model network. In a model network here, a hollow-headed arrow means that the processed image of the arrow is used as a material input of its target block, while a solid-headed arrows means that the processed image of the arrow is itself a processor, thus a solid-headed arrow represents functional entailment that yields a *transfer function* of the target block. In short, the *arrowheads* of the hollow-headed and solid-headed arrows point, respectively, to entailed material and efficient causes. In contrast, in an entailment network of a formal system with its relation diagram in graph-theoretic form, it is the *tails* of the hollow-headed and solid-headed arrows that are the formal positions of the, respectively, material and efficient causes of a mapping.

I illustrate the usage for model networks with a simple example: consider a three-component model $M = \{\langle A, \{0, f\}\rangle, \langle B, \{0, g\}\rangle, \langle X, \{0, \Phi\}\rangle\}$, where $f : A \to B$ with $f : a \mapsto b$, $g : B \to C$ with $g : b \mapsto c$, and $\Phi : X \to H(A, B)$ with $\Phi : x \mapsto f$. Then the block diagram for M is

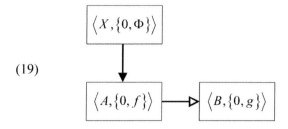

(19)

Each collection of observables of the components may be resolved into its individual mappings that are themselves represented in their relational diagrams in graph-theoretic form, resulting in a network of the solid-headed and hollow-headed arrows. The relational diagram for our example M is

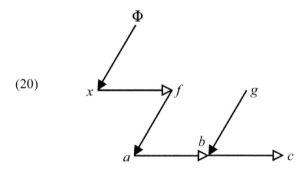

(20)

and it contracts to

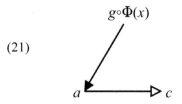

(21)

The similarity in form of the arrow usage between diagrams (19) and (21) (i.e., the isomorphism of their formal causes) demonstrates why I choose the solid-headed and hollow-headed arrow analogy for model networks.

For a model consisting of many components and many mappings, the relational diagram in graph-theoretic form is, of course, a very complicated network. Each formal-system component by itself may already be complicated (see, for example, diagram (1) in Chapter 6, and indeed the whole of the previous chapter on network topology), and now the networking process is iterated: a model is a network of component blocks, and each of these blocks is a collection of connected components, each of which is itself a network of arrows.

7.27 Definition The collection of *all* models of a natural system N is denoted $\mathbf{C}(N)$.

The lattice structure of model components $\mathbf{C}(S)$ may be extended to $\mathbf{C}(N)$. For two models $\{\langle S_i, F_i \rangle\}, \{\langle T_j, G_j \rangle\} \in \mathbf{C}(N)$, their join $\vee$ may be defined as the set-theoretic union of the two collections of components, with the exception that when $S_i = T_j$, instead of admitting $\langle S_i, F_i \rangle$ and $\langle T_j, G_j \rangle$ separately into the union one takes their join in $\mathbf{C}(S_i)$, $\langle S_i, F_i \rangle \vee \langle T_j, G_j \rangle = \langle S_i, F_i \cup G_j \rangle$. The meet of two models may be defined dually in the obvious way. Thus

7.28 Theorem *The collection* $\mathbf{C}(N)$ *of models of a natural system* N *is a lattice.*

I remarked in 1.31 that a partially ordered set $\langle X, \leq \rangle$ may itself be considered as a category, in which the objects are elements of X, and a hom-set $X(x, y)$ for $x, y \in X$ has either a single element or is empty, according to whether $x \leq y$ or not. It is in this sense that the lattice (hence poset) $\mathbf{C}(N)$ may also be considered as a category.

7.29 Corollary *The collection* $\mathbf{C}(N)$ *of models of a natural system* N *is a category.*

Thus we may speak of 'the category of models' $\mathbf{C}(N)$ in the literal category-theoretic usage.

The A and the Ω

That the binary join and meet operators of every lattice may be extended to any nonempty finite collection of elements is a matter of course (*cf.* 2.9). The meet operator of $\mathbf{C}(N)$ may also be extended to any *nonempty*, finite or infinite, collection of models, since, essentially, $\langle P_0 \cdot^s, \cup, \cap \rangle$ is a complete lattice; in other words, the meet, or infimum, of any nonempty collection of models is itself a model. I have noted above, however, that the greatest element, which is $\inf \varnothing$, does not necessarily exist for a *general* system. The join operator of $\mathbf{C}(N)$, on the other hand, may only be extended to any *countably infinite* collection of models, but not to any *arbitrary* collection: otherwise one may take the supremum of *all* the models in $\mathbf{C}(N)$ and again obtain the greatest element $\sup \mathbf{C}(N)$ which we have already excluded epistemologically for a *general* system. For a lattice to be complete, *every* subset (including the empty subset $\varnothing$ and the lattice itself) must have a supremum and an infimum. While we do have the least element $\inf \mathbf{C}(N) = \sup \varnothing = \langle N, \{0\} \rangle$, the greatest element $\sup \mathbf{C}(N) = \inf \varnothing$ does not necessarily exist; thus $\mathbf{C}(N)$ is *generally* not complete. (Note that in the notation $\langle N, \{0\} \rangle$ I have used the symbol N to denote both a natural system *and* a set that represents it. See the discussion on natural systems in 4.4.)

7.30 Definition The greatest element (if it exists) of the lattice of models $\mathbf{C}(N)$ is called the *largest model* of N.

The largest model may also be called the *greatest model*, or *maximal model*.

$\langle N,\{0\}\rangle$ is the least element of $\mathbf{C}(N)$. But $R_0 = U$ gives us no additional information other than the identification of the set N. More interesting are the models that are 'slightly larger' than $\langle N,\{0\}\rangle$ (*cf.* Definition 3.43).

7.31 Definition The join-irreducible elements in the lattice of models $\mathbf{C}(N)$ are called the *minimal model* of N.

One may also refer to minimal models as *smallest models* — but not 'least models', to avoid confusion with the least element $\langle N,\{0\}\rangle$ of $\mathbf{C}(N)$. Recall (Definition 3.25) that an element in a poset that covers the least element is called an *atom*, and that an atom is join-irreducible (Theorem 3.46). Models in $\mathbf{C}(N)$ of the form $\langle S,\{0,f\}\rangle$ that for which there are no observable h of S such that $R_f \leq R_h$ and $\langle S,\{0,h\}\rangle \in \mathbf{C}(N)$ are minimal models.

Since $\mathbf{C}(N)$ does not necessarily have a greatest element, one cannot generally speak of complements (Definition 3.9) in this lattice. One can, however, speak of *relative* complements (Definition 3.11). The lattice $\mathbf{Q}S$ of equivalence relations on S is relatively complemented (Theorem 3.14). The same constructive proof translates to $\mathbf{C}(S)$, because of the contravariant correspondence between $\mathbf{C}(S)$ and $\mathbf{Q}S$; whence the lattice $\mathbf{C}(S)$ of model components is also relatively complemented. Thus by extension, one also has the

7.32 Theorem $\mathbf{C}(N)$ *is a relatively complemented lattice.*

When one considers relative complements in the interval $[R_2, U]$ in $\mathbf{Q}S$, one has the

7.33 Corollary *If* $R_1, R_2 \in \mathbf{Q}S$ *and* $R_2 \leq R_1$ (R_2 *refines* R_1), *then there is an* $X \in \mathbf{Q}S$ *such that* $R_1 \wedge X = R_2$.

When one considers relative complements in the interval $\left[\langle S,\{0\}\rangle,\langle S,F_2\rangle\right]$ in $\mathbf{C}(S)$ (remember that the correspondence between $\mathbf{Q}S$ and $\mathbf{C}(S)$ is contravariant), one has the dual

7.34 Corollary *If* $\langle S,F_1\rangle,\langle S,F_2\rangle\in\mathbf{C}(S)$ *and* $\langle S,F_1\rangle\leq\langle S,F_2\rangle$ *, then there is an* $\langle S,G\rangle\in\mathbf{C}(S)$ *such that* $\langle S,F_1\rangle\vee\langle S,G\rangle=\langle S,F_2\rangle$.

And when one considers relative complements in the interval $\left[\langle N,\{0\}\rangle,M_2\right]$ in $\mathbf{C}(N)$, one has the corresponding

7.35 Corollary *If* $M_1,M_2\in\mathbf{C}(N)$ *and* $M_1\leq M_2$, *then there is an* $X\in\mathbf{C}(N)$ *such that* $M_1\vee X=M_2$.

Analytic Models and Synthetic Models

Next, I shall examine the inherent algebraic or topological structure of the codomains of a family of observables F of a set S. One learns about S through its model $\langle S,F\rangle$ by its *projection* into quotients

(22) $$S\to S/R_F\subset\prod_{f\in F}S/R_f\ .$$

7.36 Definition The expression of a set S as a cartesian product of quotient sets is an *analysis* of S; the corresponding model $\langle S,F\rangle$ is an *analytic model* of S.

Note that the term 'analytic model' is a description of the *expression*, or representation, of the model rather than of the model itself. *Every* model $\langle S,F\rangle$ may be represented in its cartesian-product-of-projections form $\prod_{f\in F}S/R_f$, and therefore *every model is an analytic model*. I use the term to distinguish the model from an alternate description called synthetic model that is my next topic, when the observables are *not interpreted as projections*. Note also that, for simplicity as in the construction of the lattice $\mathbf{C}(S)$ above, I have used the term 'model of S' to abbreviate the verbose but more proper term 'model component of the form $\langle S, F \rangle$ of the natural system N'. But the extension from $\mathbf{C}(S)$ to $\mathbf{C}(N)$ is trivial: a model $M = \{\langle S_i, F_i \rangle\} \in \mathbf{C}(N)$ is analytic if every $\langle S_i, F_i \rangle \in \mathbf{C}(S_i)$ is analytic.

7.37 Injection   The imputation process dual to projection is *injection* (*cf.* A.22 Product and A.33 Coproduct in the Appendix), when one reverses the arrow of an observable $f : S \to Z$, and considers properties that may be imputed onto S by '$f^{-1} : Z \to S$'. Note that 'f^{-1}' is used in the 'inverse image' sense (Definition 1.8), and is not necessarily a (single-valued) mapping. For a topological example, let Z be a *metric space*; then a pseudo-metric d_S may be defined on S by the metric d_Z on Z as

$$(23) \qquad d_S(x, y) = d_Z\big(f(x), f(y)\big).$$

For an algebraic example, let Z be a *ring*; then for $x, y \in S$ and $a \in Z$ one may define corresponding 'addition' $x + y$, 'multiplication' $x y$, and 'scalar multiplication' $a x$ in S by

$$(24) \qquad f(x + y) = f(x) + f(y),$$
$$(25) \qquad f(x y) = f(x) f(y),$$
$$(26) \qquad f(a x) = a f(x).$$

In each of these two examples, the 'new' mathematical structures in the system S on the 'left-hand side' are 'decoded' from the existing mathematical structures in the system Z on the 'right-hand side'. Obviously, the construction in S of the mathematical structures induced by observables has to be carefully done, and is indeed not always possible.

The strategy of imputing properties to S by injecting into it is not promising in epistemological terms. A general natural system S is not known *a priori*: it is the object of study, to be probed through observation and modelling. It is, therefore, natural to consider S as the domain on which observables are defined, and models established.

To treat S as codomain presupposes from the outset a knowledge of S that is difficult to phenomenologically justify. Systems for which this is possible must be special. This is the realm of *synthesis*, dual to analysis (although synthesis using analytic fragments is only a meagre part of synthesis; there is more discussion on this towards the end of this chapter). I now leave topological synthesis (the topic, *dynamical systems*, having been covered thoroughly in *FM* , *CS*, and *AS*), and concentrate on algebraic synthesis.

7.38 Algebraic Synthesis It is in human nature to fractionate and atomize. We like to break up complicated situations into simple ones, and then to take the resultant elementary pieces and put them together in various ways. Note that there is nothing wrong with this *synthetic* procedure — indeed many valuable lessons may be learned. The fatal flaw is the presumptuous reductionistic claim that this very specific kind of synthetic approach, the assembly of analytic fragments, *exhausts* reality.

> Like following life through creatures you dissect,
> You lose it in the moment you detect.
>
> — Alexander Pope: *Essay on Man*

> Humpty Dumpty sat on a wall,
> Humpty Dumpty had a great fall;
> All the King's horses and all the King's men
> Couldn't put Humpty together again.
>
> — nursery rhyme

Despite Alexander Pope's cautionary message and Humpty Dumpty's fate, reductionists continue in their futile attempt to identify the 'complete' set of elementary pieces and the 'right' way of putting them together again.

In the categorical dual of the product of the analytic model, one has the coproduct

$$(27) \qquad \coprod_\alpha U_\alpha \to S,$$

where each member in the collection of sets $\{U_\alpha\}$ may be considered to be representing a part of the whole system S. We shall specialize in categories in which the coproduct is an 'almost disjoint union' (the object generated by the disjoint union of all 'nonzero' elements, together with a common 'zero'; see the discussion in the Appendix on examples of these coproducts, A.36), whence we have the direct sum

$$(28) \qquad S = \bigoplus_\alpha U_\alpha.$$

When a system S is a direct sum, by the universal property, one sees that

7.39 Lemma *A mapping f is an observable of $S = \bigoplus_\alpha U_\alpha$ if and only if it may be expressed as a direct sum of observables f_α of the summands U_α.*

If each U_α is equipped with its own set of observables F_α, then a set of observables F of S may be constructed as the direct sums of the F_αs.

7.40 Definition The expression of a set S as a direct sum is a *synthesis* of S; the corresponding model $\langle S, F \rangle$ is a *synthetic model* of S.

(The extension from $\mathbf{C}(S)$ to $\mathbf{C}(N)$ is, again, trivial: a model $M = \{\langle S_i, F_i \rangle\} \in \mathbf{C}(N)$ is synthetic if every $\langle S_i, F_i \rangle \in \mathbf{C}(S_i)$ is synthetic.)

If $\langle S,F \rangle$ and $\langle S,G \rangle$ are two synthetic models, then so is their join; indeed,

(29) $\qquad \langle S,F \rangle \vee \langle S,G \rangle = \langle S,F \rangle \oplus \langle S,G \rangle.$

Since each model $\langle U_\alpha, F_\alpha \rangle$ is *a fortiori* an analytic model, so is its direct sum

(30) $\qquad \langle S,F \rangle = \bigoplus_\alpha \langle U_\alpha, F_\alpha \rangle.$

Thus one has

7.41 Theorem   *Every synthetic model is an analytic model.*

7.42 Corollary   *The collection of all synthetic models of N is a sublattice (whence a subcategory) of the lattice $\mathbf{C}(N)$ of all (analytic) models of N.*

The converse of Theorem 7.41 is not true: there generally exist analytic models that are not synthetic models. There are many reasons for this, and many were explained in Chapter 6 of *LI*. But above all, there is the simple mathematical reason that not every set may be expressed as a direct sum. Indeed, not every set may admit an inherently consistent *linear structure*, which is the central requisite in synthetic modelling. In other words, a synthetic model is a very special type of analytic model, in terms of the observables that define it. These observables must be expressible as linear combinations of observables of the summands. Stated yet otherwise, the values of the observables defining a synthetic model are determined, or entailed, entirely by values on summands. In category-theoretic terms, while the subcategory of synthetic models is an additive category, the category $\mathbf{C}(N)$ of all models is not necessarily so (*cf.* A.38–A.40 in the Appendix).

The Amphibology of Analysis and Synthesis

"I am not yet so lost in lexicography, as to forget that words are the daughters of earth, and that things are the sons of heaven. Language is only the instrument of science, and words are but the signs of ideas: I wish, however, that the instruments might be less apt to decay, and that signs might be permanent, like the things which they denote."

— Samuel Johnson (1755)
Dictionary of the English Language
Preface

7.43 Etymology The word 'analysis' is the Greek compound ἀνάλυσις, meaning 'an undoing'. The first component is *ana-*, 'up, on', and the second component is *lusis*, 'setting free'. The analysis of something complicated is a 'freeing up' of the thing, or resolving it into its component parts for detailed study. This technique has been in use in mathematics and logic since before Aristotle, although *analysis* as a mathematical subject is a relatively recent development as a descendent of calculus.

The word 'synthesis' is the Greek compound σύνθεσις, meaning 'putting together'. The first component is *sun-*, 'together, with', and the second component is *thesis*, 'putting, placing'. When something is 'put together' from parts, it often acquires a judgment and takes on the sense of being 'a substitute', 'an imitation', or 'artificial'. But this derogation is quite unnecessary: if one does not restrict to the dissected pieces, a synthetic approach is in no way 'inferior'. Indeed, quite the opposite is true.

7.44 Dual Analysis and synthesis are *dual* concepts; and just like other category-theoretic duals, they are 'philosophical opposites' but usually not 'operational inverses'. In analytic geometry, the space is 'cut up' by the scale of a coordinate system. In synthetic geometry (the type of geometry developed by the Greeks, i.e. 'Euclidean' geometry), shapes are treated 'together' as wholes.

The meanings and origins of the two words explain the terminology in the naming of the representation of the models (Definitions 7.36 and 7.40). A model expressed as a product resolves itself into component projections. This is the point of view of decomposition of the whole into parts; hence a product representation of a model is called analytic. A model expressed as a coproduct puts the injected summands together. This is the point of view of assembly of parts into the whole; hence a coproduct representation of a model is called synthetic.

7.45 Synthetic Models $\subset$ Analytic Models Corollary 7.42 indicates a hierarchy of models, that synthetic models are *specialized* analytic models. But we must note that this is a consequence of the *very particular definitions* of analytic and synthetic models, in terms of products and coproducts respectively. One must *not* conclude from this technical result that, in general, analysis is more generic than synthesis.

For a general natural system N, its category $\mathbf{C}(N)$ of models does not have the requisite linear structure for the component projections of an analytic model $M \in \mathbf{C}(N)$ to be injected back into an analytic model that is $\mathbf{C}(N)$-isomorphic to M. Coproduct is the category-theoretic construction *dual* to product, but not its *inverse*. Thus, in terms of Definitions 7.36 and 7.40, synthetic model and analytic model are not inverse constructions. In more general terms, analysis and synthesis are not categorical inverses of each other: synthesis of life, in particular, is more than reassembling analytic fragments. This is the lesson of Humpty Dumpty: the pieces cannot be put together again. In short,

(31)   synthesis $\circ$ analysis $\neq$ identity.

On the other hand, in the product-coproduct sense of analysis-synthesis, if one *carefully* keeps track of the parts, one can recover them by taking apart the assembled whole. So it is *possible* to have

(32)   analysis ∘ synthesis ≅ identity.

But note that this identity in (32) and the nonexistent one in (31) are in different domains. In short, (31) and (32) together demonstrate a *one-sided inverse*.

7.46 Observation < Analysis < Synthesis   James F. Danielli described the three ages in the science of modern biology as

(33)   *age of observation → age of analysis → age of synthesis*

[Danielli 1974]. The same progression may also be appropriately prescribed to science in general. It is, indeed, not a hyperbole to state that the progress of human culture also depends on the capacity to move from the second age of analysis to the third age of synthesis, i.e., from analytic machine-based technologies to synthetic biology-inspired modes of production. Paradoxically, a synthetic approach restores to our fragmented sciences the kind of integration and unity they possessed in an earlier time, when scientists regarded themselves as natural philosophers.

As I explicated in connection with Natural Law (4.7), *perception* is an integral part of science. Since science begins with observations, everything in it evolves from our physical senses. These senses interact with physical objects. It is therefore natural, as a first approximation, for scientists to assume that matter is the fundamental building blocks of the universe. The examination of material fragments, i.e. analysis, is then the next step after the accumulation of observed data, with the hope that the knowing of the parts will tell the story of the whole. The assumption is that there are certain physical laws ('equations') that all matter must obey, epitomized in the Newtonian paradigm. In sum, this is an 'upward' theory of causation.

7.47 Newtonianism

> Nature does nothing in vain, and more is in vain when less
> will serve; for Nature is pleased with simplicity and affects
> not the pomp of superfluous causes.

> — Issac Newton (1687)
> *Philosophiæ naturalis Principia mathematica*
> *De Mundi systemate Liber tertius:*
> *Regulæ Philosophandi*

The mechanistic view of the universe was what made sense to Newton. In his clockwork universe, God makes the clock and winds it up. Unlike Aristotle, Newton did not claim to have an explanation for everything (thus began the exile of *final cause* from science: see Chapter 5). For example, Newton, in his *Principia*, describes how gravity *works*, on the basis of the effects seen, but does not say what gravity *is*. On this and other 'mystery subjects', Newton said "*hypotheses non fingo*" (that he "frames no hypotheses").

While Newton himself might have framed no hypothesis, the same cannot be said of his followers. Scientists since Newton were led astray by the mechanistic viewpoint, in their attachment of synthetic significance to analytic fragments. If the world was (like) a machine, then, they reasoned, the understanding of the world had to be reduced through analogies to machines. The 'Newtonian paradigm' may be succinctly summarized thus:

  (i)   Axiomatic presentation;
 (ii)   Mathematical precision and tight logic;
(iii)   All science should have this format.

Although the paradigm bears Newton's name, the dogma was only *attributed* to him. Newton certainly demonstrated (i) and (ii) in his *Principia*, but he himself did not necessarily agree with statement (iii).

When the mechanical model is the ultimate explanation, then the emphasis is on "how?", not "why?". The misconception is that analytic knowledge (i.e. its *physiology*) can tell something about its creation (i.e. its *ontogenesis*). This is *not* to say analysis, Newtonian or otherwise, is not valuable. Quite the contrary: the scientific revolution, hence modern science, is founded on it. The error is in the *induction* that analysis is *all* of science, and therefore *everything* must be explained in analytic terms. Stated otherwise, there is nothing wrong with (i) and (ii) of the Newtonian paradigm: the effectiveness of mathematics in science is a consequence of Natural Law (*cf.* Chapter 4). It is the *generalization* (iii), the *Newtonian model of all knowledge* (the Newtonian model indeed extends far beyond physics, into philosophy, sociology, economics, etc.), that firmly epitomizes, whence stagnates, the age of analysis.

7.48 Incompleteness Newton, of course, based the 'formalization of mechanics' that is his *Principia* on Euclid's *Elements*, the very model of scientific rigour for millennia. If axiomatic presentation with mathematical precision and tight logic worked so well for geometry, the same ought to work for physics. It had even been said that "Physics is geometry." The same analogue reasoning led, two and a half centuries later, to Hilbert's program, one of the goals of which was the formalization of *all* of mathematics. Then came Gödel. It must, however, be remembered that although it is not possible to formalize *all* mathematics, it is possible to formalize almost all the mathematics that anyone uses (other than, naturally, those specifically involved in mathematical logic and foundations). In short, one acknowledges the incompleteness, and moves on.

Gödel's arguments applied to a wide range of mathematics, although his original arguments were carried through an axiomatic number-theoretic system in which a certain amount of elementary arithmetic could be expressed and some basic rules of arithmetic could be proven. In essence, what is today known as 'Gödel's incompleteness theorem' states that any such axiomatic system (as one that Gödel had considered), if consistent, is incomplete, and the consistency of the system cannot be proven within the system itself.

Succinctly, consistency and completeness of an axiomatic theory may be explicated thus:

consistency: Statement p is provable, *therefore* it is true.
completeness: Statement p is provable, *because* it is true.

I invite the reader to reflect on these two properties in connection to the "whys and wherefores" discussion in 5.3. The lesson to be learned from Gödel, however, is more importantly the metaphorical one, that "nothing works for everything": all attempts at universality or genericity in human endeavours are likely unsuccessful. Let me tersely summarize the situation in this variation of Epimenides's Paradox:

Every absolute statement is false.

What ought to be done is the reversal of this unfortunate legacy of misidentification, and separate analysis and synthesis again. Analysis and synthesis are not mutual inverses; indeed, most of our modes of analysis are inherently irreversible. Both analysis and synthesis are essential in natural philosophy. Modes of synthesis would include the entailment of existence, *immanent causation* (*cf.* 5.18).

7.49 Towards an Age of Synthesis It must be emphasized that the progression of the three ages are natural developments. A tremendous amount of *knowledge* has been gained in each of the first two ages. What is causing scientists to consider that one must go beyond analysis is their dawning realization that upward causality contains no explanation for *why* complexity increases. Note that "complex forms emerge" is not an answer: *emergence* is a descriptive concept, not an explanatory one.

The accumulation of experience and knowledge must, and will, continue, of course. But knowledge should not be the only emphasis that is passed on from generation to generation, from age to age. When one is only given the analytic fragments to assemble, one is told what one is supposed to know. Wisdom may be defined as 'experience and knowledge together with the power of applying them critically or practically'. In short, *wisdom is knowledge applied*. It is about *how* to think, instead of *what* to think. The crux is the *discovery*, not the *prescription*. The difference between analysis and synthesis is analogous to that between knowledge and wisdom.

In the age of synthesis, one recognizes that the foundational feature of the universe is not matter but *information* — the interconnecting relationships and entailment patterns among matter. The world may be considered a hierarchy of systems that convey information, and the purpose of theory is to extract as much information from these systems as possible. One does not limit oneself to the analytic fragments; information has diverse sources. This 'downward' theory of causation frees science from the reductionistic project of forcing nature into a Newtonian mould. Note that nothing of substance in mechanistic science is lost: *synthesis extends analysis* but does not replace it. Analytic tools are necessary but simply not sufficient: to progress one needs synthetic tools. Towards an age of synthesis, what one must give up is the idea that science is a 'bottom-up' affair in which knowledge of a system's parts determines knowledge of the system as a whole.

'Analysis' and 'synthesis' are examples of *amphibolous* words, those that bear two meanings that are diametrically opposed. As we saw, as expressions of the forms of models, synthetic is 'specialized analytic'; but as scientific methods, synthetic is 'generalized analytic'. The progressive generalization from analysis to synthesis in a biological context is essentially what the work of the Rashevsky-Rosen school of relational biology is about.

8

Simple Systems

Simulability

We have already met a member of the etymological family of *simulacrum*: simulation (4.10). Recall that a *simulation* of a process provides an alternate description of the entailed effects, whereas a *model* is a special kind of simulation that additionally also provides an alternate description of the entailment structure of the mapping representing the process itself.

8.1 Simulation Revisited   To recap, a simulation may be represented by the commutative element-chasing diagram

(1)

$$
\begin{array}{ccc}
y & \xrightarrow{\quad \alpha \quad} & \alpha(y) \\
\uparrow{\scriptstyle f} & & \uparrow{\scriptstyle g} \\
x & \xrightarrow{\quad \alpha \quad} & \alpha(x)
\end{array}
$$

The equality

(2) $\qquad \alpha(f(x)) = g(\alpha(x))$

may be summarized by the entailment

(3) $\qquad \alpha:\{f,x,y\} \mapsto \{g,\alpha(x),\alpha(y)\}.$

The important fact to note here is that simulation converts the efficient cause f, the processor of that being simulated, into material cause of the simulator α, and the 'simulated processor' g becomes part of the 'effect'. In particular, the process-flow distinction in the original mapping f is lost, and all become 'flow' in the simulation.

In a model, the processor f itself is mapped to a processor $\alpha(f)$, and the commutative element-chasing diagram is

(4)

$$
\begin{array}{ccc}
y & \xrightarrow{\;\;\alpha\;\;} & \alpha(y) \\[2pt]
\Big\uparrow{\scriptstyle f} & & \Big\uparrow{\scriptstyle \alpha(f)} \\[2pt]
x & \xrightarrow[\;\;\alpha\;\;]{} & \alpha(x)
\end{array}
$$

Here the equality

(5) $\qquad \alpha(f(x)) = \alpha(f)(\alpha(x))$

may be summarized by the functorial entailment

(6) $\qquad \alpha:(f:x \mapsto y) \mapsto (\alpha(f):\alpha(x) \mapsto \alpha(y)).$

Note that the 'modelled processor' $\alpha(f)$ preserves the entailment pattern (in particular, the process-flow distinction) of the original efficient cause f. Stated otherwise, a model maps efficient causes to efficient causes.

8.2 Definition An *algorithm* is a process with the following attributes:
  (i) it terminates after a finite number of steps;
  (ii) each step is unambiguously defined;
  (iii) it has zero or more input data;
  (iv) it has one or more output data; and
  (v) it must be effective, which means there must be a Turing-machine equivalent; i.e., the process must be evaluable by a mathematical (Turing) machine.

An algorithm, therefore, is a computation procedure that requires in its application a rigid stepwise mechanical execution of explicitly stated rules. It is presented as a prescription, consisting of a finite number of instructions. It may be applied to any number (including none) of members of a set of possible inputs, where each input is a finite sequence of symbolic expressions. Once the inputs have been specified, the instructions dictate a succession of discrete, simple operations, requiring no recourse to chance and ingenuity. The first operation is applied to the input and transforms it into a new finite sequence of symbolic expressions. This outcome is in turn subjected to a second operation, dictated by the instructions of the algorithm, and so on. After a finite number of steps, the instructions dictate that the process must be discontinued, and some outputs be read off, in some prescribed fashion, from the outcome of the last step.

8.3 Definition A mapping is *simulable* if it is definable by an algorithm.

If a mapping (representing a processor or efficient cause) is *simulable*, then a simulation (in the sense of diagram (1) above) exists. Note, however, the technical Definition 8.3 is somewhat more specific, and is predicated on the term 'algorithm'. In turn, the definition of 'algorithm' depends on other computing-theoretic terms: *unambiguous*, *effective*, and '*evaluable by a mathematical (Turing) machine*'. 'Simulable' is also called *computable* and *algorithmically definable*. There are fine nuances that distinguish these near-synonymous terms. I will not repeat here the thorough discussion on simulation given in Chapter 7 of *LI*. Readers interested in pursuing the computing-theoretic aspects will also find an excellent exposition in Kercel's paper *"Entailment of Ambiguity"* [2007]. For our purpose, we only need to note these three simple

8.4 Properties *If a mapping is simulable, then*
(*a*) *its corresponding Turing machine halts after a finite number of steps;*
(*b*) *its corresponding algorithmic process is of finite length; and*
(*c*) *its corresponding program, which may be considered as a word built of the alphabets of its Turing machine, is of finite length.*

The keyword is *finite*.

A formal system, an object in the universe of mathematics, may be considered a collection of mappings connected by the system's entailment pattern (i.e., its graph, which may itself be considered a mapping). (We studied this in categorical details in the previous chapter.) So one may extend Definition 8.3 and give the

8.5 Definition   A formal system is *simulable* if its entailment pattern and all of its mappings are simulable.

Note that any formal system (i.e., any mathematical structure) may or may not be the model of something, and it may or may not be simulable. If a formal system is simulable, then its entailment pattern and mappings may be replaced by their corresponding simulations, so that all processes and flows become just 'flow' (material causes and effects) for the simulator. Remember that a simulation keeps track of the 'inputs' and 'outputs', but the processors inside the 'black boxes' (i.e. the transfer functions) may be lost — unless the simulation is in fact a model.

8.6 Finitude Redux   Because of the finiteness predicated in Properties 8.4, a simulable formal system must have only finitely many observables (since, evidently, an infinite number of nonequivalent mappings requires an infinite number of algorithms). Note, however, this finitude is a *necessary, but not sufficient, condition* for simulability: it is the entailment pattern of the finitely many mappings, together with the possible computability of the mappings themselves, that determine whether or not the formal system is simulable.

While a model is a special kind of simulation, a 'simulable model' is not a tautology. This is because the requirement for a formal system to be 'simulable' is more than 'a simulation exists'. Stated otherwise, a *simulable model* is a model (of a natural system) for which the entailment pattern and all mappings are definable by algorithms. Recall (Axiom 7.20(*b*)) that a model has finitely many mappings, so it already satisfies this finitude necessity for simulability.

Finitude is a crucial property of computing (and a standard ingredient of the definition of computability) since the pioneering work of Turing. Before I leave the subject altogether, let me just illustrate with one quotation. In Kleene's *Introduction to Metamathematics* [1952], he began Chapter XIII on "Computable Functions" (i.e. our 'simulable mappings' of Definition 8.3) thus:

> § 67. **Turing machines.** Suppose that a person is to compute the value of a function for a given set of arguments by following preassigned effective instructions. In performing the computation he will use a finite number of distinct symbols or tokens of some sort. He can have only a finite number of occurrences of symbols under observation at one time. He can also remember others previously observed, but again only a finite number. The preassigned instructions must also be finite. Applying the instructions to the finite number of observed and remembered symbols or tokens, he can perform an act that changes the situation in a finite way, e.g. he adds or erases some occurrences of symbols, shifts his observation to others, registers in his memory those just observed. A succession of such acts must lead him from a symbolic expression representing the arguments to another symbolic expression representing the function value.

There are six occurrences of the word *finite* in this one paragraph.

Impredicativity

Let N be a natural system. Recall (Definition 7.27) that $\mathbf{C}(N)$ denotes the collection of all models of N, and (Theorem 7.28) that it is a lattice. I emphasized in the previous chapter (7.24 and 7.30) the fact that for a general natural system N, its lattice of models $\mathbf{C}(N)$ does not necessarily have a greatest element, whence N does not necessarily have a largest model. In this chapter I study a special class of natural systems that do have largest models.

Let $M \in \mathbf{C}(N)$; i.e., let M be a model of the natural system N. Let us consider what the inferential entailment pattern of its relational diagram in graph-theoretic form (necessarily a *finite graph*, Axiom 7.20(c)) would have to take to make M simulable.

It is clear that a tree of sequential compositions (6.13) of simulable mappings is simulable. Closed paths of *material* causation (6.14) abound, and they are also all simulable. It is standard that the output of a step in an algorithm be the input of the next sequential step. An algorithm would be quite cumbersome if it contains no closed causal loops of this type: the program length would otherwise increase proportionally with the number of computation steps. It is also obvious that a closed path with exactly one efficient cause (6.15) is simulable. Thus one may conclude with the

8.7 Theorem *A model without hierarchical cycles is simulable.*

An iteration of 'efficient cause of efficient cause' is inherently hierarchical, in the sense that a lower-level efficient cause is contained within a higher-level efficient cause; *e.g.* $H(X, H(A, B))$ is at a higher hierarchical level than $H(A, B)$. A closed path of efficient causation must form a hierarchical cycle of containment. Both the hierarchy of containment and the cycle are essential attributes of this closure. In formal systems, hierarchical cycles are manifested by *impredicativities* (i.e., entailed ambiguities). In other words, a hierarchical cycle is an impredicative cycle of inferential entailment.

8.8 Predicate   In logic, the *predicate* is what is said or asserted about an object. It can take the role as either a property or a relation between entities. Thus *predicate calculus* is the type of symbolic logic that takes into account the contents (i.e., predicate) of a statement. The defining property $p(x)$ in

(7) $P = \{x \in U : p(x)\}$

(*cf.* Axiom of Specification, 0.19) is an example of a predicate, since it *asserts* unambiguously the property that x must have in order to belong to the set P.

8.9 Self-Referencing   Contrariwise, a definition of an object is said to be *impredicative* if it invokes (mentions or quantifies over) the object itself being defined, or perhaps another set which contains the object being defined. In other words, *impredicativity* is the property of a *self-referencing definition*.

As an example, consider the definition of *supremum* (*cf.* Definition 1.27). Let $\leq$ be a partial order on a set X and let $A \subset X$. The subset A is bounded above if there exists $x \in X$ such that $a \leq x$ for all $a \in A$; such $x \in X$ is called an upper bound for A. An upper bound x for A is called the *supremum* for A if $x \leq y$ for all upper bounds y for A. Stated otherwise,

(8) $x = \sup A \iff x \leq y$ for all $y \in Y$

where $Y = \{y \in X : y$ is an upper bound for $A\}$. Note that the definition invokes the set Y and the supremum $x \in Y$, whence the definition of 'supremum' is impredicative.

Impredicative definitions usually cannot be bypassed, and are mostly harmless. But there are some that lead to paradoxes. The most famous of a problematic impredicative construction is Russell's paradox, which involves the set of all sets that do not contain themselves:

(9) $\{x : x \notin x\}$.

This foundational difficulty is only avoided by the restriction to a naive set-theoretic universe that explicitly prohibits self-referencing constructions.

A formal definition of impredicativity may be found in Kleene's *Introduction to Metamathematics* [1952]:

8.10 Impredicative Definition "When a set M and a particular object m are so defined that on the one hand m is a member of M, and on the other hand the definition of m depends on M, we say that the procedure (or the definition of m, or the definition of M) is *impredicative*. Similarly, when a property P is possessed by an object m whose definition depends on P (here M is the set of the objects which possess the property P). An impredicative definition is circular, at least on its face, as what is defined participates in its own definition."

So we see that the distinguishing feature of impredicativity is the self-referencing, cyclic constraint

$$(10) \qquad m \rightleftarrows M$$

(*cf.* the two-mapping hierarchical cycle in 6.22). This is, of course, precisely the same defining feature of hierarchical cycles.

8.11 Deadlock A *deadlock* is a situation wherein competing actions are waiting for one another to finish, and thus none ever does. It is thus a relational analogue of impredicativity. The most famous example of deadlock is 'the chicken or the egg' paradox. Another example is the following statute supposedly passed by the Kansas Legislature:

> "When two trains approach each other at a crossing, both
> shall come to a full stop and neither shall start up again
> until the other has gone."

In computer science, deadlock refers to a specific condition when two or more processes are each waiting for another to release a resource, or more than two processes are waiting for resources in a circular chain. Implementation of hierarchical cycles (or attempts to execute ambiguous codes in general) will lead a program to either a deadlock or an endless loop. In either case the program does not terminate. This is practical verification from computing science of the *inverse* of Theorem 8.7: a hierarchical cycle (i.e. a cycle in which *two or more* compositions are hierarchical, a model of a closed path of efficient causation) is different in kind from the other patterns of entailment considered above — it is *not* simulable. I state this formally as

8.12 Theorem   *A formal system that contains a hierarchical cycle is not simulable.*

Thus equivalently one also has:

8.13 Theorem   *If an impredicative cycle of inferential entailment exists in a formal system, then it is not simulable.*

'Practical verification' contributes to scientific 'proofs', but is, however, not a mathematical proof. The rest of this chapter will be a detailed examination of properties of simulable models, culminating in the proof of (an equivalent form of) Theorems 8.12 and 8.13.

Limitations of Entailment and Simulability

Let **N** be the set of all natural systems. Let $t(N)$ be the property 'there is no closed path of efficient causation in N' (recall Definition 6.16 that this means there are *no* closed paths that contain *two or more* efficient causes), and let

(11) $$T = \{N \in \mathbf{N} : t(N)\}$$

(see the Axiom of Specification 0.19 in the Prolegomena for an review of the notation). This is the

8.14 Definition A natural system is in the *subset* **T** *of* **N** if and only if it has *no closed path of efficient causation.*

8.15 In the Realm of Formal Systems Let $M \in \mathbf{C}(N)$; i.e., let M be a model of the natural system N. Let $\iota(M)$ be the property 'there is a hierarchical cycle in M', and $\pi(M)$ be the property 'M is simulable'. Theorem 8.7 says *a formal system without hierarchical cycles is simulable.* Thus, in particular,

$$(12) \qquad \forall M \in \mathbf{C}(N) \quad \neg\iota(M) \Rightarrow \pi(M).$$

The equivalent contrapositive of statement (12) is

$$(13) \qquad \forall M \in \mathbf{C}(N) \quad \neg\pi(M) \Rightarrow \iota(M),$$

which says

8.16 Corollary *A model that is not simulable must contain a hierarchical cycle.*

8.17 Implications in the Realm of Natural Systems If a natural system has no closed path of efficient causation, then none of its models can have hierarchical cycles (Lemma 6.18), so (by Theorem 8.7) all the models are all simulable. Therefore $\forall N \in \mathbf{N}$,

$$(14) \qquad \iota(N) \Rightarrow \forall M \in \mathbf{C}(N) \neg\iota(M) \Rightarrow \forall M \in \mathbf{C}(N) \pi(M).$$

Stated otherwise,

$$(15) \qquad \forall N \in \mathbf{T} \quad \forall M \in \mathbf{C}(N) \neg\iota(M) \wedge \pi(M).$$

Now let $s(N)$ be the property 'all models of N are simulable'. Thus

$$(16) \qquad s(N) = \forall M \in \mathbf{C}(N) \pi(M).$$

Let

(17) $\qquad \mathbf{S} = \{N \in \mathbf{N} : s(N)\}.$

One therefore, in view of (14) and (15), has

(18) $\qquad \mathbf{T} \subset \mathbf{S},$

and the following characterization of members of $\mathbf{T}$:

8.18 Lemma *All models of a member of $\mathbf{T}$ are simulable.*

Lemma 8.18 may alternatively be stated as

8.19 Lemma *If a natural system has no closed path of efficient causation, then all of its models are simulable.*

That is,

(19) $\qquad \forall N \in \mathbf{N} \quad t(N) \Rightarrow s(N).$

Note that the property $t(N)$ is a characterization of a natural system in the natural domain, whereas the property $s(N)$ characterizes a natural system through its models in the formal domain. The implication (19) is a quintessential property of the functorial encoding in a modelling relation.

Lemma 8.19 proclaims the consequences in the universe of formal systems, when a natural system has no closed path of efficient causation, in terms of limitations on its models. It is a very important fact that the *converse* of the lemma is also true. That is, one also has

(20) $\qquad \forall N \in \mathbf{N} \quad s(N) \Rightarrow t(N),$

and

(21) $S \subset T,$

stated explicitly as the

8.20 Theorem   *If all models of a natural system* N *are simulable, then there can be no closed path of efficient causation in* N.

Theorem 8.20 says that certain modes of entailment are *not* available to a natural system when all its models are simulable. This is the most important theorem in *LI*, and as such, most far-reaching and hence most controversial. Chapter 9 of *LI* is a detailed apagogical argument that proves it, albeit in the 'illustrative' Rosen form. Towards the end of this chapter, I shall provide an alternate proof using the mathematical tools we have accumulated heretofore in this monograph. But before we get there, let us discover more of what the property 'all models are simulable' entails.

The Largest Model

For the remainder of this chapter, unless otherwise stated, let N denote a natural system all models of which are simulable; i.e., $N \in \mathbf{S}$.

8.21 Lemma   *The lattice* $\mathbf{C}(N)$ *satisfies the ascending chain condition.*

PROOF I shall show that a strictly increasing chain in $\mathbf{C}(N)$ must terminate, whence the equivalence in Lemma 3.34 entails the desired conclusion. Consider

(22) $M_1 < M_2 < M_3 < \cdots < M_k < \cdots$

in $\mathbf{C}(N)$. Each M_k must have a program of finite length. I can form the join of the countably infinite family

(23) $M = \bigvee_k M_k \in \mathbf{C}(N),$

which is itself simulable, whence its program must also be of finite length. Since there are only finitely many programs of a fixed finite length (*cf.* Property 8.4(*c*)), a strictly increasing infinite sequence of models must have a corresponding subsequence of program lengths monotonically increase to infinity. So unless the chain terminates, the lengths of the programs of M_k would force the program length of M to be infinite, because $M_k < M$ for all k. The contradiction thus entails that the strictly increasing chain must terminate. □

By Lemma 3.34, $\mathbf{C}(N)$ therefore also satisfies the maximum condition, so in particular $\mathbf{C}(N)$ itself has a maximal element, whence also the greatest element (Theorem 2.4).

8.22 Theorem   *N has a unique largest model M^{max}.*

Epistemologically, this model M^{max} contains everything knowable about N, according to Natural Law. With the existence of the greatest element $M^{\text{max}} = \sup \mathbf{C}(N) = \inf \varnothing$ secured, Theorem 2.11 gives us the

8.23 Theorem $\mathbf{C}(N)$ *is a complete lattice.*

If a natural system has a *simulable* largest model, then every model, being a submodel of the largest one, is simulable. Whence the converse to Theorem 8.22 is also true, and one has this important

8.24 Theorem   *All models of a natural system N are simulable if and only if N has a simulable largest model.*

Minimal Models

8.25 Lemma *The lattice* $\mathbf{C}(N)$ *satisfies the descending chain condition.*

PROOF I shall show that a strictly decreasing chain in $\mathbf{C}(N)$ must terminate, then Lemma 3.35 leads to the desired result. Consider

(24) $$M_1 > M_2 > M_3 > \cdots > M_k > \cdots$$

in $\mathbf{C}(N)$. Each M_k must have a program of finite length, with the length a decreasing function of k. There are only finitely many programs of a fixed finite length (*cf.* Property 8.4(*c*)), and one obviously cannot have a strictly decreasing infinite sequence of natural numbers (*cf.* the method of infinite descent, 3.36); thus the strictly decreasing chain must be finite, *i.e.* terminate. □

By Lemma 3.45, one has the following important theorem for a natural system N with all simulable models:

8.26 Theorem *Every element of* $\mathbf{C}(N)$, *i.e. every model of* N, *can be expressed as a join of a finite number of join-irreducible elements.*

The set $\left\{ M_i^{\min} \right\}$ of all join-irreducible elements of $\mathbf{C}(N)$, *i.e.* minimal models of N, must be finite: otherwise the strictly ascending chain

(25) $$M_1^{\min} < M_1^{\min} \vee M_2^{\min} < M_1^{\min} \vee M_2^{\min} \vee M_3^{\min} < \cdots$$

would be non-terminating. So in particular, one has

8.27 Corollary N *has a finite set* $\left\{ M_i^{\min} \right\}$ *of minimal models.*

8.28 Corollary *The maximal model is the join of the finite number of minimal ones,*

(26) $$M^{\max} = \bigvee_i M_i^{\min}.$$

The keyword, again, is *finite*.

Sum of the Parts

Corollary 8.28 says that the maximal model of N is the *join* of the minimal ones; one can, in fact, claim a bit more:

8.29 Theorem *The maximal model is equivalent to the direct sum of the minimal ones,*

(27) $$M^{\max} = \bigoplus_i M_i^{\min},$$

and is therefore a synthetic model.

PROOF The direct sum $\bigoplus_i M_i^{\min}$ of *all* the minimal models $\left\{ M_i^{\min} \right\}$ is clearly itself a model. Suppose it is not $M^{\max}$, whence $\bigoplus_i M_i^{\min} < M^{\max}$. Corollary 7.35 says that there is a model $X \in \mathbf{C}(N)$ such that $\bigoplus_i M_i^{\min} \vee X = M^{\max}$. By Corollary 8.28 the model X must be the join of minimal models different from those in $\left\{ M_i^{\min} \right\}$, contradicting the fact that the latter is supposed to be the collection of *all* the minimal models. □

8.30 Theorem *Analytic and synthetic models coincide in the category* $\mathbf{C}(N)$.

PROOF In view of Theorem 7.41, what remains to be shown is that when all models of N are simulable, every model is synthetic. So let

$M \in \mathbf{C}(N)$. Then $M \leq M^{\text{max}} = \bigoplus_i M_i^{\text{min}}$. Let $\left\{ M_{i_k}^{\text{min}} \right\}$ be the *smallest* subset of the minimal models $\left\{ M_i^{\text{min}} \right\}$ for which $M \leq \bigoplus_k M_{i_k}^{\text{min}}$. If $M \neq \bigoplus_k M_{i_k}^{\text{min}}$, by Corollary 7.35 there is a model $X \in \mathbf{C}(N)$ such that $M \vee X = \bigoplus_k M_{i_k}^{\text{min}}$. But that means X itself must be the join of some of the minimal models in the collection $\left\{ M_{i_k}^{\text{min}} \right\}$. These components of X may then be removed from $\left\{ M_{i_k}^{\text{min}} \right\}$ and the direct sum of the remaining collection would still be greater than or equal to M, contradicting the minimality of the collection $\left\{ M_{i_k}^{\text{min}} \right\}$. Thus $M = \bigoplus_k M_{i_k}^{\text{min}}$ □

I have just shown that if all models of N are simulable, any model is equivalent to a synthetic model. Hence in particular, any analytic model must be a synthetic model. As we have seen in the discussion following Theorem 7.42, this cannot be *generally* true for all natural systems. The situation may be summarized succinctly as

Direct sum and direct products coincide in $\mathbf{C}(N)$.

The fact that it is true for a natural system N when all its models are simulable illustrates how special N itself must be.

In the proof of Theorem 8.30, one sees that any $M \in \mathbf{C}(N)$ may be represented as a direct sum $M = \bigoplus_k M_{i_k}^{\text{min}}$ for a subset $\left\{ M_{i_k}^{\text{min}} \right\}$ of all the minimal models $\left\{ M_i^{\text{min}} \right\}$. Stated otherwise, any property or characteristic of N embodied in a model $M \neq M^{\text{max}}$ may be *localized*, in the sense that it may be expressed as a direct summand of the largest model M^{max}; *i.e.* one may write

(28) $\qquad M^{\text{max}} = \bigoplus_i M_i^{\text{min}} = \bigoplus_k M_{i_k}^{\text{min}} \oplus \bigoplus_{j \neq i_k} M_j^{\text{min}} = M \oplus \bigoplus_{j \neq i_k} M_j^{\text{min}}.$

I give the

8.31 Definition A property of a natural system S is *fractionable* if S can be separated into two parts modelled by disjoint direct summands, such that the property is manifest in one of these parts.

Note that fractionability implicitly implies that the property may be embodied in a *synthetic* model. One considers a property embodied in the largest model $M^{\max}$ trivially fractionable. One says a natural system S can be *fractionated* if every property is fractionable. Thus

8.32 Theorem *Every property of N is fractionable.*

and

8.33 Theorem *The natural system N can be fractionated.*

The Art of Encoding

Robert Rosen, in Section 8B of *LI*, gave the

8.34 Definition A natural system is a *mechanism* if and only if all of its models are simulable.

And in Chapter 19 of *EL*, gave the synonymous

8.35 Definition A natural system N is a *simple system* if and only if all of its models are simulable.

The collection of all simple systems is, therefore, our set **S** (definition in line (17)). Note the characterization of simple applies to natural systems. In other words, a simple system, and a mechanism, according to Rosen, is a natural system with the property that every formal system that encodes it through the modelling relation is simulable.

218

Definition 8.35 of 'simple system', characterizing a natural system in terms of properties of its models, is a *relational* definition. The term 'simple system' is not an 'everyday term', and has no 'standard definition', and so may be used according to the Rosen Definition 8.35 without too often encountering problems. On the other hand, while it may be argued that Definition 8.34 as one of 'mechanism' agrees well with its common kinematic *structural* definition — for example as in 'an assemblage of bodies formed and connected to move upon one another with definite relative motion' — it still endows Rosen's mechanisms with very specific properties. Since the word 'mechanism' does have its common-usage meaning, one must be careful not to fall into the trap of the fallacy of semantic equivocation.

The usage of 'mechanism' to mean neither more nor less than what Rosen means is part of Rosen's art (an art of naming, if you will), his encoding arrow ε of the modelling relation diagram (4.14). Feel free to find the art congenial or uncongenial. The indisputable fact, however, is that a natural system all models of which are simulable has certain inherent properties that may be mathematically proven (viz. from Lemma 8.21 to Theorem 8.33). This is the inferential entailment arrow i that once proven becomes a certainty.

8.36 Conclusions In Section 8B of *LI* we find five conclusions stated. These are properties of simple systems (called 'mechanisms' in *LI*) and are sequentially proven in the remainder of Chapter 8 of *LI*. I have now just completed an alternate set of proofs in terms of lattice theory. In summary, I list these five important conclusions:

If a natural system N is a simple system, then

Conclusion 1 [Theorem 8.22]: *N has a unique largest model $M^{\max}$.*

Conclusion 2 [Corollary 8.27]: *N has a finite set $\left\{ M_i^{\min} \right\}$ of minimal models.*

Conclusion 3 [Theorem 8.29]: *The maximal model is equivalent to the direct sum of the minimal ones,* $M^{\text{max}} = \bigoplus_i M_i^{\text{min}}$, *and is therefore a synthetic model.*

Conclusion 4 [Theorem 8.30]: *Analytic and synthetic models coincide in the category* $\mathbf{C}(N)$.

Conclusion 5 [Theorem 8.32]: *Every property of* N *is fractionable.*

8.37 Equivalent Definitions   Recall our notation that $\mathbf{N}$ is the collection of all natural systems, $\mathbf{S}$ is the collection of all natural systems every model of which is simulable (i.e., all simple systems), and $\mathbf{T}$ is the collection of all natural systems with no closed path of efficient causation.

Statements (18)–(21) together give

(29) $\forall N \in \mathbf{N} \quad t(N) \Leftrightarrow s(N)$

whence

(30) $\mathbf{T} = \mathbf{S}$.

[At this point I have not yet proven statements (20) and (21). This I shall do very shortly.] In particular, I could have given my Definition 8.35 as

8.38 Definition   A natural system is a *simple system* if and only if it has no closed path of efficient causation.

Indeed, the purpose of Chapter 9 of LI is precisely to establish the *equivalence* of the two definitions 8.35 and 8.38: the former characterizes a natural system through its models in the universe of formal systems, while the latter stays within the universe of natural systems.

We may summarize our lexicon succinctly thus:

$$\begin{aligned} simple\ system\ &=\ mechanism \\ &=\ no\ closed\ path\ of\ efficient\ causation \\ &=\ all\ models\ are\ simulable \end{aligned}$$

8.39 Mathematical Logic Let

(31)
$$\mathbf{Q} = \{\, N \in \mathbf{N} : \text{ the collections of analytic models} \\ \text{and synthetic models coincide} \\ \text{in the category } \mathbf{C}(N) \text{ of models of } N \,\}.$$

Then Theorem 8.30, which I have proven, says

(32) $\mathbf{S} \subset \mathbf{Q}$.

So unless an error is found in the proof of $\mathbf{S} \subset \mathbf{Q}$, it remains indisputable.

Rosen defined *mechanism* (Definition 8.34) as a synonym of simple system. That is, if $\mathbf{M}$ denotes the collection of all mechanisms, then it is the set

(33) $\mathbf{M} = \{\, N \in \mathbf{N} : \text{all models of } N \text{ are simulable} \,\}$,

and one has

(34) $\mathbf{M} = \mathbf{S}$.

Combining (32) and (34), one therefore obtains

(35) $\mathbf{M} \subset \mathbf{Q}$.

Now the statement (34), $\mathbf{M} = \mathbf{S}$, is a *definition* made by Rosen. The fact that he chose to define 'mechanism' thus is the art of his encoding. Humpty Dumpty's privilege allows one to define 'mechanism' to mean whatever one chooses it to mean, in which case the set **M** of all mechanisms *under another definition* may not be equivalent to (33), whence **M**≠**S**, and so with this *alternative* **M** one may have

(36)   **M** ⊄ **Q**.

Stating the obvious otherwise, Theorem 8.30 says **S** ⊂ **Q**; the fact **M** ⊂ **Q** only follows when **M** = **S**. When a new **M** is defined such that **M**≠**S**, one may *not* have **M** ⊂ **Q**. So even if one happens to show that **M** ⊄ **Q** with a new definition of **M**, it in no way implies that Rosen's original **M** ⊂ **Q** is wrong, let alone by gross generalization from the dubious **M** ⊄ **Q** that *all* of Rosen's results are suspect! The mathematical logic here may appear elementary, but it is surprising that some people did erroneously (and perhaps misleadingly or even maliciously) reach such conclusions.

8.40 Zen Kōan

ROSEN   Suppose x is a member of A.
NOSER   Suppose x is not a member of A.

The Limitations of Entailment in Simple Systems

Chapter 9 of *LI* is a detailed *reductio ad absurdum* argument that *proves* that certain modes of entailment are *not* available in a simple system:

8.41 Theorem   *There can be no closed path of efficient causation in a simple system.*

Its contrapositive statement is

8.42 Theorem   *If a closed path of efficient causation exists in a natural system N, then N cannot be a simple system.*

Taking Definition 8.35 of simple system into account, this is equivalent to

8.43 Theorem   *If a closed path of efficient causation exists in a natural system, then it has a model that is not simulable.*

The nonsimulable model contains a hierarchical cycle that corresponds to the closed path of efficient causation in the natural system being modelled. The hierarchical cycle in the model is what renders it nonsimulable (*cf.* Theorems 8.12 and 8.13). Note that Theorem 8.43 is precisely the contrapositive statement of our Theorem 8.20.

Theorem 8.41 may be rephrased in graph-theoretic terms. Because of the isomorphism between an efficient cause and its representation as a solid-headed arrow [Theorem 6.1], one has

8.44 Theorem   *In (the relational diagram of) a simple system there cannot be a cycle that contains two or more solid-headed arrows.*

Theorems 8.20 and 8.41–8.44 are five equivalent forms of the same statement. I now proceed with the

8.45 Proof   Let M be a model of a simple system N. I consider a path of inferential entailment in M that represents a path of efficient causation in N, and investigate what form this path can take.

I cast the semantics in a general setting in the language of algebraic topology. The path of inferential entailment means one has a sequence of sets $\{A_0, A_1, A_2, ...\}$, on which one may define a sequence of hom-sets $\{H_1, H_2, ...\}$ by

$$
\begin{aligned}
H_1 &= H(A_1, A_0) \\
H_2 &= H(A_2, H(A_1, A_0)) = H(A_2, H_1) \\
&\ \vdots \\
H_k &= H(A_k, H_{k-1}) \\
&\ \vdots
\end{aligned}
$$

(37)

For each k, the formal system $\langle A_k, H_k \rangle$ is then a component of the model M. I may also form a sequence of submodels of M defined by

(38) $\qquad M_k = \bigoplus_{i=1}^{k} \langle A_i, H_i \rangle.$

This is a strictly ascending chain:

(39) $\qquad M_1 < M_2 < \cdots < M_k < \cdots \ (\leq M)$

Since the lattice $\mathbf{C}(N)$ satisfies the ascending chain condition (Lemma 8.21), this chain must terminate after a finite number of steps, say n. With $x_i \in A_i$ and $f_j \in H_j$, the path of hierarchical composition then has the relation diagram

(40)

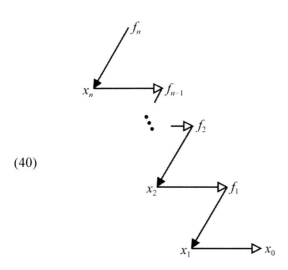

The graph corresponding to the entailment pattern of the model M is, of course, not necessarily a single hierarchical chain. It may, indeed, have very complicated branching; but one topology that it *cannot* have is a *closed path*. In other words, one cannot have $H_k \cap H_{k+m} \neq \emptyset$, *i.e.* the existence of some mapping $h \in H_k \cap H_{k+m}$, for some $m > 0$. For ease of illustration I assume, without loss of generality, that $k = 1$ and $m = 3$ (the argument being the same for arbitrary k and $m > 0$). This means one has three mappings in a hierarchical cycle:

(41)

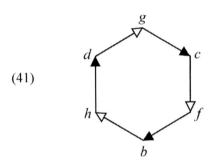

where

(42)	$f \in H(B, A)$	$f : b \mapsto h$	$f \vdash h$
(43)	$g \in H(C, H(B, A))$	$g : c \mapsto f$	$g \vdash f$
(44)	$h \in H(D, H(C, H(B, A)))$	$h : d \mapsto g$	$h \vdash g$

with the entailment cycle

(45)

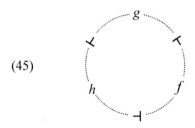

Hidden in these innocent-looking mappings is the impredicative structure. When I close the loop at h, it takes on two identities:

(46) $h \in A$

and

(47) $h \in H\big(D, H\big(C, H\big(B, A\big)\big)\big).$

Thus there is an entailed ambiguity in h: that which is entailed and that which entails. (See the discussion on the final cause of a mapping in 5.10.) The two nonidentical yet noncontradictory statements (46) and (47) are not *algorithmically derivable* from each other.   Since algorithms are, by definition, forbidden to include ambiguous steps or data, this ambiguous entailment demonstrates the inherent noncomputability of hierarchical cycles. The correspondence between A and $H(D, H(C, H(B, A)))$ — in general between H_k and H_{k+m}, hom-sets at different hierarchical levels — is something that cannot be derived from *syntax* alone. One needs to know something *about* the maps involved, *i.e.* the *semantics*, to reach this identification.   The closing of the hierarchical chain is what renders it noncomputable.

I may also reach this noncomputability conclusion in an alternate fashion. The two identities of h must *split into two direct summands*: h_1 and h_2 encoding the morphisms (46) and (47) respectively; otherwise, the property encoded in h would be nonfractionable, contradicting Theorem 8.32. In other words, since N is a simple system, one must have

(48) $h = h_1 + h_2$

in the sense of direct sum. I can similarly consider the loop to close at either f or g, whence they also fractionate into

(49) $f = f_1 + f_2$

226

and

(50) $g = g_1 + g_2.$

Graphically, one has

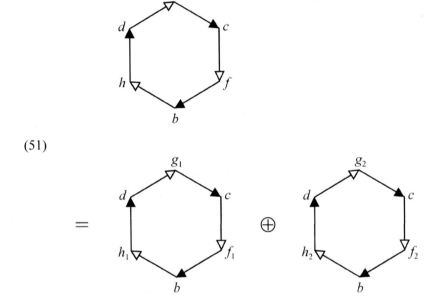

(51)

But then one obtains *two* hierarchical cycles. The splitting process may logically continue *ad infinitum*, resulting in smaller and smaller models but without a terminating process. This contradicts Lemma 8.25 that the lattice $C(N)$ also satisfies the descending chain condition.

This completes the proof of Theorem 8.41 that there can be no closed path of efficient causation in a simple system.   □

Lemma 8.19 and Theorem 8.20 together give the central

8.46 Theorem   *A natural system has no closed path of efficient causation if and only if all of its models are simulable.*

8.47 *Explanatio*   In view of Theorem 8.46, every appearance of the characterization 'all models are simulable' may be replaced by 'has no closed path of efficient causation', or equivalently 'has no hierarchical cycle' (taking care, obviously, in rephrasing to avoid tautologies). So this whole monograph (and indeed *LI* itself) may be written without ever mentioning simulability (or computability, or any other computing-theoretic concepts). In fact, the only property of simulability that is used in the proofs (of Lemmata 8.21 and 8.25) is 8.4(*c*), the obvious fact and almost-tautological statement that the program of a simulable model must be of finite length.

The point is that although I have proven in this chapter (as Rosen has shown in Chapter 9 of *LI*) that certain processes are not simulable, it is really beside the point! The important conclusion is that causal entailment patterns *with* and *without* closed paths of efficient causation are *different in kind*, and that the barrier between the two classes is 'non-porous': "there are no purely syntactic operations that will take us across the barrier at all". This dichotomy is my next topic.

9

Complex Systems

Dichotomy

I shall begin this chapter with Robert Rosen's formal definition of complex systems. With the groundwork heretofore laid, the definition is in fact exceedingly simple. Complex systems are objects in the set-theoretic complement of the collection of simple systems in the universe of natural systems:

9.1 Definition A natural system is a *complex system* if it is not a simple system.

As we discussed in the previous chapter, in the universe **N** of all natural systems, the subset **S** of simple systems may alternatively be defined (*cf.* Definition 8.38) by the property $t(N)$ = 'there is no closed path of efficient causation in N':

(1) $S = \{N \in \mathbf{N} : t(N)\}$

Thus

9.2 Theorem *A natural system is complex if and only if it contains a closed path of efficient causation.*

(which is the complementary statement of Theorem 8.46). See Chapter 18 of *EL* for a more detailed discussion of Theorem 9.2 and its consequences.

In terms of relational diagrams, one has the complementary theorem to Theorem 8.44:

9.3 Theorem *In (the relational diagram of) a complex system there is a cycle that contains two or more solid-headed arrows.*

With the equivalent Definition 8.35 of simple system, one has

$$(2) \qquad \mathbf{S} = \{N \in \mathbf{N} : s(N)\}$$

where $s(N)$ = 'all models of N are simulable' (*cf.* (17) in 8.17). Its complementary set, the subset $\mathbf{I}$ of complex systems, is thus

$$(3) \qquad \mathbf{I} = \mathbf{S}^c = \{N \in \mathbf{N} : \neg s(N)\}$$

(*cf.* (29) in Definition 0.21). (Complexity is *implicatio* in classical Latin. I am using $\mathbf{I}$ instead of $\mathbf{C}$ for the collection of complex systems to avoid confusion with $\mathbf{C}(N)$, the category of models of a natural system N. I am preserving the notation $\mathbf{C}(\cdot)$ for category of models, which Rosen introduced in Section 6F of *LI*.)

Now let $M \in \mathbf{C}(N)$; i.e., let M be a model of the natural system N. Let $\pi(M)$ be the property 'M is simulable'. Then

$$(4) \qquad s(N) = \forall M \in \mathbf{C}(N) \; \pi(M)$$

(*cf.* (16) in 8.17). Using the Law of Quantifier Negation (0.22) $\neg \forall x \; p(x) \Leftrightarrow \exists x \; \neg p(x)$, the negation of the property in (4) is

$$(5) \qquad \neg s(N) = \exists M \in \mathbf{C}(N) \; \neg \pi(M);$$

i.e., the negation of $s(N) =$ 'all models of N are simulable' is $\neg s(N) =$ 'there exists a model of N that is not simulable'. This characterizes the collection of complex systems as those natural systems that have at least one nonsimulable model. Thus one has the

9.4 Lemma *A natural system is a complex system if and only if it has a nonsimulable model.*

Any natural system has many different models that do not contain impredicative structures of inferential entailment, whence they are simulable. The limitation for a simple system is that this impoverishment applies to all of its models. A simple system may have a finite hierarchy of efficient causes that does not form a loop, or it may have a 'flat' sequential loop of material causes that are on the same 'hierarchical level'. The defining property of a complex system is that there exists at least one model that does contain an impredicative structure of entailment, a *hierarchical cycle* that corresponds to the closed path of efficient causation in the complex system being modelled.

Let me re-emphasize the exposition at the end of Chapter 6 here. The defining property of a complex system, that it contains a closed path of efficient causation, is not 'closed to efficient causation'. The latter is more stringent than simply 'containing a hierarchical cycle in its entailment pattern'. A complex system only requires *some*, but not necessarily all, efficient causes to be part of a hierarchical cycle. On the other hand, 'closure to efficient causation' requires all efficient causes to be in hierarchical cycles. Stated otherwise, one has the

9.5 Theorem *The collection of natural systems that are closed to efficient causation form a proper subset of the set of complex systems.*

This special subset of **I** is the topic of Chapter 11.

9.6 The Taxonomy Because of the defined dichotomy $\mathbf{I} = \mathbf{S}^c$, a natural system is either complex or simple, but cannot be both: it either contains a

232

closed path of efficient causation or it does not. Rosen explains this taxonomy of natural systems in Chapter 19 of *EL* thus:

> ...the barrier between simple and complex is not porous; it cannot be crossed at all in the direction from simple to complex; even the opposite direction is difficult. There are certainly no purely syntactic operations that will take us across the barrier at all. That is, no given finite number of repetitions of a single rote operation will take us across the barrier in either direction; it can produce neither simplicity from complexity, nor the reverse.

The dichotomic taxonomy may be represented by the diagram

(6)

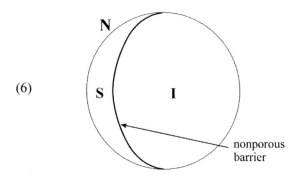

Note this diagram (6) showing partitioning of **N** into the complementary parts **S** and **I** is *not* area-proportional. Indeed, simple systems form a *meagre* (i.e. nongeneric) subset of natural systems, so the subset **I** is *almost all* of **N**.

Relational Biology

9.7 What is an Organism? The principles of relational biology may be considered the operational inverse of reductionistic ideas. The essence of reductionism in biology is to keep the matter of which an organism is made, and throw away the organization, with the belief that, since physicochemical structure implies function, the organization can be effectively reconstituted from the analytic material parts. Relational biology, on the other hand, keeps the organization and throws away the matter; through the process of realization, material aspects are recaptured. In short,

an organism is a material system
that realizes a certain kind of relational pattern,

whatever the particular material basis of that realization may be.

An organism (remember that this term is used in the sense of an 'autonomous life form', a general living system) is, of course, a natural system. Thus the collection **O** of organisms is a subset of **N**, so it has a place somewhere in diagram (6). In the next chapter, I shall explore a property of organisms that would place **O** as a proper subset of **I**. For now, I shall present the statement as

9.8 Rosen's Conjecture *An organism must be complex; a complex system may (or may not) be an organism.*

While 'complexity' is a popular scientific topic these days, I must emphasize that it is somewhat apart from our direct line of inquiry of life itself. Also, it must be noted that Rosen's Definition 9.1 of complex system differs essentially from most others' usage. There are, indeed, almost as many definitions of complexity as there are schools involved in the study of the topic. An evidence of the power of Rosen's articulation of his science is our realization that it "has seeped into every aspect of everything else". I am delighted that scholars from many diverse disciplines find causes from relational biology to formulate conceptions that are of use in their respective subjects. But one must not be sidetracked, go astray, and lose sight that *our* subject is mathematical biology. So, let me iterate: complexity is not our main interest. It is one of our means to an end; it is just a corollary in relational biology.

Complexity is a necessary condition of life, but not life itself.

9.9 Necessity and Sufficiency Rosen's Conjecture 9.8, stated in set-theoretic terms, is

(7) $$\mathbf{O} \subset \mathbf{I} \text{ but } \mathbf{O} \neq \mathbf{I}.$$

Thus

(8)

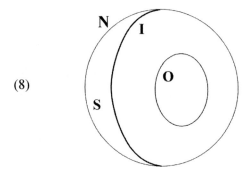

I is a superset of **O** (i.e. **I** contains **O** as a subset); but complexity by itself is not sufficient for biology. A subset A of a set X may be described as the infimum in the poset $\langle \mathbf{P}X, \subset \rangle$ taken over the collection of all its supersets:

(9) $$A = \inf \{ B \in \mathbf{P}X : A \subset B \}$$

With the notational convention

(10) $P = \{x \in X : p(x)\}$

of the Axiom of Specification 0.19, the infimum (9) is

(11) $A = \inf \{B \in PX : \forall x \in X \; a(x) \Rightarrow b(x)\}.$

In other words, a set is defined by the infimum of the collection of all its necessary conditions (whence the definition becomes sufficient).

     Complexity is one of the necessities of life. I now proceed to tighten the necessary conditions.

(12)

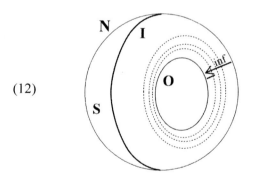

PART IV

Hypotheses fingo

Copiare il vero può essere una buona cosa
ma inventare il vero è meglio, molto meglio.

[It may be a good thing to copy reality;
but to invent reality is better, much better.]

— Giuseppe Verdi (1876)
Letter to Clarina Maffei

All the tools are now in our hands. From our present plateau, we are in a good position from which we may ascend to the summit of life itself. So let us set out on this next leg of our journey.

10

Anticipation

Anticipatory Systems

An anticipatory system's present behaviour depends upon 'future states' or 'future inputs' generated by an internal predictive model. This apparent violation of causality is, however, simply an illusion. Robert Rosen instituted a rigorously mathematical study of the subject in the second book of his trilogy, *Anticipatory Systems* [*AS*]. This chapter is an expository introduction of the concepts I need to tighten the necessary conditions for life. The interested reader should, naturally, read *AS* in the original to further pursue the topic.

10.1 Ought "What should we do now?"

To one degree or another, this 'question of *ought*' is the same question the biologist, the economists, the political scientists, the urban planners, the futurists, and many others want to know. However different the contexts in which these questions are posed, *they are all alike in their fundamental concern with the making of policy, and the associated notions of forecasting the future and planning for it*. What is sought, in each of these diverse areas, is in effect a technology of decision making. But underlying any technology there must be an underlying substratum of basic principles: a science, a *theory*. What is the theory underlying a technology of policy generation? Rosen proposed that this is the theory of anticipatory systems. Note that the *concept* of 'anticipation' had not been new, but the *systemic study* of it was when Rosen wrote *the* book on the subject.

Now what is an anticipatory system? Here is Robert Rosen's

10.2 Definition An *anticipatory system* is a natural system that contains an internal predictive model of itself and of its environment, which allows it to change state at an instant in accord with the model's predictions pertaining to a later instant.

Note, in contrast, that a *reactive system* can only react, in the present, to changes that have already occurred in the causal chain, while an *anticipatory system*'s present behaviour involve aspects of past, present, and future. The presence of a predictive model serves precisely to pull the future into the present; a system with a 'good' model thus behaves in many ways as if it can anticipate the future. In other words, *a predictive model permits anticipation*. Indeed, to use teleological language, the *purpose* of a predictive model is to anticipate. Model-based behaviour requires an entirely new paradigm, an 'anticipatory paradigm', to accommodate it. This paradigm *extends — but does not replace —* the 'reactive paradigm' which has hitherto dominated the study of natural systems. The anticipatory paradigm allows us a glimpse of new and important aspects of system behaviour.

True to the spirit of relational biology, the crux in Definition 10.2 is not what an anticipatory system itself *is*, but the embedded internal predictive model itself, i.e. the entailment *process* of anticipation.

10.3 Predictor There is an intimate anticipatory relationship between the formal and exemplary causes (*cf.* 5.8 and 5.20). One may recognize that Aquinas's exemplary cause is the morphism of anticipation, the *predictor*. An exemplary cause itself is an actuality in the agent, but it is also a potentiality that *anticipates* another actuality, the becoming and being of the formal cause of something else. A natural system with an exemplary cause model of an entailed formal cause *is* an anticipatory system. When a morphism $f \in H(A,B)$ is functionally entailed (*cf.* 5.15), the morphism

$g \in H\left(X, H\left(A, B\right)\right)$ that entails it may be considered its exemplary cause. Thus the statement

(1) $\qquad \left(\vdash f\right) \vdash \left(\exists g : g \vdash f\right).$

(*cf.* 5.18) is as much about immanent causation as exemplary causation.

Note that an exemplary cause, in anticipation, implies that something else is imminent. While the statement (1) is thus an alligation of *immanence* and *imminence*, the two similar words have distinct etymological roots. The Latin *immanere* means 'to remain in', and evolves into 'inherent', whence 'to naturally *exist*'. The Latin *imminere* means 'to project over', and therefore 'impending'. With respect to the entailment symbol $\vdash$, immanence and imminence are, indeed, on opposite ends: in essence, that which entails and that which is entailed, the initial and the terminal in the category of causation, the alpha and the omega.

In Section 6.8 of *AS*, Rosen summarized thus:

> The point of departure for our entire development was the recognition that most of the behavior we observe in the biological realm, if indeed not all of the behavior which we consider as characteristically biological, is of an anticipatory rather than a reactive character. In fact, if it were necessary to try to characterize in a few words the difference between living organisms and inorganic systems, such a characterization would not involve the presence of DNA, or any other purely structural attributes; but rather that organism constitute the class of systems which can behave in an anticipatory fashion. That is to say, organisms comprise those systems which can make predictive models (of themselves, and of their environments) and use these models to direct their present actions.

In other words, anticipation is a necessary condition for life. In short, this is the

10.4 Axiom of Anticipation   *Life is anticipatory.*

Let **N** be, as before, the collection of natural systems, and let **O** be the collection of organisms. Define

(2) $\mathbf{A} = \{\, N \in \mathbf{N} : N \text{ is an anticipatory system} \,\}$,

then

(3) $\mathbf{O} \subset \mathbf{A}$.

But anticipation by itself is not sufficient to define organisms: thus **O** is a proper subset of **A**; i.e.

(4) $\mathbf{O} \neq \mathbf{A}$.

The idea of anticipation in science is controversial, because of 'objective causality' pronounced in the

10.5 Zeroth Commandment   *Thou shalt not allow future state to affect present change of state.*

Anticipation is almost always excluded from study at every level of system theory. The reasons for this rest on certain basic methodological presuppositions which have underlain 'science' in the past few centuries:

I. the essential basis on which "genuine scientific inquiry" rests is the principle of *causality* (which an anticipatory systems apparently violates);

and

II. "true objective science" cannot be argued from final cause (but an anticipatory system seems to embody a form of *teleology*).

I shall debunk these two characterization of science in some detail below. But let us first consider a few examples of anticipatory systems.

Biology is replete with situations in which organisms can generate and maintain internal predictive models of themselves and their environments, and use the predictions of these models about the future for purpose of control in the present. Much, if not most, biological behaviour is model-based in this sense. This is true at every level, from the molecular to the cellular to the physiological to the behavioural, and this is true in all parts of the biosphere, from microbes to plants to animals to ecosystems. But it is not restricted to the biological universe; anticipatory behaviour at the human level can be multiplied without end, and may seem fairly trivial: examples range from avoiding dangerous encounters, to any strategy in sports, and even to Linus's waiting for the Great Pumpkin in the pumpkin patch on Halloween. Model-based behaviour is the essence of social, economic, and political activity. An understanding of the characteristics of model-based behaviour is thus central to any technology one wishes to develop to control such systems, or to modify their model-based behaviour in new ways.

10.6 Information It should be clarified that anticipation in Rosen's usage does not refer to an ability to 'see' or otherwise sense the immediate or the distant future — there is no prescience or psychic phenomena suggested here. Instead, Rosen suggests that there must be information about self, about species, and about the evolutionary environment, encoded into the organization of all living systems. He observes that this *information*, as it behaves through time, is capable of acting causally on the organism's present behaviour, based on relations projected to be applicable in the future. Thus, while not violating time established by external events, organisms seem capable of constructing an internal surrogate for time as part of a model that can indeed be manipulated to produce anticipation. In particular, this "internal surrogate of time" must run *faster than real time*. It is in this sense that degrees of freedom in internal models allow time its multi-scaling and reversibility to produce new information. At no point in such a picture is 'causality' ever violated; the future is never involved directly, but only the *image* of the future as embodied in an internal predictive model. The future

244

still has not yet happened: the organism has a *model* of the future, but not definitive knowledge of future itself.

10.7 Feedforward Anticipatory behaviour involves the concept of *feedforward*, rather than feedback. (A more proper contrastive word of 'feedback' should have been 'feedforth'.) The distinction between feedforward and feedback is important, and is as follows.

The essence of feedback control is that it is *error-actuated*; in other words, the stimulus to corrective action is the discrepancy between the system's actual present state and the state the system should be in. Stated otherwise, a feedback control system must already be departing from its nominal behaviour before control begins to be exercised.

In a feedforward system, on the other hand, system behaviour is *preset*, according to some model relating present inputs to their predicted outcomes. The essence of a feedforward system, then, is that present change of state is determined by an anticipated future state, derived in accordance with some internal model of the world.

We know from introspection that many, if not most, of our own conscious activities are generated in a feedforward fashion. We typically decide what to do *now* in terms of what we perceive will be the consequences of our action at some *later* time. The vehicle by which we anticipate is in fact a *model*, which enables us to pull the future into the present. We change our present course of action in accordance with our model's prediction. The stimulus for our action is not simply the present percepts; it is the prediction or output of our model under these conditions. Stated otherwise, our present behaviour is not just *reactive*; it is also *anticipatory*.

10.8 Behaviour The essential novelty in Rosen's approach to anticipatory systems is that he considers them as single entities, and relate their overall properties to the character of the models they contain. There have, of course, been many approaches to planning, forecasting, and decision-making, but these tend to concentrate on *tactical aspects* of model synthesis and model deployment in *specific circumstances*. Rosen's *AS* is not at all concerned with tactics of this type. It deals, instead, with the behavioural correlates arising throughout a system simply from the fact that present behaviour is generated in terms of a predicted future situation. It does not consider, for instance, the various procedures of extrapolation and correlation which dominate much of the literature concerned with decision-making in an uncertain or incompletely defined environment. *AS* is concerned rather with global properties of model-based behaviour, irrespective of how the model is generated, or indeed of whether it is a 'good' model or not. In other words, *AS* looks at properties of an anticipatory system, not how to build an anticipatory system.

Causality

The concept of anticipation has been rejected out of hand in formal approaches to system theory, because it appears to violate causality. We have always been taught that we must not allow present changes of state to depend on future states; the future cannot affect the present. I now show that this restriction is simply an artefact of the Newtonian reactive paradigm.

10.9 Dynamical System   However much the languages that one uses to construct system models of whatever kind may differ, in detail and emphasis, they all represent paraphrases of the language of Newtonian mechanics. Two separate ingredients are necessary for the process of system description; they are: (i) a specification of what the system is like at any particular instant of time, with the associated concept of the *instantaneous state* of the system, and (ii) a specification of how the system changes state, as a function of present or past states and of the forces imposed on the system, i.e. the *dynamics*. The characterization of the instantaneous state involves the specification of an appropriate set of *state variables*, while the characterization of how the system changes state involves a specification of the *equations of motion* of the system. Another name of this Newtonian reactive system is 'dynamical system'.

The universe with which a natural scientist deals is that of events in space and time. A physical system is a certain sequence of such events, and a system behaviour is some property of such a sequence. This universe of events can be effectively divided into two distinct domains. The first of these, which is characterized by regularity and order, is the province of Natural Law (see Chapter 4, *cf.* 4.7 in particular). The second domain, in which no perceptible regularity is discernible, is the realm of initial conditions. The basic task in approaching any particular system or phenomenon is to specify those laws which govern the system, and to determine the initial conditions which, in conjunction with the system laws, determine the behaviours of the system as sequences of events.

10.10 Constitution The state variables of a system may be partitioned into two subsets: (i) the set of constitutive variables $a(t)$, those that are not predictable from the equation of motion describing the system, and (ii) the nonconstitutive variables $x(t)$ (often called degrees of freedom for the system), those with values that can be predicted, given the initial conditions $x(0)$, from the dynamical laws. Thus a Newtonian dynamical system may be written in the form

$$(5) \qquad x(t) = G\big[t, a(t), x(0)\big].$$

Note that an equation of motion like equation (5) can be regarded either as an explanation of a present event $x(t)$ in terms of a past event $x(0)$, or as a prediction of a future event $x(t)$ in terms of a present event $x(0)$. The Newtonian paradigm, restricting itself entirely to system laws like equation (5), is thus completely 'causal', since causality in this forward-temporal sense, $x(0) \rightarrow x(t)$, is inextricably built directly into the form of the dynamical laws that are selected for study.

By definition, if one knows the time course of the state variables, one also knows the time course of any other system observable b. Combining this fact with the system law (5), one finds that

(6) $\qquad b(t) = F\big[t, a(t), x(0)\big].$

In this context, the time sequence $b(t)$ of the observable b is called an *output* (or response) of the system to the *input* (or force) $a(t)$. The relation F in equation (6), which involves both the specific observable b in question and the dynamical relation G governing change of (nonconstitutive) state variables, expresses the relation between output and input; it is essentially a transfer function for the system. It should be noted that there will be a different such function F for each observable b. A relation like (6) can be regarded still more abstractly; namely, it can be regarded as establishing a relation R between mappings $a(t)$ (inputs) and $b(t)$ (outputs):

(7) $\qquad R\big[a(t), b(t)\big] = 0;$

two mappings being R-related if there is an initial state $x(0)$ such that equation (6) holds. In other words, the initial physical picture of systems, as time sequences of events, has been transformed to an equivalent view of systems, as relations between input-output pairs of time mappings. This last characterization (7) of systems clearly lends itself to vast generalization and abstraction; in fact, it provides the basis for most approaches to abstract general system theory.

As long as we restrict ourselves to dynamical equations of the form (5) or (6), which as we have seen inextricably involve the traditional view of causality, anticipatory systems are clearly excluded from discussion. However, when we proceed to consider systems in terms of relations (7) between input-output pairs of mappings of time, we find that causality needs only dictate natural regularities relating causes and effects, without necessarily including a built-in forward-temporal restraint. Thus anticipatory behaviour not only is possible, but is actually less restrictive and therefore in some sense generic, because relations (7) contain (5) and (6) as special cases. [The mathematical theory involved is the Implicit Function Theorem.]

Teleology

I now consider the assertion that anticipatory systems involve teleology or final causes in an essential way, and thus must be excluded from science. Feedforward behaviour seems telic, or goal-directed. The goal is in fact built in as part of the model that connects predicted future states and present changes of state. But the very suggestion that a behaviour is goal-directed is repellent to many scientists, who regard it as a violation of the Newtonian paradigm.

10.11 Aristotelian Causality The formulation of this 'teleophobic' assertion goes back to Aristotle's conception of causality (*cf.* Chapter 5), in which four distinct kinds of 'causes' for any physical event are recognized. Adapting this Aristotelian parlance to the above discussion: if one regards the value $b(t)$ of an observable b at an instant t as such an event, and if one allows only dynamical laws of the form (6) to express relations between events, then one may say that

(i) $x(0)$ is the *material cause* of the event $b(t)$;
(ii) $a(t)$ is its *efficient cause*;
(iii) F is its *formal cause*.

This assignment of three of the causes clearly exhausts all the quantities and relations in the expression (6); hence the event $b(t)$ can have no room for the fourth, *final cause*. This observation is essentially the entire basis for asserting that scientific explanation (which is posited in advance to be exclusively embodied in relations of the form (6)) cannot involve final causes. Moreover, since final causes presuppose future states and/or future inputs, one must according to this argument *a fortiori* exclude anticipatory systems.

10.12 Hidden Teleology in Physics However, already in physics one finds numerous situations in which present events appear to be determined by subsequent ones. Of course, such situations are not directly governed by laws of the form (6). An obvious example is any system that obeys an 'optimality principle', such as Fermat's principle in optics or Hamilton's principle in mechanics; here *the actual path described by a physical process is as much determined by its terminal state as by its initial one.* A similar teleological aspect can be seen in Le Chatelier's principle in physical chemistry and in Lenz's law of electricity. These principles express that in case of disturbance, the system develops forces which counteract the disturbance and restore a state of equilibrium; they are derivations from *the principle of minimum effect.* Further, the transition of a system to a state of 'minimal free energy', 'maximum entropy', etc, involves a tacit characterization of such a state as the final cause of motion toward it. Precisely the same situation is encountered in probability theory, where the family of convergence arguments collectively called the law of large numbers asserts that limiting probabilities exert an apparent attractive force on the successive steps of a random process, even though those steps are independent. In sum, even though dynamical laws in physics express conventional views regarding causality, they are mathematically equivalent to principles in which a future state acts retroactively on a present change of state.

We should note that hidden teleology by itself is not sufficient to define an anticipatory system. An optimality- or otherwise-determined future still constitutes a reactive system. An anticipatory system needs to use the information from its predictive model to change the present, so that a possibly different future from one that is originally predicted may result.

The misguided need to exclude finality in the name of "preserving objectivity" has often been carried to ludicrous lengths in biology. Some would even go so far as to entirely do away with the concept of 'function', a very pillar of biology, on the grounds that it is finalistic and therefore not 'objective'. Statements such as "the function of the heart is to pump blood" and "the function of the lungs is for gaseous exchange" would hence become heresy. Carried still further, many consider illegitimate for science to seek to understand anything about a system in terms of (its relations and interactions with) a larger system of which it is a part. The reductionistic idea is that one must only seek answers of larger wholes in terms of 'objective', context-independent constituent parts; but never the reverse. And worse: any method that is not based on the 'scientific method' of physicochemical, mechanistic dogma (i.e., 'their' way) cannot possibly be 'objective'.

The characterization of 'scientific knowledge' (as opposed to other kinds of knowledge) with the adjective 'objective' is usually meant to indicate that scientific knowledge pertains to its object alone, devoid of any information about the specificities of its obtainment. Stated otherwise, this is the description that neither the observer nor the observation process plays a causal role in entailing what is observed. Final causation, i.e. teleology, has long been regarded as the quintessence of subjectivity, and therefore incompatible with objective science itself. But this is simply an equivocation. As a final note, let me point out that even if the final causation of an effect is accepted, the effect is still not entailed by the process of a teleological answer of its "why?". The fact that an effect has a final cause can still be itself an objective fact: its acquisition plays no role in its entailment.

Synthesis

Having analyzed and dispensed with those formal arguments adduced to justify excluding anticipatory systems from system theory, I shall now be positive, and construct a model anticipatory system with some synthetic arguments.

10.13 Construction   Let us begin with a system S that is of interest: an individual organism, or an ecosystem, or a social or economic system. For simplicity I shall suppose that S is an ordinary (i.e. non-anticipatory) dynamical system, which is therefore described by some dynamical equation of the form (5). As we have seen, this fact allows us to make predictions about the future states of S, from a knowledge of an initial state and of the system input. Indeed, the dynamical law (5) itself already expresses a predictive model of S.

But let us embody a predictive model of S explicitly in another physical system M. For M to be 'predictive', the requirement is that if the trajectories of S are parameterized by real time, then the corresponding trajectories of M are parameterized by a time variable that goes *faster than real time*. For example, one can arrange matters so that the present state $m(t)$ of M (in 'real time' t) describes the state $s(h(t))$ of S at some later instant of real time $h(t) > t$. Thus, any observable $f[m(t)]$ serves as a predictor for the behaviour of some corresponding observable of S at that later instant.

I shall now allow M and S to be coupled; i.e. allow them to interact in specific ways. For the simplest model, one may simply allow the output $f[m(t)]$ to be an input to the system S. This then creates a situation in which a future state $s(h(t))$ of S is controlling the present state transition in S. But this is precisely what is characterized above as anticipatory behaviour. It is clear that the above construction does not violate causality; indeed, we have invoked causality in an essential way in the concept of a predictive model, and hence in the characterization of the system M. Although the composite system $(M + S)$ is completely causal, it nevertheless will behave in an anticipatory fashion.

Similarly, we may construct a system M with outputs that embody predictions regarding the inputs $a(t)$ to the system S. In that case, the present change of state of S will depend upon information pertaining to future inputs to S. Here again, although causality is in no sense violated, our system will exhibit anticipatory behaviour.

From the above remarks, we see that anticipatory behaviour will be generated in any system that: (i) contains an internal predictive model of itself and/or of its environment; and (ii) is such that its dynamical law uses the predictions of its internal model in an essential way. From this point of view, anticipatory systems can be viewed as a special class of adaptive control systems.

There are many other modes of coupling, discussed in *AS*, which will allow *S* to affect *M*, and which will amount to updating or improving the model system *M* on the basis of the activity of *S*. I shall for the present example suppose simply that the system *M* is equipped with a set *E* of *effectors* that operate either on *S* itself or on the environmental inputs to *S*, in such a way as to change the dynamical properties of *S*. We thus have a situation of the type in the diagram, formulated as an input-output system.

(8)   Input

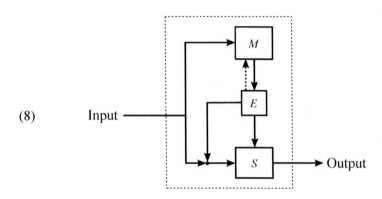

The abstract formalism is how *we describe* the predictive model, not an anthropomorphic imputation that the anticipatory system *S* itself, which may after all be a primitive organism, has to somehow *formulate M* and *E*. While it is true that without a modeller, there is no modelling, there may not be intentional effort involved on the modeller's part.

Let me use the same symbols for the object, model, and effector systems, respectively *S*, *M*, and *E*, to denote their efficient causes. In other words, let each symbol represent the *processor* associated with the block (the 'black box') as well as the block itself. If one traces the path of an input element *a*, the diagram of the anticipatory system (8) becomes

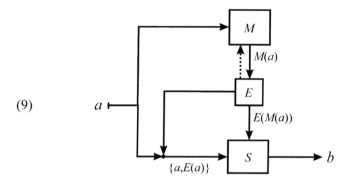

(9) $\quad a$

and the corresponding output b will be of the form

(10) $\qquad b(t) = S\big[a(t), E\big(a(t)\big), E\big(M\big(a(t)\big)\big)\big],$

which is the anticipatory analogue to the reactive relation (6). Within such generality, it is easy to see that it is possible to define many different time scales.

10.14 Errors A natural system is almost always more than any model of it. In other words, a model is, by definition, incomplete. As a consequence, under appropriate circumstances, the behaviour predicted by a model will diverge from that actually exhibited by the system. This provides the basis for a theory of error and system failure on the one hand, and for an understanding of emergence on the other. It is crucial to understand this aspect in any comprehensive theory of control based on predictive models.

Anticipation can fail in its purpose. A study of how planning can go wrong is illustrative; indeed the updating of models from lessons learned is the essence of an anticipatory system. Rosen discussed errors in anticipation in Section 1.1 of *AS*, and also in Rosen [1974], to which the reader is referred for details. I shall only give a brief summary here. The causes of errors in anticipation may be categorized into (i) bad models, (ii) bad effectors, and (iii) side effects.

A bad model can result from technical, paradigmatical, or state-correspondence errors, all due to improper functorial imaging of mappings. In short, faulty encodings lead to faulty models. A proper choice of the internal predictive model M and the fine tuning of its updating processes are evidently crucial to an anticipatory system's success.

An effector E is defective when it is incapable in steering S, when it cannot appropriately manipulate the state variables, or simply when it fails to accordingly react to the information from M. Thus the careful construction of an anticipatory system also depends on the selection, design, and programming of the effector system E, as well as on the partitioning of the 'desirable' and 'undesirable' regions of response.

Side effects arise because, essentially, structures have multiple functions and functions may be carried out by multiple structures. Combined with the fact of incomplete models, the consequence is that, in general, an effector E will have additional effects on S to those planned, and the planned modes of interaction between E and S will be modified by these extraneous effects.

The diagnosis and treatment of erroneous anticipatory systems are frequently analogous to the procedures used in neurology and psychology.

We may further ask, how does a system generate predictive models? On this point we may invoke some general ontogenic principles, by means of natural selection, to achieve some understanding (see Chapter 13). And finally, given a system that employs a predictive model to determine its present behaviour, how should we observe the system so as to determine the nature of the model it employs? This last question raises fundamental and new questions of importance to the empirical sciences, for it turns out that most of the observational techniques we traditionally employ actually destroy our capability to make such underlying models visible. Just think how often one kills an organism to study its living processes. Rosen often joked that 'molecular biology' is an oxymoron.

Lessons from Biology

10.15 Examples   The conscious generation and deployment of predictive models for the purpose of control is one of the basic intuitive characteristics of intelligence.   However, precisely the same type of model-based behaviour appears constantly at lower levels of biological organization as well.   For instance, many simple organisms are negatively phototropic; they tend to move away from light.   Now darkness in itself is physiologically neutral; it has no intrinsic biological significance (at least for non-photosynthetic organisms).   However, darkness tends to be correlated with other characteristics that are not physiologically neutral, such as moisture and the absence of sighted predators.   The tropism can be regarded biologically as an exploitation of this correlation, which is in effect a predictive model about the environment.   Likewise, the autumnal shedding of leaves and other physiological changes in plants, which are clearly an adaptation to winter conditions, are not cued by ambient temperature, but rather by day length. There is an obvious correlation between the shortening day, which again is physiologically neutral in itself, and the subsequent appearance of winter conditions, which again constitutes a predictive model exploited for purposes of adaptive control.   Innumerable other examples of such anticipatory preadaptation can be found in the biosphere, ranging from the simplest of tropisms to the most complex hormonal regulatory processes in physiology.

10.16 To Do or Not to Do   The behaviours exhibited by an anticipatory system will be largely determined by the nature of its internal models. Understanding such a system means knowing its models.   From this viewpoint, the modelling relation is not simply established between us and a system; it is also established between the system and itself.   When viewed in this perspective, many of the baffling problems posed by complexity, as manifested especially in the behaviours of organisms and societies, appear in an entirely new light.   For instance, the employment of a predictive model for control purposes brings with it an almost ethical aspect to the system's behaviour.   There is an avoidance of certain future states as bad or undesirable; a tendency towards others as good or favourable.   Such a system will behave as if it knew the meaning of the word 'ought'.   Further, the availability of several models always raises the possibility that they will predict distinct futures, and hence invoke incompatible responses. Such *conflict* can arise within a single system, or it can arise between systems; from this perspective, the *resolution* of conflict consists in an adjustment of the models giving rise to it. As a final remark, we may note that the intrinsic limitations of models, which arise from the fact that in complex systems they must be abstractions, themselves give rise to behaviours which can be characterized as *senescent* — maladaptations that grow in time, without any localizable structural cause.

In dealing with these issues, properties of biological systems will provide crucial insights. Robert Rosen was fond of saying that the first lesson to be learned from biology is that there are lessons to be learned from biology. Biology, incidentally, is the study of special types of adaptive anticipatory systems, and *not* the memorization of the names of structural parts and biochemical molecules that passes for the subject in schools. Biology provides us with existence proofs, and specific examples, of cooperative rather than competitive activities on the part of large and diverse populations. Indeed, considered in an evolutionary context, biology represents a vast encyclopaedia of how to effectively solve complex problems; and also of how not to solve them. Biology is the science of the commonality of relations; and relationships contain the essential meaning of life. These insights represent natural resources to be harvested, resources perhaps even more important to our ultimate survival than the more tangible biological resources of food and energy. But to reap such a harvest, we need to fabricate proper tools. It is my belief that the conceptions of nature arising from relational biology will help us learn how to make it so.

An Anticipatory System is Complex

10.17 Anticipatory Cycle   The entailment diagram for the anticipatory system (10) is

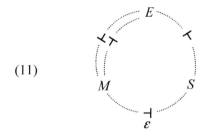

(11)

The map $\varepsilon : S \to M$, completing the hierarchical cycle, is the *encoding* of the object system S into its model M. The entailment of the three maps $\{M, E, S\}$ in cyclic permutation, i.e., the hierarchical cycle $\{ S \vdash M , E \vdash S , M \vdash E \}$, renders this anticipatory system complex.

Note that an anticipatory system has more structure in its entailment pattern than the existence of the cycle (11). What characterizes an anticipatory system is that its maps have a feedforward aspect. Also, the model-updating map $E \vdash M$ is not necessarily present in a hierarchical cycle of a complex system. Stated otherwise, an anticipatory system is a special kind of complex system.

10.18 Corollary Rosen concluded *AS* with:

> [One] final conceptual remark is also in order. As we pointed out above, the Newtonian paradigm has no room for the category of final causation. This category is closely tied up with the notion of anticipation, and in its turn, with the ability of systems to possess internal predictive models of themselves and their environments, which can be utilized for the control of present actions. We have argued at great length above that anticipatory control is indeed a distinguishing feature of the organic world, and developed some of the unique features of such anticipatory systems. In the present discussion, we have in effect shown that, in order for a system to be anticipatory, it must be complex.

Thus, our entire treatment of anticipatory systems becomes a corollary of complexity. In other words, complex systems can admit the category of final causation in a perfectly rigorous, scientifically acceptable way. Perhaps this alone is sufficient recompense for abandoning the comforting confines of the Newtonian paradigm, which has served us so well over the centuries. It will continue to serve us well, provided that we recognize its restrictions and limitations as well as its strengths.

The corollary, as I demonstrated with the anticipatory cycle 10.17, is:

10.19 Theorem *An anticipatory system must be complex; a complex system may (or may not) be anticipatory.*

In other words, the collection **A** of anticipatory systems is a proper subset of the collection **I** of complex systems:

(12) $A \subset I$ but $A \neq I$.

Thus, one has, in view of Axiom 10.4 and Theorem 10.19, the hierarchy:

(13) $O \subset A \subset I$,

in which both inclusions are proper. Thus

(14)

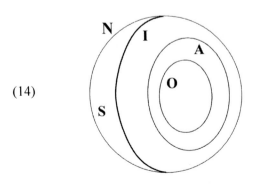

11

Living Systems

> Hierarchical order is found both in "structures" and in "functions". In the last resort, structure (i.e. order of parts) and function (order of processes) may be the very same thing: in the physical world matter dissolves into a play of energies, and in the biological world structures are the expression of a flow of processes.

> — Ludwig von Bertalanffy (1968)
> *General System Theory*

A Living System is Complex

Rosen created the theory of anticipatory systems as a stepping-stone towards the ultimate goal of the characterization of life. There is no question that the subject of Chapter 10, *anticipation* itself, just as *complexity* described in Chapter 9, is of independent interest, far-reaching, and tremendously worthy of study. It must, however, be remembered that the *raison d'être* of biology, hence of our relational approach to the subject, is *life* itself. The final causes of complexity and anticipation, in this regard, are the zeroth step and the first step, respectively, in the tightening of the necessary conditions that define life.

The important conclusion one draws from the proper inclusions

(1) $\mathbf{O} \subset \mathbf{A} \subset \mathbf{I}$

that conclude the previous chapter, that a living system is anticipatory and an anticipatory system is complex, is

(2) $\mathbf{O} \subset \mathbf{I}$ but $\mathbf{O} \neq \mathbf{I}$.

In short, Rosen's Conjecture 9.8 may now be restated as

11.1 Rosen's Theorem   *An organism must be complex; a complex system may (or may not) be an organism.*

11.2 "Nothing comes from nothing."   In any deductive system of logic, after the definition of the primitive terms, one must begin with a collection of statements that by nature cannot be proven. These are the *axioms* of the theory. The Greek word *ἀξίωμα* means 'that which is deemed worthy; self-evident principle'.

Rosen's Theorem 11.1 ($\mathbf{O} \subset \mathbf{I}$) is deduced from the postulated Axiom of Anticipation 10.4 ($\mathbf{O} \subset \mathbf{A}$) and the proven Theorem 10.19 ($\mathbf{A} \subset \mathbf{I}$). As I explained in the Preface and in Chapter 4, modelling is more an art than a science. A major part of this art of modelling is the careful choice of what the axioms of the theory are. For natural systems, all one has are perceptions and interpretations: one has to begin somewhere; not everything can be *mathematically proven.* I have chosen, in my formulation of relational biology that is this monograph, to state as axiom the more self-evident "life is anticipatory". The less self-evident "life is complex" then follows as a theorem.   While the Axiom of Anticipation, the statement "life is anticipatory", cannot be mathematically proven, it may well be considered as being scientifically 'proven': there is plainly abundant evidence for it. That is the best one can do with scientific 'proofs' and biological 'laws'. It has been said that the only law in biology is that there are exceptions to every possible 'law' in biology.

A living system is complex, whence inherits all properties of complex systems. As consequences of Theorems 9.2 and 9.3 and Lemma 9.4, therefore, one has the following

11.3 Theorem *A living system must contain a closed path of efficient causation.*

11.4 Corollary *A living system must have a model that contains an impredicative cycle of inferential entailment.*

11.5 Theorem *In (the relational diagram of) a living system there is a cycle that contains two or more solid-headed arrows.*

11.6 Theorem *A living system must have noncomputable models.*

11.7 Finale on Simulability Note that our (i.e., the relational-biology school's) interest is in life itself. The only reason the issue of simulability makes an appearance in relational biology is that it turns out to be a derivative of what we have to say about living systems. Simulability is a not-insignificant scientific subject of investigation, but computing science is simply not congenial and less interesting to me personally.

Biology-envy is the curse of computing science. In some languages, the term for 'computer' is 'electric brain'. It may be argued that the Holy Grail of computing, its ultimate final cause, is to successfully model biological and cognitive processes. The point of the Turing Test, indeed, is to see that if a computing machine's programming may be sophisticated enough to fool us into thinking that it may not be nonhuman. But what if life itself is, even in principle, nonsimulable? There are, of course, many things that mechanization by rote does better than life , in terms of speed, repeatability, precision, and so forth. On the other hand, a living system is driven by final causation, and may be characterized by its ability to handle ambiguities and take chances, indeed, its ability to err. These are precisely the processes that cannot, by definition (*cf.* Definition 8.2), be modelled algorithmically.

Algorithms can at best simulate. A simulation of life is, alas, not life itself. An impredicative cycle is, in particular, a representation of processes in the modelling relation such that there is no algorithm for using the representation itself to gain novel insight about the processes being modelled. The existence of the impredicative cycle is the lesson of complexity. In short, intuition, insight, and creativity are not computable.

(M,R)-Systems

11.8 Necessity versus Sufficiency In Chapter 1 of *EL*, after explaining that a living system must contain a closed path of efficient causation, hence must be complex, Rosen added:

> To be sure, what I have been describing are necessary conditions, not sufficient ones, for a material system to be an organism. That is, they really pertain to what is not an organism, to what life is not. Sufficient conditions are harder; indeed, perhaps there are none. If so, biology itself is more comprehensive than we presently know.

And in the final, concluding Section 11H of *LI*, he wrote:

> But complexity, though I suggest it is the habitat of life, is not itself life. Something else is needed to characterize what is alive from what is complex.

That "something else" is the 'closure to efficient causation' property found in (M,R)-systems, the subject of this chapter and the next.

11.9 The Next Step Robert Rosen introduced (M,R)-systems to the world in 1958, in his very first published scientific paper [Rosen, 1958]. They began as a class of metaphorical, relational paradigms that define cells. The M and R may very well stand for 'metaphorical' and 'relational' in modelling terms, but they are realized as 'metabolism' and 'repair'. The comprehensive reference is Rosen [1972].

Rosen subsequently discussed (M,R)-systems in many of his publications, notably in Section 3.5 of *AS*, Sections IV and V of *NC*, Section 10C of *LI*, and Chapter 17 of *EL*. The reader may refer to any or all of the above for further details.

In Rosen [1971], he listed three basic kinds of problems arising in the study of (M,R)-systems:

a. To develop the formal properties of such systems, considered in the abstract, and interpret them in biological terms;
b. To determine the methods by which the abstract organization which defines the (M,R)-system may be realized in concrete terms;
c. To determine whether a particular concrete biological system is in fact a realization of an (M,R)-system (i.e. to identify the functional components in a real biological system); this is basically the inverse problem to (b).

And he wrote:

Almost all of my published scientific work has arisen from a consideration of these three problems, although this is perhaps not always immediately apparent.

This last statement is in fact as true today, when we study Rosen's whole lifetime's work, as it was when he wrote it in 1971.

11.10 Metabolism and Repair   The simplest (M,R)-system may be represented by the diagram

(3) $A \xrightarrow{\ f\ } B \xrightarrow{\ \Phi\ } H(A,B).$

The mapping f represents *metabolism*, whence its efficient cause, an *enzyme*, with material input and output represented by the sets A and B. Thus metabolism is a morphism $f \in H(A,B) \subset B^A$. Members of $H(A,B)$ are mappings that model metabolic process, so clearly not all mappings in B^A qualify; thus $H(A,B)$ is a proper subset of B^A. The element trace is

(4) $f : a \mapsto b$

with relational diagram

(5)

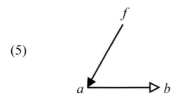

and entailment diagram

(6) $f \vdash b$.

In form (3), the morphism Φ represents *repair*. Its codomain is $H(A,B)$, so it may be considered as a mapping that creates new copies of enzymes f, hence a *gene* that 'repairs' the metabolism function. In other words, repair is a morphism Φ with the prescribed codomain $H(A,B)$; i.e. $\Phi \in H\left(\bullet, H(A,B)\right) \subset H(A,B)^{\bullet}$. Repair in cells generally takes the form of a continual synthesis of basic units of metabolic processor (i.e. enzymes), using as inputs materials provided by the metabolic activities themselves. Stated otherwise, the domain of the repair map Φ is the codomain of metabolism f, its 'output set' B. Thus $\Phi \in H(B, H(A,B)) \subset H(A,B)^B$, and its element-chasing, relational, and entailment diagrams are, respectively,

(7) $\Phi : b \mapsto f$

(8)
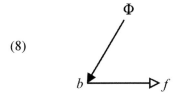

(9) $\Phi \vdash f .$

Metabolism and repair combine into the relational diagram

(10)
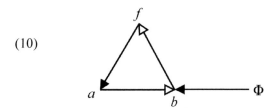

and entailment diagram

(11) $\Phi \vdash f \vdash b .$

This hierarchical entailment is the essence of the simplest (M,R)-system in form (3): Φ is the repair component, f is the metabolism component, and b is the output of the metabolic activity.

Note the adjective *simplest* I use for the (M,R)-system in form (3). This form already entails the impredicative cycle in (M,R)-systems. But a general (M,R)-system is actually a network of formal systems that are the metabolism and repair components (and their outputs). While form (3) may capture the essence of all (M,R)-systems (and indeed it is possible in principle to abbreviate every abstract (M,R)-system to this simple form by making the sets and mappings involved sufficiently complex), one must, nevertheless, not lose sight of the network aspect of (M,R)-systems. An *(M,R)-network*, i.e., a network of (a necessarily *finite* family of) metabolism and repair components, contains many fine nuances of inferential entailment that are not reflected in the simplest model. I shall come back to the exploration of the very rich mathematical structure of (M,R)-networks in Chapter 13.

11.11 Replication What if the repair components themselves need repairing? New mappings representing replication (i.e. that serve to replicate the repair components) may be defined. A replication map must have as its codomain the hom-set $H(B, H(A, B))$ to which repair mappings Φ belong, so it must be of the form

(12) $\beta : Y \to H\big(B, H\left(A, B\right)\big)$

for some set Y, whence the relational diagram

(13)

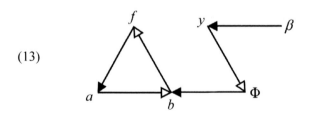

For the convenience of iterative combination (for illustrative purposes), one may choose $Y = H\left(A, B\right)$; so (12) and (13) become

(14) $\beta : H\left(A, B\right) \to H\big(B, H\left(A, B\right)\big)$

and

(15)

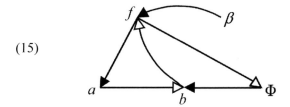

The replication morphism (14) may be combined with the repair morphism Φ in (3) to give a new (M,R)-system from the old one; *viz.*

(16) $\qquad B \xrightarrow{\Phi} H(A,B) \xrightarrow{\beta} H(B, H(A,B)),$

which has the property that the 'metabolic' part of system (16) is the 'repair' part of system (3), and the 'repair' part of system (16) is the 'replication' part of system (3) (i.e. form (14)). Indeed, one may sequentially extend this formalism ad infinitum, the next system being

(17) $\quad H(A,B) \xrightarrow{\beta} H(B, H(A,B)) \xrightarrow{\Xi} H(H(A,B), H(B, H(A,B))).$

The arrow diagrams may be extended on either side, rightward shown above as well as leftward.

11.12 Closure   If this were all there is to it with (M,R)-systems, it would have been pretty pointless. The magic of an (M,R)-system is that the replication mapping β may already be entailed in the original form (3). On the basis of what are already present in (3), "under stringent but not prohibitively strong conditions, such replication essentially comes along for free." The apparent infinite sequence of maps that may arise with the iteration of 'repair the repair' is truncated by a mathematical argument that turns it into a hierarchical cycle of maps instead. So there is no infinite graph of arrows here: the finite arrow diagram (3) alone suffices.

Not all (M,R)-networks satisfy the stringent requirements for entailment closure. Those that do may acquire an adjective and be called *replicative (M,R)-systems*. The hierarchical cycle is the closure that provides the 'self-sufficiency in efficient causes' that defines replicative (M,R)-systems. The defining characteristic, in other words, is the self sufficiency in the networks of metabolism-repair-replication components, in the sense that every mapping is entailed within; in short, closure in efficient causation. Henceforth I shall use the term *(M,R)-network* to describe a network of metabolism and repair components that is not necessarily closed to efficient causation. I shall drop the adjective 'replicative' for (M,R)-systems whence all (M,R)-systems are replicative. I state this explicitly as the formal

11.13 Definition
(*a*) An *(M,R)-network* is an entailment network of a finite collection of metabolism and repair components.
(*b*) An *(M,R)-system* is an (M,R)-network that is closed to efficient causation.

11.14 Nominalism Revisited   A note on Rosen's terminology is in order. Some people have pointed out that Rosen's usage of 'repair' and 'replication' do not conform to current standards in molecular biology, where these terms are mostly applied to nucleic acids, DNA in particular. While this non-conformation may be true, one must consider the chronology of events.

The Watson-Crick model of the structure of the DNA macromolecule was published in *Nature* in 1953. Francis Crick proclaimed his Central Dogma in 1958. The concepts of DNA repair and DNA replication in molecular biology were gradually formulated and developed in the decades thence. On the other hand, Robert Rosen introduced 'metabolism' and 'repair' components of his (M,R)-systems in 1958, as I have previously mentioned, in his first published scientific paper, entitled "A relational theory of biological systems". 'Replication' in (M,R)-systems first appeared in 1959, in Rosen's fourth paper [Rosen 1959], entitled "A relational theory of biological systems II". Thus, when Rosen wrote of 'repair' and 'replication', their modern biological senses had not been well established and certainly not standardized. In short, Rosen defined them first.

Words mutate and their usage morphs, of course. So we must remind ourselves that Rosen's 'repair' is 'replenishment', 'resynthesis', or 'replacement' (of enzymes) in modern biological terms.

Similarly, note that Rosen's 'replication' is strictly limited to the notion of a mapping in the model that makes copies of the repair process. Thus it is *not* (self-)replication in the modern biological sense. Rosen's 'replication' is the efficient cause of an (M,R)-system's inherent 'autonomy', a kind of 'relational invariance' in terms of its entailment pattern. This is a concept of relational biology that has no obvious counterpart in molecular biology. I emphasize: replication in an (M,R)-system is *not* how the genetic material is replicated, *not* a description of how a cell makes copies of itself, and *not* organismal reproduction. In one synthesis, however, of an alternate (M,R)-system, which I shall introduce in the epilogue, the replication of the repair process is functionally identical to (i.e. has an analogous interpretation as) the replication of the genetic components in a cell; i.e. nucleic acid replication.

11.15 Evaluation Map   There are many ways to construct the mapping β in form (12) from nothing else but what are already in the arrow diagram (3). Rosen has always used the simplest way, chosen his replication map β to have domain $Y = H(A,B)$, and made it an *inverse evaluation map*. (I shall explore other ways in the next chapter). True to the spirit of relational biology, we must recognize that the most important aspect of a replication map is *not* its *form*, i.e. not the exact details of how the map is defined. Rather, the most important is its *function*, that it needs to produce repair mappings Φ, which belong to the hom-set $H(B,H(A,B))$. Therefore the codomain of a replication map β must be $H(B,H(A,B))$; stated otherwise, one must have $\beta \vdash \Phi$.

Here is how one constructs Rosen's β. An element $b \in B$ defines an 'evaluation map' (*cf.* Examples A.19(i) and (ii), and A.52)

(18) $\hat{b} \in H\left(H\left(B, H\left(A, B\right)\right), H\left(A, B\right)\right)$

by

(19) $\hat{b}(\Phi) = \Phi(b)$ for $\Phi \in H\left(B, H\left(A, B\right)\right)$.

The map

(20) $\alpha : b \mapsto \hat{b}$

defines an embedding of B into $H\left(H\left(B, H\left(A, B\right)\right), H\left(A, B\right)\right)$. Rosen mentioned (for example in Rosen [1972]) that this "is the abstract version of the familiar embedding of a vector space into its second dual space". I shall further explore this concept, in the interlude below, after I finish constructing Rosen's inverse evaluation map.

11.16 Inverse Evaluation Map   The mapping $\hat{b}$ is invertible if it is monomorphic; *viz.* for every pair of repair maps $\Phi_1, \Phi_2 \in H(B, H(A, B))$,

(21) $\hat{b}(\Phi_1) = \hat{b}(\Phi_2) \;\Rightarrow\; \Phi_1 = \Phi_2$;

i.e.

(22) $\Phi_1(b) = \Phi_2(b) \;\Rightarrow\; \Phi_1 = \Phi_2$.

This implication (22) is a condition on the repair maps $\Phi \in H(B, H(A, B))$: if two repair maps agree at b, then they must agree everywhere. In other words, a repair map Φ [gene] is uniquely determined by its one value $\Phi(b) \in H(A, B)$ [enzyme]. This result may be regarded as the abstract version of the *one-gene-one-enzyme hypothesis*. These are essentially one set of the "stringent but not prohibitively strong conditions" required to make the inverse evaluation map a replication map with nothing but the ingredients of arrow diagram (3).

Note the inverse evaluation map $\hat{b}^{-1}$ maps thus:

(23) $\qquad \hat{b}^{-1} : H(A,B) \rightarrow H(B, H(A,B)),$

(24) $\qquad \hat{b}^{-1}(\Phi(b)) = \Phi.$

It takes one image value $f = \Phi(b) \in H(A,B)$ to the whole mapping $\Phi \in H(B, H(A,B))$: this is the sense in which it 'replicates'. But the stringent condition, requiring a repair map Φ to be uniquely determined by the one value $\Phi(b)$ in its range, neatly overcomes this $\Phi = \Phi(b)$ identification problem!

11.17 Remarks Let me paraphrase the dictum of relational biology in the current context. When the replication map β has domain $Y = H(A,B)$ and one constructs it as an inverse evaluation map, the important aspect is *not* that it *is* an inverse evaluation map. The fact that Rosen's regular example has $\beta = \hat{b}^{-1}$ is entirely incidental. Rather, the important aspect is that this particular replication map *has the property* that it is uniquely determined by one value in its range. The crux is $\beta : \Phi(b) \mapsto \Phi$. There are other ways to define $\beta \in H(H(A,B), H(B, H(A,B)))$ such that $\beta : \Phi(b) \mapsto \Phi$; choosing $\beta = \hat{b}^{-1}$ is just the simplest way, one specific example of how such a map may arise naturally. In other words, the emphasis is not on replication's *efficient cause*, but on its *final cause*. So when one seeks material realizations of the replication map thus constructed, the question to ask is not, say, "What is the physical interpretation of the inverse evaluation map?" One ought to ask, instead, "What biochemical processes are uniquely determined by their products?" One possible answer here is that one gene controls the production of one enzyme, or conversely, a gene is uniquely determined by which enzyme it produces. This is, of course, the one-gene-one-enzyme hypothesis.

Interlude: Reflexivity

11.18 Evaluation Map Revisited Rosen usually constructed his 'evaluation map' in two steps. He would begin with two arbitrary sets X and Y, and then define for each element $x \in X$ a mapping

(25) $\qquad \hat{x} : H(X,Y) \rightarrow Y$

by

(26) $\qquad \hat{x}(f) = f(x)$ for all $f \in H(X,Y)$.

Next he would put $X = B$ and $Y = H(A,B)$. Then an element $b \in B$ defines an evaluation map $\hat{b}$ as in lines (18) and (19) above, where I have defined the evaluation map in one single step.

The map $x \mapsto \hat{x}$ that sends an element to its corresponding evaluation map defines an embedding of X into $H(H(X,Y),Y)$. It is analogous to *the embedding of a vector space into its second dual space* (*cf.* Example A.19(ii)). The main subject here is linear algebra; two standard references are Halmos [1958] and Hoffman & Kunze [1971]. The counterpoint of reflexivity is found in the topic of functional analysis; two good references are Brown & Page [1970] and Rudin [1973].

11.19 Dual Space and Dual Transformation Let X and Y be two vector spaces over the field F. I shall restrict F to either the real field $\mathbb{R}$ or the complex field $\mathbb{C}$. The hom-set from X to Y in the category **Vct** of vector spaces consists of linear transformations, and is denoted $L(X,Y)$, a standard notation in linear algebra in lieu of the category-theoretic **Vct**(X,Y). Note that $L(X,Y)$ is itself a vector space over F, **Vct** being an additive category (*cf.* Definition A.39). Also, the scalar field F is a one-dimensional vector space over itself, so one may speak of $L(X,F)$. An element of $L(X,F)$, a linear transformation of X into F, is called a *linear functional*. This special vector space $L(X,F)$ is called the *dual space* of X, and one writes X^* in place of $L(X,F)$.

The concept of 'dual' applies to linear transformations as well. For any linear transformation $T:X \to Y$ one may define a linear transformation $T^*:Y^* \to X^*$ by

(27) $\qquad T^*(g) = g \circ T \quad \text{for all} \quad g \in Y^*,$

or diagrammatically

(28)

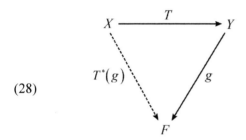

The linear transformation $T^* \in L(Y^*,X^*)$ is called the *dual transformation* of $T \in L(X,Y)$.

Let D be the operation of forming the dual space and the dual transformation. In other words, define $DX = X^*$ for each vector space X, and $DT = T^* \in L(Y^*,X^*)$ for each linear transformation $T \in L(X,Y)$. Then D is a contravariant functor on the category **Vct** of vector spaces and linear transformations, called the *dual functor*. Note that D is *not* the same as its namesake, the dual functor $I_{\mathbf{A}}^{\mathrm{op}}$ that sends a category $\mathbf{A}$ to its dual $\mathbf{A}^{\mathrm{op}}$ (*cf.* Example A.12(i)). In particular, $I_{\mathbf{A}}^{\mathrm{op}}$ is an involution ($I_{\mathbf{A}}^{\mathrm{op}} \circ I_{\mathbf{A}}^{\mathrm{op}} = I_{\mathbf{A}}$, the identity functor), but $D^2 = D \circ D$ is not necessarily equivalent to I_{Vct}, as we shall see presently.

11.20 Second Dual   The dual process may be iterated. Since X^* is itself a vector space, one may consider its own dual. For simplicity one writes X^{**} in place of $(X^*)^*$, and one calls X^{**} the *second dual (space)* of X. Note that an element of X^{**} is a 'linear functional of linear functionals', $X^{**} = L(L(X,F),F)$.   Similarly, the second dual transformation of $T \in L(X,Y)$ may be defined as $T^{**} \in L(X^{**}, Y^{**})$.

Repeated applications of the dual operation on a given vector space X result in a sequence of vector spaces $X, X^*, X^{**}, X^{***}, \ldots$ If X is a *finite-dimensional* vector space over F, then each vector space of the sequence is finite-dimensional and has the same dimension as X. This means they are all isomorphic (because each one is isomorphic to F^n, where n is the dimension). There does not exist, however, any *canonical* isomorphism from X to X^* (unless X has certain additional algebraic structures — we shall encounter one in the next chapter).

But from a *finite-dimensional* vector space X over the field F to its second dual X^{**}, there is an isomorphism that distinguishes itself from all the others. Define for each element $x \in X$ a mapping

(29) $\hat{x} : X^* \to F$

by

(30) $\hat{x}(f) = f(x)$ for all $f \in X^*$.

($\hat{x}$ is, of course, the now familiar evaluation map.) The mapping

(31) $\alpha_X : X \to X^{**}$

defined by

(32) $\alpha_X : x \mapsto \hat{x}$ for all $x \in X$

is an isomorphism, called the *natural isomorphism* between X and X^{**}. For every linear transformation $T \in L(X,Y)$, one has

(33) $T^{**} \circ \alpha_X = \alpha_Y \circ T$,

i.e. the diagram

(34)
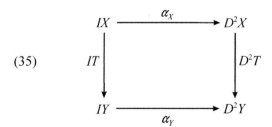

commutes.

11.21 Second Dual Functor   The *second dual functor* $D^2 = D \circ D$ is a covariant functor on the category of vector spaces defined by $D^2 X = X^{**}$ and $D^2 T = T^{**}$. Let the identity functor on **Vct** be denoted by I; i.e. $IX = X$ and $IT = T$. Then diagram (34) may be rewritten as

(35)

$$
\begin{array}{ccc}
IX & \xrightarrow{\ \alpha_X\ } & D^2 X \\
{\scriptstyle IT}\downarrow & & \downarrow{\scriptstyle D^2 T} \\
IY & \xrightarrow[\ \alpha_Y\ ]{} & D^2 Y
\end{array}
$$

Thus the natural isomorphism may be regarded as a morphism $\alpha : I \mapsto D^2$ of functors. It is, for finite-dimensional vector spaces, a natural isomorphism in the sense of category theory; indeed, it is the Example A.19(ii).

Each finite-dimensional vector space X can thus be identified with its second dual X^{**}, and consequently $T = T^{**}$ for each linear transformation $T : X \to Y$ of finite-dimensional vector spaces. Therefore in the sequences

$$X, X^*, X^{**}, X^{***}, \ldots$$
$$T, T^*, T^{**}, T^{***}, \ldots$$

one needs only consider the first pairs of terms X, X^* and T, T^*. The remaining ones, being *naturally* isomorphic copies, may be identified with them. [The first two members of the hierarchy suffice: here is another level of analogy with (M,R)-systems.]

Let me make one other remark before leaving *finite-dimensional* vector spaces. From the fact that X and its second dual X^{**} have the same finite dimension it follows that they are isomorphic; i.e. there exists an isomorphism $\phi : X \to X^{**}$. This unspecified isomorphism, however, may not satisfy the condition that is satisfied by the *natural* isomorphism when $\phi = \alpha_X$, that

(36) $(\phi(x))(f) = f(x)$ for all $x \in X$ and $f \in X^*$.

11.22 Reflexive Vector Space When the vector space X is *infinite-dimensional*, the mapping α_X defined in (32) is still injective, and it still satisfies (33) (and so the arrow diagram (34) still commutes). But the range of α_X may not be all of X^{**}. Thus α_X is an embedding of X *into*, but not necessarily *onto*, its second dual space X^{**}. Since for an infinite-dimensional X, α_X is not necessarily an isomorphism from X to its codomain X^{**}, one changes its name, from the 'natural isomorphism', and calls it the *canonical mapping* of X into X^{**}. The canonical mapping is an isomorphism of X

onto its range, the subspace $\hat{X} = \{\hat{x} : x \in X\}$ of X^{**}. In general, however, $\hat{X} \neq X^{**}$.

A vector space X is called *reflexive* if and only if the canonical mapping $\alpha_X : x \mapsto \hat{x}$ maps X *onto* X^{**}; i.e. iff $\hat{X} = X^{**}$; in other words, if and only if the canonical mapping *is* the natural isomorphism between X and X^{**}. [Here is polysemy at work again: this 'reflexive' is obviously different from the reflexive 'self-relating' property for relations (*cf.* Definition 1.10(*r*)).] All finite-dimensional vector spaces are reflexive, but some infinite-dimensional vector spaces are not. Let me emphasize that for X to be reflexive, the existence of *some* isomorphism from X onto X^{**} is not enough: the vector space and its second dual must be *isomorphic under the canonical mapping*. It is possible for a vector space X to be isomorphic to its second dual X^{**} without being reflexive.

11.23 Inverses As a final note of this interlude in linear algebra, I would like to point out the difference between two kinds of inverse mappings that one encounters when these linear algebra concepts extend to (M,R)-systems. Since the canonical mapping α_X is injective, its inverse exists with domain $\hat{X}$, defined by

(37) $\qquad \alpha_X^{-1}(\hat{x}) = x.$

But note that

(38) $\qquad \alpha_X^{-1} \in L(\hat{X}, X).$

It is completely different from the 'inverse' of the evaluation map $\hat{x} = \alpha_X(x)$, which may not exist. Since $\hat{x} \in X^{**} = L(X^*, F)$, it is a linear transformation from, generally, a higher-dimensional space into a one-dimensional space, thus highly singular. To make it invertible, "stringent but not prohibitively strong conditions" are required, just like for its counterpart $\hat{b}$ in (M,R)-

systems. Here, the conditions are restrictions on its domain and codomain. If the inverse exists, it would be a mapping

(39) $\qquad \hat{x}^{-1} \in L\left(F, X^{*}\right).$

A comparison of (38) and (39) shows how different the two inverses are: there is no general entailment between the inverse of a mapping $[\alpha_X]$, and the inverse of the image of one single element $[x]$ of the domain that mapping, when that image $[\hat{x} = \alpha_X(x)]$ happens to be a mapping in its own right. The situation is summarized succinctly as

(40) $\qquad \exists \alpha_X^{-1}(\hat{x}) \not\approx \exists\left(\alpha_X(x)\right)^{-1}.$

Traversability of an (M,R)-System

11.24 Completing the Cycle The inverse evaluation map $\beta = \hat{b}^{-1}$ establishes a correspondence between $H(H(A,B), H(B,H(A,B)))$ and B, whence $\beta: f \mapsto \Phi$ may be replaced by the isomorphic

(41) $\qquad b: f \mapsto \Phi$

with relational diagram

(42)

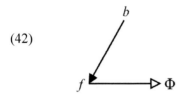

and entailment diagram

(43) $b \vdash \Phi.$

The cyclic entailment pattern when one combines lines (11) and (43) is the impredicative, hierarchical cycle of the (M,R)-system. The three maps $\{b, \Phi, f\}$ of replication, repair, and metabolism entail one another in a cyclic permutation. The three maps form the trivial traversable simple diagraph

(44)

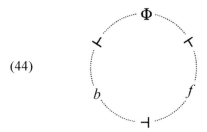

The Eulerian circuit may begin at any of the three vertices: $b \to \Phi \to f \to b$, $\Phi \to f \to b \to \Phi$, or $f \to b \to \Phi \to f$.

In terms of relational diagrams, the identification '$\hat{b}^{-1} = b$' transforms (15) into

(45)

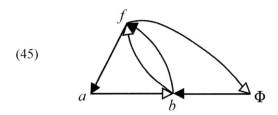

which is our multiple-connections example 5.17.

11.25 Cytoplasm and Nucleus A typical biological (eukaryotic) cell is compartmentalized into two observably different regions, the cytoplasm and the nucleus. Metabolic activities mainly occur in the cytoplasm, while repair processors (i.e. genes) are contained in the nucleus. Let me suggest an alternate depiction of the digraph (45) of the simplest (M,R)-system. I change the geometry to enclose the repair map Φ within. This gives a graphic representation of the metabolism component as the abstract equivalent of 'cytoplasm' and the repair component as the abstract counterpart of 'nucleus'. After I additionally label the arrows, digraph (45) becomes the equivalent digraph

(46)

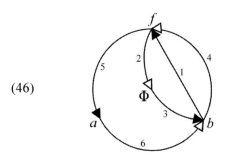

Both vertices a and Φ have indegree 1 and outdegree 1, while vertices b and f have indegree 2 and outdegree 2. Thus by Theorem 6.6(a), diagram (46) is traversable as a digraph; its Eulerian circuit in our context is precisely the hierarchical cycle containing all the solid-headed arrows, whence the (M,R)-system is closed to efficient causation (*cf.* Definition 6.23 and Theorem 6.28), therefore complex (Theorem 9.5). The closed path may begin at any vertex; in particular, the Eulerian circuits (1,2,3,4,5,6), (3,4,5,6,1,2) and (5,6,1,2,3,4), correspond to the Eulerian circuits in diagram (44).

Note that these three Eulerian circuits of diagram (46) respect the solid-headed-arrow–hollow-headed-arrow ordered-pairing of each morphism: the solid-headed arrows and hollow-headed arrows are in an alternating sequence. In strictly digraph-theoretic terms, circuits such as (3,1,5,6,4,2) and (6,1,2,3,4,5) are Eulerian as well; such 'out-of-phase' circuits, however, have no corresponding Eulerian circuits in the entailment digraph (44), and hence do *not* represent the hierarchical cycle. In particular, the fact that the Eulerian circuit (3,1,5,6,4,2) happens to 'segregate' the solid-headed arrows and the hollow-headed arrows is a graphic-theoretic coincidence that has no entailment implications.

11.26 Traversability as a Relation Diagram As a relational diagram, (46) may have the degrees of its vertices enumerated thus:

$$(47) \quad \begin{cases} \left(\varepsilon_i(a),\tau_i(a),\varepsilon_o(a),\tau_o(a)\right)=(1,0,0,1) \\ \left(\varepsilon_i(b),\tau_i(b),\varepsilon_o(b),\tau_o(b)\right)=(1,1,1,1) \\ \left(\varepsilon_i(f),\tau_i(f),\varepsilon_o(f),\tau_o(f)\right)=(1,1,1,1) \\ \left(\varepsilon_i(\Phi),\tau_i(\Phi),\varepsilon_o(\Phi),\tau_o(\Phi)\right)=(0,1,1,0) \end{cases}$$

(*cf.* 6.8 for the notation of the four degrees of a vertex in a relational diagram, and Example 6.9 for the enumeration of the diagram (45) which is isomorphic to (46)). Thus diagram (46) satisfies the conditions of Theorem 6.12(*a*), whence *as a relational diagram* it is traversable and has an Eulerian circuit.

What is Life?

Rosen's idea behind (M,R)-systems was, as he explained in Chapter 17 of *EL*, "to characterize the minimal organization a material system would have to manifest or realize to justify calling it a *cell*". Whence Rosen defined a cell thus:

11.27 Definition A *cell* is (at least) a material structure that realizes an (M,R)-system.

Recall that a *realization* of a formal system is a natural system obtained from decoding that formal system; i.e., a natural system that is a realization of a formal system has the latter as a *model* (*cf.* 4.14). Note that the word 'cell' in the definition is used in the generic sense of 'autonomous life form'. This

282

class of relational cell models can just as well describe organisms, indeed all living systems.

In Section 10C of *LI* one finds (The "graph" is Rosen's arrow diagram [10C.6] in *LI* of an (M,R)-system, which is an alternate version of my diagrams (45) and (46) above.):

> Any material system possessing such a graph as a relational model (i.e., which *realizes* that graph) is accordingly an organism. From our present perspective, we can see that [10C.6] is not the only graph that satisfies our conditions regarding entailments; there are many others. A material realization of any of them would likewise, to that extent, constitute an organism.

Definition 11.27 says that 'having an (M,R)-system as a model' is a necessary condition — that is what the 'at least' in the definition signifies — for a natural system to be an autonomous life form. Rosen, for emphasis, added the adjectival phrase "under the condition that at least one of the appropriate inverse evaluation maps exists" to his description of an (M,R)-system in his original definition in Chapter 17 of *EL*. The requisite inverse evaluation map is what completes the impredicative cycle in Rosen's standard construction of an (M,R)-system. I shall have more to say on other means of closure (*cf.* "there are many others" in the quote above) in the next chapter.

Immediately after Definition 11.27, in the same paragraph in Chapter 17 of *EL* in fact, Rosen added:

> *Making a cell means constructing such a realization.* Conversely, I see no grounds for refusing to call such a realization an autonomous life form, whatever its material basis may be.

The converse statement provides the sufficiency. So I may *define* 'organism', meaning any 'living system', as:

11.28 Postulate of Life   A natural system is an *organism* if and only if it realizes an (M,R)-system.

Note that Postulate 11.28 is not a contradiction to the quote in the necessity-versus-sufficiency discussion in 11.8 that there may not be sufficient conditions that characterize life. Rosen had established the necessity; he chose to *state* the sufficient condition in his *definition* of life. 'Having an (M,R)-system as a model' is the necessary and sufficient condition for a natural system to be an autonomous life form, on a relational level, even if one may not readily recognize the natural system as 'alive' on the material level.

Rosen's answer to the question "What is life?" (in its epistemological form of "What are the defining characteristics of a natural system for us to perceive it as being alive?") is given in Chapter 10 of *LI*:

11.29 Theorem   *A material system is an organism if, and only if, it is closed to efficient causation.*

An (M,R)-system is a relational model of a living organism that captures this necessary and sufficient condition.   Definition 11.13(*b*) establishes the equivalence of Postulate 11.28 and Theorem 11.29. The important point to note for the purposes of relational biology is that life is characterized through the use of *efficient causation*, one of Aristotle's four categories.   The characterization of life is not what the underlying physicochemical *structures* are, but by its entailment *relations*, what they *do*, and to what *end*. In other words, life is not about its material cause, but is intimately linked to the other three Aristotelian causes, formal, efficient, and final.

Explicitly in terms of efficient causes, one has

11.30 Theorem   *A natural system is an organism if and only if it has a closed path containing all of its efficient causes.*

An efficient cause is identified with its corresponding solid-headed arrow in the relational diagram in graph-theoretic form. So equivalently:

11.31 Theorem *In the relational diagram of (a formal system model of) a living system, there is a cycle that contains all the solid-headed arrows.*

Functional entailment is identified with the entailment symbol ⊢. So one also has

11.32 Theorem *In the entailment diagram of (a formal system model of) a living system, there is a cycle that contains all the ⊢.*

The New Taxonomy

11.33 From Necessity to Sufficiency The journey to identify the distinguishing features of a living system began with the collection **N** of natural systems. Let **O** be the collection of organisms (i.e. living systems), and let < be the relation 'less than' (*cf.* Definition 1.22) in the poset $\langle \mathbf{PN}, \subset \rangle$, *viz.* the relation 'is a proper subset of':

(48) $X < Y$ if and only if $X \subset Y \subset \mathbf{N}$ and $X \neq Y$.

Clearly

(49) $\mathbf{O} < \mathbf{N}$,

i.e., an organism is necessarily a natural system. Thus

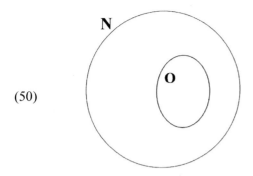

(50)

The strategy is to keep tightening the necessarily conditions, to eventually arrive at a set of conditions r that is both necessary and sufficient to characterize $\mathbf{O}$; in other words,

$$(51) \qquad \mathbf{O} = \mathbf{R} = \{N \in \mathbf{N} : r(N)\} < \cdots < \mathbf{N}.$$

After the partitioning of $\mathbf{N}$ into the complementary sets $\mathbf{S}$ of simple systems and $\mathbf{I}$ of complex systems, we established that an organism is complex, whence

$$(52) \qquad \mathbf{O} < \mathbf{I}.$$

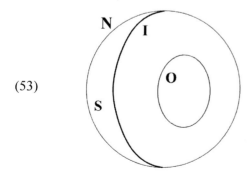

(53)

Anticipation provides a further constraint: if **A** is the collection of anticipatory systems, then

(54) $\mathbf{O} < \mathbf{A}$

(55)

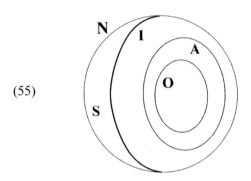

In this chapter, we have finally reached our goal, and established that the necessary and sufficient condition is

(56) $r(N) = N$ realizes an (M,R)-system,

and the equivalent

(57) $k(N) = N$ is closed to efficient causation.

Thus, with $\mathbf{R} = \{N \in \mathbf{N} : r(N)\}$ and $\mathbf{K} = \{N \in \mathbf{N} : k(N)\}$, we have

(58) $\mathbf{O} = \mathbf{R} = \mathbf{K}$.

This is the new taxonomy of natural systems in the school of relational biology:

(59)

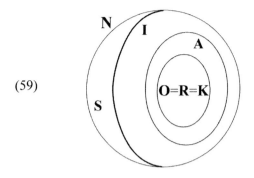

11.34 Realization   The realization of an (M,R)-system is a difficult problem. It is also a central problem, in view of the very definition of life as realization of an (M,R)-system. The realization postulate 11.28 is completely in keeping with the crux of relational biology, to *throw away the matter and keep the underlying organization*. So the building of realizations assumes the central role in the recapture of 'matter from bauplan'. Rosen himself has made several attempts in the realization of (M,R)-systems: for example Rosen [1971], Rosen [1973], and Chapter 17 of *EL*. He has taken formal, dynamic, inverse, and synthetic approaches. In Rosen [1971] he wrote "we are nowhere near having anything like a solution", and in Chapter 17 of *EL* the conclusion was that the answer "takes a lot more than we presently have. That is why the problem is so hard, but also why it is so instructive."

The final section (11H) of *LI* is, indeed, entitled "Relational Biology and Its Realizations". There, Rosen summarizes the realization problem of relational biology this way:

> Organization [in living systems] in its turn inherently involves *functions* and their interrelations; the abandonment of fractionability, however, means that there is no kind of 1 to 1 relationship between such relational, functional organizations and the structures which realize them. These

> are the basic differences between organisms and mechanisms or machines.

This lack of one-to-one correspondence between functions and structures is inherent in the nature of these two classes of alternate descriptions. A functional organization cuts across physical structures, and a physical structure is simultaneously involved in a variety of functional activities. So an (M,R)-system is not realized by identifying its components and maps in a 'concrete' biological example. To tackle the biological realization problem of (M,R)-systems, one ought not to be seeking physicochemical implementations of what the relations *are*, but, rather, one ought to be seeking interpretations of what the relations *do*. The journey continues.

12

Synthesis of (M,R)-Systems

Alternate Encodings of the Replication Component in (M,R)-Systems

Rosen's theory of the metabolism-repair representation of organisms, i.e. (M,R)-systems, rests on the capacity of the system to synthesize the replication mapping from what was already available among the M and R components. Rosen demonstrated this capacity with his classic 'inverse evaluation map' encoding. He noted cryptically, however, that there were many other encodings that led to replication from the interaction of M and R (but had never shown what they were in any of his writings). Knowing what some of those other ways may be is useful, since it provides further insight into what properties are allowed, required, or forbidden in the metabolism-repair paradigm.

I shall in this chapter construct two additional encodings of (M,R)-systems with replication represented by morphisms that are not the classic 'inverse evaluation map'. I shall describe how these synthetic systems may be realized biologically, and study these alternate descriptions in graph-theoretic terms.

12.1 Domains and Codomain Recall that a replication map must have as its codomain the hom-set $H(B, H(A, B))$ to which repair mappings Φ belong, whence it must be of the form

(1) $\qquad \beta : Y \to H(B, H(A, B))$

for some set Y. How many choices does one have for Y? Since the most important feature of an (M,R)-system is the closure of its entailment structure, one must choose Y to be a set already present in the form

(2) $\qquad A \xrightarrow{\ f\ } B \xrightarrow{\ \Phi\ } H(A, B).$

So one may have $Y = A$, B, or $H(A, B)$.

12.2 Inverse Evaluation Map In the previous chapter, the choice for Y is $H(A, B)$, and it leads to Rosen's replication map β as an inverse evaluation map. The evaluation map from linear algebra inspires, for an element $b \in B$, through the natural transformation

(3) $\qquad \alpha : B \to H\big(H(B, H(A, B)), H(A, B)\big),$

the (M,R)-system's evaluation map

(4) $\qquad \alpha(b) = \hat{b} \in H\big(H(B, H(A, B)), Y\big) = H\big(H(B, H(A, B)), H(A, B)\big),$

defined by

(5) $\qquad \alpha(b) = \hat{b} : \Phi \mapsto \Phi(b)$

The replication map is then defined as its inverse

(6) $\qquad \beta = \hat{b}^{-1} \in H\big(Y, H(B, H(A, B))\big) = H\big(H(A, B), H(B, H(A, B))\big),$

which is required to exist by the "stringent but not prohibitively strong conditions". The resulting replication map

(7) $$\beta = \hat{b}^{-1} : \Phi(b) \mapsto \Phi$$

identifies the repair map Φ with one value $\Phi(b)$ in its *range*, which is the chosen $Y = H(A, B)$. Note that this construction hinges on the definition of the evaluation map (5); the rest follows as a matter of course. Note also that the evaluation map in linear algebra is

(8) $$\hat{x} \in X^{**} = L(X^*, F) = L(L(X, F), F),$$

while the evaluation map here is

(9) $$\hat{b} \in H(H(B, H(A, B)), H(A, B)).$$

Comparing (8) and (9), one thus sees that the functorial encoding of an (M,R)-system into linear algebra is $B \mapsto X$ and $H(A, B) \mapsto F$.

Replication as a Conjugate Isomorphism

Now let me try an alternate construction and choose $Y = B$. I would like to have the replication map as

(10) $$\beta \in H(B, H(B, H(A, B))).$$

So I ought to seek a well-defined mapping, an embedding of B into $H(B, H(A, B))$, that maps

(11) $$\beta : b \mapsto \Phi \quad \text{for} \quad b \in B.$$

The repair map Φ is hence identified with one value b in its *domain*, which is the chosen $Y = B$.

12.3 Hilbert Space Where in mathematics does one encounter a map that naturally identifies a mapping with one value in its domain? Again, linear algebra and functional analysis provide the analogy. The embedding in this case is a little more straight-forward than inverse evaluation maps, and the balance is that, correspondingly, the objects of the category need a little more structure. This time one turns to the category of Hilbert spaces. I shall not explain here what a Hilbert space is, other than mention in passing that it is a vector space equipped with an inner product, and is complete in the metric associated with this inner product. See Rudin [1973] and Brown & Page [1970] for a good introduction to Hilbert space theory.

Consider a Hilbert space X over the field F (which I shall restrict to either the real field $\mathbb{R}$ or the complex field $\mathbb{C}$). Its inner product $\langle \cdot, \cdot \rangle : X \times X \to F$ is linear in the first argument, and conjugate-linear in the second argument (which means linear in the second argument when $F = \mathbb{R}$). Such a bivariate mapping is sometimes called *conjugate-bilinear*, or *sesquilinear* (i.e. '$1\frac{1}{2}$-linear'). As a simple example, a finite-dimensional Euclidean space (i.e., $\mathbb{R}^n$) with the standard inner product is a Hilbert space.

For each $y \in X$, the mapping $\Lambda_y : X \to F$ defined by

(12) $\Lambda_y(x) = \langle x, y \rangle$ for all $x \in X$

is a continuous linear functional on X, i.e. $\Lambda_y \in L(X, F) = X^*$. In tensor theory, Λ_y is called the *covector* of y. The map $\gamma_X : X \to X^*$ that sends a vector to its covector, i.e. defined by

(13) $\gamma_X : y \mapsto \Lambda_y$ for all $y \in X$,

is a *canonical embedding* of X into X^*, in the sense that it preserves the inner product space structure: the definition

(14) $\qquad \langle \Lambda_x, \Lambda_y \rangle = \overline{\langle x, y \rangle} = \langle y, x \rangle$

satisfies the properties of an inner product, whence equipping X^* into an inner product space. Indeed, X^* is itself a Hilbert space. Recall that I have mentioned in 11.20, for a general vector space X, there is *no* canonical embedding of X into X^*, *unless* X is endowed with additional algebraic structures. So one sees here that having an inner product is one such equipment.

It turns out that in Hilbert space theory, *all* continuous linear functionals are of this type, 'inner product with a fixed vector':

12.4 Theorem *If g is a continuous linear functional on X, then there is a unique $y \in X$ such that for all $x \in X$, $g(x) = \Lambda_y(x) = \langle x, y \rangle$.*

This theorem thus says, in particular, that the mapping $g : X \to F$ is identified with one value $y \in X$ in its domain. It also says that the embedding $\gamma_X : y \mapsto \Lambda_y$ from X into X^* is bijective, hence invertible. Indeed, one has $\gamma_X^{-1} : \Lambda_y \mapsto y$, whence for all $x \in X$ and $g \in X^*$,

(15) $\qquad g(x) = \langle x, \gamma_X^{-1}(g) \rangle.$

Note that, because of the conjugacy property of the *complex* inner product (i.e. when $F = \mathbb{C}$)

(16) $\qquad \langle y, x \rangle = \overline{\langle x, y \rangle},$

the inner products in X and X^* are related by

(17) $\qquad \langle x, y \rangle = \overline{\langle \gamma_X(x), \gamma_X(y) \rangle} = \overline{\langle \Lambda_x, \Lambda_y \rangle} = \langle \Lambda_y, \Lambda_x \rangle$ for all $x, y \in X$

(*cf.* (14)); or alternatively,

(18) $\langle g,h \rangle = \overline{\langle \gamma_X^{-1}(g), \gamma_X^{-1}(h) \rangle}$ for all $g,h \in X^*$.

For the *real* inner product, i.e. when $F = \mathbb{R}$, one has the symmetric relation

(19) $\langle x,y \rangle = \langle y,x \rangle$,

whence this issue of conjugacy does not occur, and one has simply

(20) $\langle x,y \rangle = \langle \Lambda_x, \Lambda_y \rangle$ for all $x,y \in X$.

Thus when $F = \mathbb{C}$, $\gamma_X : X \to X^*$ is not a linear mapping, only a *conjugate-linear* mapping. When $F = \mathbb{R}$, however, γ_X is a linear mapping. So γ_X preserves the inner product structure either conjugately or directly, whence it is a [*conjugate-*]*linear isomorphism*. In both the complex and real cases, one has

(21) $\|\Lambda_y\| = \|y\|$,

whence γ_X is a [*conjugate-*]*linear isometry*.

In sum, a Hilbert space X is isomorphic and isometric, under the *conjugate isomorphism* γ_X, to its dual space X^*.

12.5 Second Dual When X is a Hilbert space, so is X^*. So one has iteratively a conjugate isomorphism $\gamma_{X^*} : X^* \to X^{**}$. It is now interesting to compare the composite linear transformation

(22) $\gamma_{X^*} \circ \gamma_X : X \to X^{**}$

with the canonical mapping from linear algebra,

(23) $\qquad \alpha_X : X \to X^{**}$

defined by

(24) $\qquad \alpha_X : x \mapsto \hat{x} \quad$ for all $\quad x \in X$

(*cf.* 11.20). One may speak of the canonical mapping because a Hilbert space is in particular a vector space. A little algebra (using observation (15) and the definition (24)) leads to the conclusion that

(25) $\qquad \gamma_{X^*} \circ \gamma_X = \alpha_X .$

In sum: for Hilbert spaces, the canonical mapping is a composite of two conjugate isomorphisms. This also means, of course, that the canonical mapping α_X is a natural isomorphism, whence a Hilbert space is reflexive.

12.6 Adjoint Recall from 11.18 that the dual transformation of a linear transformation $T \in L(X,Y)$ is the linear transformation $T^* \in L(Y^*, X^*)$ such that $T^*(g) = g \circ T$ for all $g \in Y^*$. Now let both X and Y be Hilbert spaces. Then for each linear transformation $T \in L(X,Y)$ one may define a linear transformation

(26) $\qquad \tilde{T} = \gamma_X^{-1} \circ T^* \circ \gamma_Y \in L(Y,X),$

called the [*Hilbert space*] *adjoint* of the linear transformation T :

(27)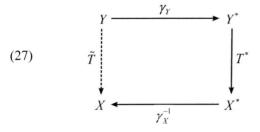

For each pair of vectors $x \in X$ and $y \in Y$, one has an inner product $\langle x, \tilde{T}(y) \rangle$ of X and an inner product $\langle T(x), y \rangle$ of Y. [Note that the last two 'of's signify that the inner products have *domains* in their respective Hilbert spaces; the *values* of the inner products are, of course, scalars, i.e. $\in F$.] The adjoint is, indeed, characterized by the equality of these two inner products:

(28) $\langle T(x), y \rangle = \langle x, \tilde{T}(y) \rangle$ for all $x \in X$ and $y \in Y$.

Instead of defining the adjoint using conjugate isomorphisms as in (26), given a linear transformation $T \in L(X,Y)$, the adjoint is often defined as the unique linear transformation $\tilde{T} \in L(Y,X)$ that satisfies (28). Note that the form of the defining equality (28) of the Hilbert space adjoint generalizes to adjunction in category theory (*cf.* A.48).

Let us now examine the formation of the Hilbert space adjoint in the language of category theory. Define in the category of Hilbert spaces $AX = X$ for each Hilbert space X, and $AT = \tilde{T} \in L(Y,X)$ for each linear transformation $T \in L(X,Y)$. Then A is a contravariant functor on the category of Hilbert spaces, called the *adjoint functor* (note that this *Hilbert space* adjoint functor, while a namesake, is different from the *left* and *right* adjoint functors, although in certain contexts there is an analogy). Further, it is trivial to verify that $\tilde{\tilde{T}} = T$, so $A^2 = I$, the identity functor, whence A is an involution.

Finally, let us compare the adjoint functor A with the dual functor D from 11.19, defined by $DX = X^*$ for each [Hilbert space as a] vector space X, and $DT = T^* \in L(Y^*, X^*)$ for each linear transformation $T \in L(X,Y)$. Diagram (27) may be redrawn as

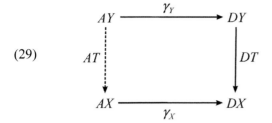

(29)

Thus the conjugate isomorphism may be regarded as a morphism $\gamma : A \mapsto D$ of functors. It is, therefore, another natural transformation.

12.7 Replication My required embedding of B into $H\left(B, H\left(A, B\right)\right)$,

$$(30) \qquad \beta : b \mapsto \Phi \quad \text{for} \quad b \in B,$$

may be considered as the abstract version of the conjugate isomorphism of a Hilbert space onto its dual space. For $b \in B$, let Φ be the image of b under the conjugate isomorphism γ_B from B to $H\left(B, H\left(A, B\right)\right)$, i.e.

$$(31) \qquad \Phi = \gamma_B\left(b\right) = \Lambda_b \in H\left(B, H\left(A, B\right)\right)$$

defined by

$$(32) \qquad \Phi\left(x\right) = \Lambda_b\left(x\right) = \left\langle x, b \right\rangle \in H\left(A, B\right) \quad \text{for all} \quad b \in B,$$

(*cf.* (12) and (13)). The 'generalized inner product' in (32) is a sesquilinear mapping

$$(33) \qquad \left\langle \cdot, \cdot \right\rangle : B \times B \rightarrow H\left(A, B\right).$$

The conjugate isomorphism in Hilbert space theory is

$$(34) \qquad \gamma_X \in L\big(X, X^*\big) = L\big(X, L(X, F)\big),$$

while the corresponding embedding here is

$$(35) \qquad \gamma_B \in H\big(B, H\big(B, H(A, B)\big)\big).$$

Comparing (34) and (35), one thus sees that the functorial encoding of an (M,R)-system into Hilbert spaces remains the same $B \mapsto X$ and $H(A, B) \mapsto F$ as in the inverse evaluation map construction (*cf.* 12.2).

12.8 Realization When one seeks material realizations of the replication map here, the question to ask is neither "How may the conjugate isomorphism be interpreted in biological terms?", nor "Can anything biological possibly be encoded as a Hilbert space?" (although the latter question does have surprisingly positive answers; see the next paragraph). Instead of these efficient-cause questions, one should be posing final-cause ones. The requirement that a repair map Φ [gene] be uniquely determined by a metabolic product $b \in B$ in its domain may be realized thus. A metabolic product in fact determines the enzyme $f \in H(A, B)$ required in the biochemical reaction that produces it. This is the concept of *enzyme specificity*. The one-gene-one-enzyme hypothesis then completes the entailment path to the gene $\Phi \in H\big(B, H(A, B)\big)$.

12.9 Recognition For $b \in B$ and $\Phi \in H\big(B, H(A, B)\big)$, the mapping notation $\Phi(b)$ is itself sometimes represented in bracket form $\langle b, \Phi \rangle$, whence this 'generalized inner product' is a sesquilinear mapping

$$(36) \qquad \langle \bullet, \bullet \rangle \colon B \times H\big(B, H(A, B)\big) \to H(A, B).$$

It is in this bracket form $\langle b, \Phi \rangle$ that (M,R)-systems are fully realized into the realm of enzyme catalysis. In Louie, Richardson, & Swaminathan [1982], using enzyme-substrate recognition as an example, a phenomenological calculus for recognition processes was developed. We first employed the Hilbert space $X = X^* = L^2$ of square-integrable functions. Then we specialized into the space of continuous functions $C(K)$ and its dual, the space of normalized functions of bounded variation $X^* = NBV(K)$, where K was a compact subset of Euclidean space. In this latter formulation, the recognition of a substrate $s \in C(K)$ by an enzyme $\alpha \in NBV(K)$ resulted from the evaluation of a Stieltjes integral of the form

$$(37) \qquad \langle s, \alpha \rangle = \int_K s \, d\alpha .$$

In Louie & Somorjai [1984], Stieltjes integration was connected to differential geometry, when the protein backbone space curve of an enzyme molecule was represented by its complex curvature-and-torsion function. In these two papers, many formal features of a metabolism-repair-replication system were decoded and realized in biological terms. Multi-enzyme system, cofactor, apoenzyme, holoenzyme, activation-inhibition, active-site location, etc., all have relational encodings. The reader is encouraged to seek out these two relics and explore.

Hilbert space theory is the language of quantum mechanics, and forms the foundation of biological imaging. It would, however, be idle to enter here into a more detailed discussion of these, and indeed any other of its many biophysical applications. The intricate connections among (M,R)-systems, quantum mechanics, and tomography have been some of the topics explored in the sequence of Richardson-Louie phenomenological calculus papers, most notably in Richardson & Louie [1983, 1986] and Louie [1983].

Replication as a Similarity Class

12.10 Similarity Class The third and final choice for the domain of the replication map is $Y = A$. Now I would like to have

(38) $\qquad \beta \in H\big(A, H\big(B, H\big(A, B\big)\big)\big).$

I require an embedding of A into $H\big(B, H\big(A, B\big)\big)$, that maps

(39) $\qquad \beta : a \mapsto \Phi \quad$ for $\ a \in A$.

When I trace the path of the element $a \in A$ as it is mapped through the arrow diagram (2) of the (M,R)-system, I get

(40) $\qquad a \mapsto b = f\big(a\big) \mapsto \Phi\big(b\big) = \Phi\big(f\big(a\big)\big) = f.$

So *formally*, from $\Phi\big(f\big(a\big)\big) = f$, I can write

(41) $\qquad \Phi = f\,a^{-1}f^{-1}.$

This says Φ and a^{-1} are *similar* to each other; in other words, Φ is in the *similarity class* of a^{-1} (similarity being an equivalence relation).

I, however, still need a rigorous mathematical encoding of this formalism. This time, the analogy is provided in the algebra of linear operators.

12.11 Similitude The equivalence relation of similarity appears in many topics in mathematics. In particular, we may stay within linear algebra. Let X be a vector space over the field F (either the real field $\mathbb{R}$ or the complex field $\mathbb{C}$ as before). A linear transformation from X into itself, i.e., a member of $L\big(X, X\big)$, is called a *linear operator*. In addition to the vector space operations, $L\big(X, X\big)$ admits a binary 'multiplication' operation on its members, that of composition of mappings. All these operations satisfy the properties that make $L\big(X, X\big)$ into a *linear associative algebra*. One denotes $L\big(X, X\big)$, the algebra of linear operators on X, as $\mathcal{A}\big(X\big)$.

The linear operators $T, T' \in \mathcal{A}(X)$ are said to be *similar* if there exists an *invertible* element $P \in \mathcal{A}(X)$ such that

(42) $T' = P T P^{-1}.$

The relation on $\mathcal{A}(X)$ defined by similarity is an equivalence relation; let me denote it by S. The equivalence class of a linear operator T is called its *similarity class*, denoted by $[T]_S$. Thus the similarity relation (42) may be written as

(43) $[T']_S = [T]_S.$

Note also that $T' \in [T]_S$ iff there exists an invertible element $P \in \mathcal{A}(X)$ such that (42) holds. The whole subject area of *canonical forms* in linear algebra is the selection, from a similarity class, of linear operators (hence matrices) of particularly nice forms (which, in terms of matrices, are those with a lot of zero entries, and with the nonzero entries arranged in simple geometric patterns).

The collection of all similarity classes is the quotient algebra

(44) $\mathcal{A}(X)/S = \{ [T]_S : T \in \mathcal{A}(X) \}$

(*cf.* Definition 1.13). The map that sends a linear operator to its similarity class, i.e.

(45) $\pi_S : \mathcal{A}(X) \to \mathcal{A}(X)/S$

defined by

(46) $\pi_S(T) = [T]_S$

is called the *natural projection* (*cf.* Theorem 2.20).

I will not continue further with my brief detour into equivalence relation and similarity. As I mentioned in the beginning of Part I, Rosen's book *FM* may equally well be entitled "Epistemological Consequences of the Equivalence Relation". In particular, its Chapter 1 provides the mathematical background of the equivalence relation, Chapter 6 is on the linkage between similitude and symmetry, and the final Chapter 7 explores many topics on "Similarity in Physics and Biology". Seek and read!

12.12 Generalized Inverse In mathematics, one tends not to distinguish between members of the same equivalence class, since they are 'identical up to an equivalence relation'. Instead of setting the repair map Φ to be *in* the similarity class of a^{-1}, one may simply define Φ to *be* the similarity class of a^{-1}. The embedding of A into $H(B, H(A,B))$,

(47) $\beta : a \mapsto \Phi$ for $a \in A$.

may then be defined as the generalized natural projection

(48) $\beta(a) = \pi_S(a^{-1}) = \left[f \, a^{-1} \, f^{-1} \right]_S = \left[a^{-1} \right]_S = \Phi$

(*cf.* (46)). Thus the repair map Φ defined by (48) may be interpreted as a generalized inverse.

The repair map Φ is hence identified with, indeed anticipated by, one value a from the set A, which seems to have only a remote connection to it. The set A is not the domain of $\Phi \in H(B, H(A,B))$, and is only related to its codomain by being the domain of *members* of the latter. The material realizations of this particular replication map

(49) $\beta = \pi_S \circ (\cdot)^{-1} : A \to H(B, H(A,B))$

are not found in answers to the efficient-cause questions "What does a^{-1} mean when a is supposed to be a substrate of a metabolic reaction?" and

"What does similarity have to do with biology?" (The answer to the latter question is in fact 'a lot'; read *FM*.) The final cause, that a repair map is identified with an equivalence class of substrates, may be realized thus. The concept of enzyme specificity applies just as well from substrates $a \in A$ to enzymes $f \in H(A, B)$ required in the biochemical reactions that metabolize them. The one-gene-one-enzyme hypothesis then again completes the entailment path to the gene $\Phi \in H(B, H(A, B))$. Also, because of the self-referencing nature of the map $\beta : a \mapsto \left[a^{-1} \right]_S$, the set of metabolism-repair-replication maps for this $Y = A$ (M,R)-system may be decoded into the set of pathways of *protein biochemistry*. In particular, the enzymes involved act on enzymes themselves, and may be realized among peptide synthases, protein polymerases, protein kinases, and peptidases.

Traversability

As we saw in the previous chapter, a graph-theoretic analysis of the traversability of (M,R)-systems illustrates succinctly the underlying topological structure of impredicative hierarchical cycles.

12.13 The Metabolism and Repair Components   The relation diagram that corresponds to the (M,R)-system (2), with metabolism and repair maps

(50) $f : a \mapsto b$ and $\Phi : b \mapsto f$,

is

(51)

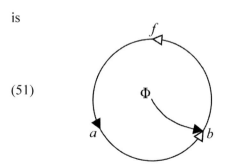

304

That the replication map for an (M,R)-system must already be entailed in the form (2) is equivalent to the graph-theoretic requirement that digraph (51) be completed so that it has a closed path containing all the solid-headed arrows.

12.14 The Standard (M,R)-System   With the classical inverse evaluation map representing replication,

(52) $b: f \mapsto \Phi,$

the hierarchical cycle is completed thus:

(53)
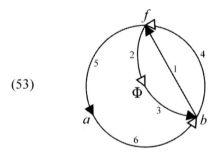

which unfolds into the entailment digraph

(54)
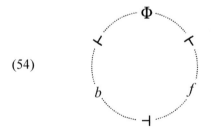

The traversability, both as a digraph and as a relational diagram, of this standard, first (M,R)-system was discussed in the previous chapter (11.24–11.26).

12.15 The Second (M,R)-System When replication is a 'conjugate isomorphism', its depiction is

(55) $\qquad b: b \mapsto \Phi$.

Comparing (55) with (52), one sees that only the material cause of the replication morphism is changed. Thus (52) and (55) have the same entailment diagram

(56) $\qquad b \vdash \Phi$,

whence the same entailment digraph (54). The relational diagram for this alternate (M,R)-system is

(57)

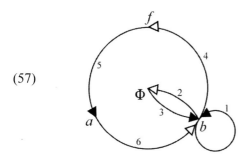

Note the distinction between digraphs (53) and (57): (53) is a multigraph, while (57) has a self-loop $1 = (b,b)$ and is therefore a pseudograph (*cf.* 6.3 for a review of these graph-theoretic terms). In digraph (57), vertices a, f, and Φ have indegree 1 and outdegree 1, while vertex b has indegree 3 and outdegree 3. Thus, by Theorem 6.6(*a*), (57) has an Eulerian circuit as a digraph, which in our context is precisely the hierarchical cycle containing all the solid-headed arrows, whence equipping this (M,R)-system with the requisite closure to efficient causation.

The closed path may begin at any vertex; the Eulerian circuits are (1,2,3,4,5,6), (3,4,5,6,1,2) and (5,6,1,2,3,4). These three Eulerian circuits of diagraph (57) respect the solid-headed-arrow–hollow-headed-arrow ordered-pairing of each morphism: the solid-headed arrows and hollow-headed arrows are in an alternating sequence. All these conclusions on Eulerian circuits are identical between diagraphs (53) and (57).

The degrees of the vertices of (57) may be enumerated thus:

(58)
$$\begin{cases} \left(\varepsilon_i(a),\tau_i(a),\varepsilon_o(a),\tau_o(a)\right)=(1,0,0,1) \\ \left(\varepsilon_i(b),\tau_i(b),\varepsilon_o(b),\tau_o(b)\right)=(2,1,1,2) \\ \left(\varepsilon_i(f),\tau_i(f),\varepsilon_o(f),\tau_o(f)\right)=(0,1,1,0) \\ \left(\varepsilon_i(\Phi),\tau_i(\Phi),\varepsilon_o(\Phi),\tau_o(\Phi)\right)=(0,1,1,0) \end{cases}$$

(*cf.* 6.8 for the notation). Thus diagram (58) satisfies the conditions of Theorem 6.12(*a*), whence as a relational diagram it is traversable and has an Eulerian circuit.

12.16 The Third (M,R)-System When replication is a 'similarity class', its depiction is

(59) $a: a \mapsto \Phi$.

Comparing (59) with (52), one sees that this time both the material cause and the efficient cause of the replication morphism are changed. (The formal cause, the categorical structure of a morphism, cannot change; neither can the final cause: replication has to entail Φ.) The entailment diagram is

(60) $a \vdash \Phi$,

and the corresponding relational diagram is

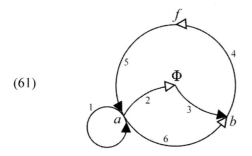

(61)

Because of the presence of the self-loop $1=(a,a)$, digraph (61) is a pseudograph. Vertices f and Φ have indegree 1 and outdegree 1, vertex b has indegree 2 and outdegree 1, and vertex a has indegree 2 and outdegree 3. This time one has to invoke Theorem 6.6(b) and conclude that the digraph (61) has an Eulerian path that begins at vertex a and ends at vertex b, but no Eulerian circuit. The Eulerian path $\{1,2,3,4,5,6\}$, however, still respects the ordering of the solid-headed arrows and hollow-headed arrows in an alternating sequence.

The absence of an Eulerian circuit in this (M,R)-system does not, however, necessarily imply that it is not closed to efficient causation. Note that the requirement in Theorem 6.28 is only that *there is a cycle that contains all the solid-headed arrows*, but not necessarily *all* the arrows, solid-headed and hollow-headed. In our two previous (M,R)-systems the cycles also happen to contain *all* the arrows. That it is the case for digraph (53) is a consequence of its being a multigraph. When the relational diagram is a pseudograph (*i.e.* has self-loops), the cycle that contains all the solid-headed arrows may or may not be an Eulerian circuit. For digraph (57) it happens to be. For digraph (61), its Eulerian path $\{1,2,3,4,5,6\}$ is not a circuit, but it does include the cycle $(1,2,3,4,5)$ that contains all the solid-headed arrows. This is the requisite hierarchical cycle for this third (M,R)-system.

The four degrees of the vertices of (61) are:

(62)
$$\begin{cases} \left(\varepsilon_i(a),\tau_i(a),\varepsilon_o(a),\tau_o(a)\right)=(2,0,1,2) \\ \left(\varepsilon_i(b),\tau_i(b),\varepsilon_o(b),\tau_o(b)\right)=(1,1,0,1) \\ \left(\varepsilon_i(f),\tau_i(f),\varepsilon_o(f),\tau_o(f)\right)=(0,1,1,0) \\ \left(\varepsilon_i(\Phi),\tau_i(\Phi),\varepsilon_o(\Phi),\tau_o(\Phi)\right)=(0,1,1,0) \end{cases}.$$

So one sees that

(63) $\varepsilon_i(v)=\tau_o(v)$ for $v=a,b,f,\Phi$;

(64) $\tau_i(f)=\varepsilon_o(f)$ and $\tau_i(\Phi)=\varepsilon_o(\Phi)$,

while

(65) $\varepsilon_o(a)-\tau_i(a)=1$ and $\tau_i(b)-\varepsilon_o(b)=1$.

Thus diagram (61) satisfies the conditions of Theorem 6.12(*b*), whence as a relational diagram it is traversable and has an Eulerian path, which begins from vertex a and ends at vertex b.

PART V

Epilogus

Il n'y a pas de citadelles imprenables.
Il n'y a que des citadelles mal attaquées.

[There are no impregnable fortresses.
There are only fortresses that are badly attacked.]

> — narration written by Roger Vailland in
> Roger Vadim's 1960 film adaptation of
> Pierre Choderlos de Laclos (1782)
> *Les liaisons dangereuses*

This final Part V is a collection of vignettes. These biological topics of interest and importance are only touched upon herein, and shall be pursued further in other publications.

13

Ontogenic Vignettes

(M,R)-Networks

13.1 Metabolism and Repair Components Recall (*cf.* 11.10) that the simplest (M,R)-system may be represented by the diagram

(1) $\qquad A \xrightarrow{\ f\ } B \xrightarrow{\ \Phi\ } H(A,B).$

The mappings combine into the relational diagram

(2)

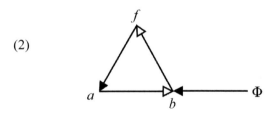

and entailment diagram

(3) $\qquad \Phi \vdash f \vdash b \,.$

    Metabolism may be considered an input-output system, with the mapping f representing the transfer function of the 'block', the domain A as the set of inputs, and the codomain B as the set of outputs. Thus I may define a *metabolism component* as the formal system $M = \langle A, H(A,B) \rangle$. (Remember that $H(A,B)$ denotes a proper subset of B^A. Here it can be as small as $H(A,B) = \{0,f\}$.) Similarly, *repair* may be considered an input-output system, with the mapping Φ representing the transfer function of the block, the domain B as the set of inputs, and the codomain $H(A,B)$ as the set of outputs. Thus I may define a *repair component* as the formal system $R = \langle B, H(B, H(A,B)) \rangle$. Then the model network diagram (*cf.* 7.26 for the graphic notation) of this simplest (M,R)-system is

(4)

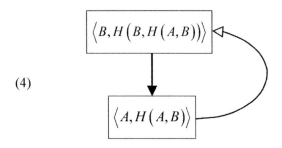

With the addition of entailment arrows for environmental inputs and outputs, and the representation by the symbols M and R of the components (instead of their notation $\langle S, F \rangle$ as formal systems), I arrive at the simplest example of what I call an *(M,R)-network*, i.e., a network of metabolism and repair components:

(5)

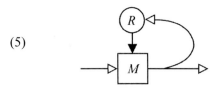

Network (5) is a modified form of the abstract block diagrams that Rosen started using in his introductory (M,R)-systems papers [1958 & 1959] from half a century ago.

I now summarize the discussion heretofore in the

13.2 Definition *Metabolism* and *repair* are input-output systems that are connected as *components* into a network. They are formal systems with the following further category-theoretic structures.

(a) A *metabolism component* is a formal system $M_i = \langle A_i, H(A_i, B_i) \rangle$.

(b) A *repair component* is a formal system $R_i = \langle Y_i, H(Y_i, H(A_i, B_i)) \rangle$.

(c) A *metabolism-repair network*, i.e., an (M,R)-network, is a finite collection of pairs of metabolism and repair components $\{(M_i, R_i) : i \in I\}$, connected in a model network. In particular, the output of a repair component R_i are observables in $H(A_i, B_i)$ of its corresponding metabolism component M_i. The metabolism components may be connected among themselves by their inputs and outputs (i.e., by $B_k \subset A_j$ for some $j, k \in I$). Repair components must receive at least one input from the outputs of the metabolism components of the network (i.e., $Y_i = \prod_{k=1}^{n} B_{i_k}$ with $n \geq 1$ and where each $i_k \in I$).

I have, of course, already defined *(M,R)-network* in 11.13(*a*). The current definition 13.2(*c*) my be considered its verbose version. Note that the connections specified in 13.2(*c*) are the *requisite* ones; an (M,R)-network may have additional interconnections among its components and with its environment.

13.3 Example For illustrative purposes, here is an (M,R)-network with six pairs of metabolism-repair components.

(6)

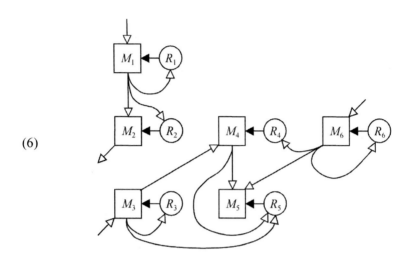

Note that a solid-headed arrow initiates from every repair component R_i and terminates at the latter's *corresponding* metabolism component M_i. These representations of functional entailment in the (M,R)-network are the only solid-headed arrows. Each repair component R_i receives input (hollow-headed arrows that terminate at R_i) from at least one output of the metabolism components. The metabolism components are interconnected in a network of hollow-headed arrows. A hollow-headed arrow that either initiates from or terminates in the ambience is, respectively, an environmental input or output.

Metabolism and repair components may be viewed as 'little factories' for making and deploring biologically active things ('bioactivities'). Their arrangement in an (M,R)-network may be considered analogous to that in biochemical reaction mechanisms. In such a 'network of bioactivities', some very surprising things can emerge. I shall, however, be treating these topics elsewhere.

13.4 Dependency We may now study the dependency structure in (M,R)-networks and see how they react when various components are removed. For example, consider, in the network (6), what happens when the metabolism component M_2 is damaged and ceases to function (and hence may be considered as removed from the network). Since its corresponding repair component R_2 receives input from M_1, the absence of M_2 does not affect the function of R_2, which is to replenish copies of M_2. So an absent component M_2 gets *repaired*, and the (M,R)-network continues to function properly.

Now consider what happens if the metabolism component M_1 is destroyed or otherwise inhibited. Since its corresponding repair component R_1 receives input from M_1 itself, without input from M_1, the repair component R_1 will cease to function, and therefore cannot reproduce copies of M_1.

These two distinct kinds of behaviour may be named thus:

13.5 Definition A metabolism component in an (M,R)-network is *reestablishable* if the network has the capacity to replace it in the event of its absence. Otherwise, the metabolism component is *nonreestablishable*.

So in our sample (M,R)-network (6), the component M_2 is reestablishable, and the component M_1 is nonreestablishable. In graph-theoretic terms, one has the

13.6 Lemma *A metabolism component is reestablishable if and only if there is no directed path from it to its corresponding repair component.*

The removal of M_1 in (6) in fact has further consequences. Its output also supplies the components M_2 and R_2; without M_1, therefore, M_2 and R_2 will, along with R_1, cease to function. Thus the whole connected subnetwork of $\{(M_1,R_1),(M_2,R_2)\}$ dies.

13.7 Definition A metabolism component in an (M,R)-network is *central* if its absence inhibits all activities of a connected subnetwork.

A central component evidently must be nonreestablishable. In our example, the component M_1 is central. If an (M,R)-network is connected (i.e., consists of only one connected subnetwork), then the removal of a central component kills the whole system.

I leave it as an exercise for the reader to verify that in our sample (M,R)-network (6), components M_4 and M_5 are reestablishable, while components M_3 and M_6 are nonreestablishable, although neither is central.

One interesting property of (M,R)-networks is the

13.8 Theorem *Every (M,R)-network must contain a nonreestablishable component.*

PROOF Choose a reestablishable component. Assume, for the ease of labelling but without loss of generality, that it is M_1. The corresponding repair component R_1 cannot receive input from M_1, so assume, again without loss of generality, that the output from M_2 is an input to R_1. If M_2 is nonreestablishable the proof is done. If not, then R_2 must receive input from the output of a metabolism component other than M_1 or M_2; say M_3.

Proceeding inductively, one must eventually, since the number of components is finite, reach a nonreestablishable component, else one shall run out of the supply of reestablishable components and arrive at a contradiction. □

It has an immediate

13.9 Corollary *If an (M,R)-network has exactly one nonreestablishable component, then that component is central.*

PROOF Otherwise one may remove the single nonreestablishable component and a surviving (M,R)-network containing only reestablishable components remains, whence contradicting the theorem. □

A connected subnetwork of an (M,R)-network is an (M,R)-network in its own right. Thus one also has

13.10 Corollary *Every connected subnetwork of an (M,R)-network must contain a nonreestablishable component.*

13.11 Corollary *If a connected subnetwork of an (M,R)-network has exactly one nonreestablishable component, then that component is central.*

For the simplest (M,R)-network (5), since there is only one metabolism component and one repair component, the latter must receive as its input the output of the former. So there is a directed path from the metabolism component to its corresponding repair component, whence the former is nonreestablishable. This fact also follows from Theorem 13.8: an *only* metabolism component must be nonreestablishable, whence by Corollary 13.9 it is therefore central. This is another illustration that while the simplest (M,R)-system captures the closure to efficient causation aspect that characterizes life, a three-map hierarchical cycle loses many internal inferential entailment structures of more elaborately networked (M,R)-systems.

13.12 The Biology of (M,R)-Networks Theorem 13.8 says that as a simple consequence of interconnected metabolism and repair components, there must be metabolism components the loss of which is not repairable by the system, even when the repair components are not directly damaged. There must always be at least one component that is not reestablishable. The topology of the network determines what the nonreestablishable components are. A component may be reestablishable in one (M,R)-network, but when the same configuration is embedded in another (M,R)-network, the component may become nonreestablishable.

Theorem 13.8 and its corollaries also entail a subtle interplay between reestablishability and centrality. It may seem beneficial for an (M,R)-network to maximize the proportion of its reestablishable components. But as a consequence, the number of nonreestablishable components diminishes, whence increasing the chance that a nonreestablishable component is the only one in a connected subnetwork, hence central. So while an (M,R)-network with a large number of reestablishable components may survive many kinds of injuries and recover, certain specific injuries will cripple an entire subsystem or even the whole network. Thus as a balance it may be better to have a large number of nonreestablishable components. While damage to them leads to their removal, the overall effect to the entire (M,R)-network is not as serious. The optimality of reestablishability is, indeed, the efficient cause of selective advantage in the evolutionary biology of (M,R)-networks.

Anticipation in (M,R)-Systems

13.13 Internal Time Scales If the concept of separate internal time scales for metabolism and repair components is introduced, then reestablishability takes on a new characterization. Even when a directed path does lead from a metabolism component M_i to its corresponding repair component R_i, the component M_i may still be replenished by its repair component R_i if R_i has a longer operational lifetime. In such a case, M_i may be repaired by R_i before R_i perishes due to lack of input from M_i, but then once M_i is repaired the input line to R_i is reestablished, so that no irreversible damage in done. In other words, the presence of 'finite time lags' (often manifest in natural systems as *hysteresis*) allows M_i to be rebuilt into the (M,R)-network although M_i is graph-theoretically nonreestablishable.

We have, of course, encountered the multiple scaling of time before, in the context of anticipatory systems. Recall that an internal predictive model has a time scale that runs faster than real time (*cf.* 10.6). I shall now show that the entailment pattern of an anticipatory system may be represented as a relational network of metabolism and repair components.

13.14 Effectors as Repair Components The simple anticipatory system (*cf.* the construction in 10.13)

(7)   Input

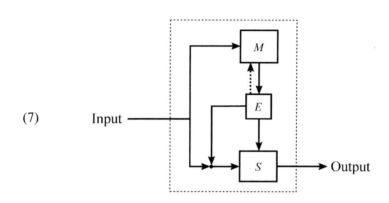

may be redrawn in graph-theoretical form as the model network

(8)

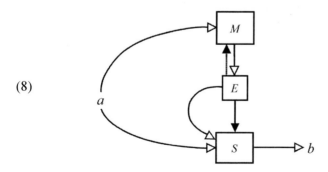

Note that the set E of effectors functionally entails both the system S and the internal predictive model M. If I fractionate E into the functional

components E_S that acts on S and E_M that acts on M, the model network (8) becomes

(9)

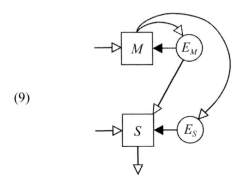

which is recognizably an (M,R)-network $\{(S, E_S), (M, E_M)\}$, with two pairs of metabolism and repair components. The pair (M, E_M) is the internal predictive model of the anticipatory system (9), and has an internal time scale that runs faster than real time (or at least faster then the clock of (S, E_S)).

Semiconservative Replication

13.15 Self-Replication   In 11.11, when I introduced replication in an (M,R)-system, I emphasized that it was a process of generating the repair component (i.e. the entailment ⊢ Φ). Replication in an (M,R)-system is *not* a process by which a thing may make a copy of *itself*. Thus it is not a description of cell division, and *not* a description of DNA replication.

Self-replication of a mapping Φ is the entailment of existence Φ ⊢ ∃Φ, not Φ ⊢ Φ (*cf.* the examination of the self-entailed ouroboros in 5.12). Thus if one were to model replication of the genetic component, one does *not* attempt to fit into the diagram of metabolism and repair

(10)

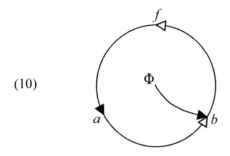

the impossibility

(11)

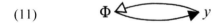

13.16 DNA Replication There is one defining characteristic, common to (almost) all living organisms on earth, of the fundamental process to make copies of the genetic material: the process of nucleic acid replication is *semiconservative*. Each strand of the original double-stranded DNA molecule serves as template for the reproduction of the complementary strand, producing two copies that each contained one of the original strands and one entirely new strand. Thus to model this semiconservative replication process, I need to find a mapping with the property that 'half the mapping determines the complementary half, hence the whole'.

It turns out that a continuous linear functional on a Hilbert space, from my conjugate isomorphism construction of the second (M,R)-system, provides the perfect analogy.

In what follows, let X be a Hilbert space over the field F.

322

13.17 Definition Let E be a nonempty subset of X. The set

(12) $$E^{\perp} = \left\{ g \in X^* : g(x) = 0 \ \text{ for all } x \in X \right\}$$

is called the *annihilator* of E.

Thus $E^{\perp}$ consists of all continuous linear functionals on X that vanish on E. $E^{\perp}$ is a closed linear subspace of X^*.

13.18 Definition A point $x \in X$ is *orthogonal* to a point $y \in X$ if and only if $\langle x, y \rangle = 0$.

One sees that x is orthogonal to y if and only if y is orthogonal to x; thus one may say without ambiguity that 'x and y are orthogonal'. It is clear that $0 \in X$ is orthogonal to every point of X.

13.19 Definition Let E be a nonempty subset of X. The set

(13) $$E^{\perp} = \left\{ x \in X : \langle x, y \rangle = 0 \ \text{ for all } y \in E \right\}$$

is called the *orthogonal complement of E in X*.

Thus $E^{\perp}$ consists of points in X that are orthogonal to every point in E. For any subset E of X, $E^{\perp}$ is a closed linear subspace of X, and that $E \subset \left(E^{\perp} \right)^{\perp}$. One has, indeed, the following

13.20 Theorem *Let E be a closed linear subspace of X. Then*

(14) $$X = E \oplus E^{\perp}$$

and

(15) $$E = \left(E^{\perp} \right)^{\perp}.$$

(*Direct sum* in the context of vector spaces is $X = V \oplus W$ iff $X = V + W$ and $V \cap W = \{0\}$; *cf.* A.36 and A.38)

13.21 Conjugate-Linear Isometry Comparing Definitions 13.17 and 13.19, we see that I have used the symbol $E^\perp$ to denote two different objects that are subspaces of X^* and X respectively. This symbolic polysemy for $(\cdot)^\perp$ causes no confusion, because there is an isomorphic relation between an annihilator and an orthogonal complement, as follows.

Theorem 12.4 says that $\gamma_X^{-1} : \Lambda_y \mapsto y$ is a conjugate-linear isometry from X^* to X, so that for all $x \in X$ and $g \in X^*$,

$$(16) \qquad g(x) = \langle x, \gamma_X^{-1}(g) \rangle.$$

For a nonempty subset E of X, one may verify that

$$(17) \qquad \gamma_X(E^\perp) = E^\perp.$$

Thus the orthogonal complement of E in X (the $E^\perp$ on the left-hand side of (17)) is isomorphic to the annihilator of E in X^* (the $E^\perp$ on the right-hand side of (17)) under the conjugate-linear isometry $\gamma_X : X \to X^*$.

13.22 Half Determines Whole Let g be a nonzero, continuous linear functional on X. The set

$$(18) \qquad E = \{x \in X : g(x) = 0\},$$

the *null space* of g, is a closed linear subspace of X, whence by Theorem 13.20

$$(19) \qquad X = E \oplus E^\perp.$$

If z is any non-zero element in $E^{\perp}$, then

$$(20) \qquad g(x) = \frac{\langle x, z \rangle}{\langle z, z \rangle} g(z) \quad \text{for all } x \in X.$$

Thus $g(x)$ depends on $g(z)$, scaled by the ratio of the values of two inner products; stated otherwise, g is completely determined by its values on $E^{\perp}$. In yet other words, one only needs to know g on $E^{\perp}$, and its values on the rest of X are replicated semiconservatively.

The analogy with the semiconservative replication of DNA may now be made. With the same functorial encoding $B \mapsto X$ and $H(A, B) \mapsto F$ as that of the first two kinds of (M,R)-systems, the self-replication of the genetic component $\Phi \in H(B, H(A, B))$ now acquires the characteristic 'half the mapping determines the complementary half, hence the whole'.

The Ontogenesis of (M,R)-Systems

13.23 The Category of (M,R)-Systems Let N be a natural system and let $\mathbf{C}(N)$ be the category of its models (*cf.* Definition 7.27). Recall Definition 7.17 that a model of N is a finite collection of formal systems with certain entailment requirements. An (M,R)-network, as defined in 13.2, has further entailment requirements, and is thus a *specialized* model. Rosen's Postulate of Life (11.28) says that a natural system is an organism if and only if it realizes an (M,R)-system. Stated otherwise, the category of (M,R)-systems that model an organism N is a *subcategory* of $\mathbf{C}(N)$ (hence inherits the latter's categorical structures).

13.24 Cartesian Closure $\mathbf{C}(N)$ is a category of sets and mappings with further structures. In **Set**, it being a cartesian closed category (*cf.* A.53 and Example A.19(iii)), one has

$$(21) \qquad H(X \times Y, Z) \cong H(X, H(Y, Z))$$

In a general (M,R)-network, a repair map in a repair component R_i is

$$(22) \qquad \Phi_i \in H\left(\prod_{k=1}^{n} B_{i_k}, H(A_i, B_i)\right).$$

The natural equivalence (21) gives

$$(23) \qquad H\left(\prod_{k=1}^{n} B_{i_k}, H(A_i, B_i)\right) \cong H\left(\prod_{k=1}^{n} B_{i_k} \times A_1, B_i\right).$$

For the simplest (M,R)-system (1), the repair map is

$$(24) \qquad \Phi \in H(B, H(A, B)),$$

whence the natural equivalence (21) gives

$$(25) \qquad H(B, H(A, B)) \cong H(B \times A, B).$$

Thus one sees that a functional entailment of metabolism may be described by an isomorphic mapping that has a more complicated cartesian product set as domain, but a simpler set as codomain.

Similarly, in a general (M,R)-system, a replication map that replenishes a repair map Φ_i in a repair component R_i is

$$(26) \qquad \beta_i \in H(Z_i, H(Y_i, H(A_i, B_i))),$$

where $Y_i = \prod_{k=1}^{n} B_{i_k}$ and Z_i = cartesian product of sets already present in the network. The natural equivalence (21) then yields

$$(27) \qquad H\Big(Z_i, H\Big(Y_i, H\big(A_i, B_i\big)\Big)\Big) \cong H\Big(Z_i \times Y_i, H\big(A_i, B_i\big)\Big).$$

For the simplest (M,R)-system (1), this simplifies to

$$(28) \qquad \beta \in H\Big(Y, H\big(B, H\left(A, B\right)\big)\Big)$$

and

$$(29) \qquad H\Big(Y, H\big(B, H\left(A, B\right)\big)\Big) \cong H\big(Y \times B, H\left(A, B\right)\big),$$

with $Y = H(A, B)$, B, or A, for the three kinds of replication we studied in detail in Chapters 11 and 12.

13.25 The Genesis of (M,R)-Systems The natural isomorphism

$$(30) \qquad \mathbf{C}\big(X \times Y, Z\big) \cong \mathbf{C}\big(X, Z^Y\big)$$

in a cartesian closed category (*cf.* A.52 and A.53) defines as the right adjoint the exponential object Z^Y. When the exponential may be interpreted as (i.e., is **C**-isomorphic to) the hom-set $\mathbf{C}(Y, Z)$, the right-hand side of (30) posits the existence in the category **C** of the entailment of morphisms, i.e. functional entailment

$$(31) \qquad \Phi \in \mathbf{C}\big(X, \mathbf{C}(Y, Z)\big).$$

Since one can only speak of closure to efficient causation when functional entailment exists, one may conclude from the above discussion that the natural isomorphism

$$(32) \qquad \mathbf{C}\big(X \times Y, Z\big) \cong \mathbf{C}\big(X, \mathbf{C}(Y, Z)\big)$$

equips a category **C** for possible embeddings of (M,R)-systems. Indeed, it turns out that in a suitably equipped category, any sufficiently large finite family of morphisms must contain an (M,R)-system. Note the implication for the origin of life: *Complexitas viventia producit.* What this 'suitable equipment' is will be a topic of another book.

13.26 Fabrication of Life   Rosen's answer to the epistemological form of the question "What is life?" (i.e., "What are the defining characteristics of a natural system for us to *perceive* it as being alive?") is (Theorem 11.29) "A material system is an organism if, and only if, it is closed to efficient causation." This 'self-sufficiency' in efficient causation is what we implicitly recognize as the one feature that distinguishes a living system from a nonliving one.

The ontogenetic form of the question "What is life?" is "What *makes* a natural system alive?" The characterization of 'closure to efficient causation' again provides the answer, in the form thus. When the entailment pattern in an (M,R)-network, enriched by the presence of replication maps, attains a structure such that all efficient causes are functionally entailed within the network, then it becomes an (M,R)-system, i.e., a model of a living system. In short, the closure in efficient causation is what generates the living being, what makes a natural system come alive.

If one constructs the maps of metabolism, repair, and replication meticulously, one can indeed *fabricate* an (M,R)-system that has all the features of being alive. The fact that $\bullet \times Y$ and $H(Y, \bullet)$ are adjoint functors have astonishing ramifications for (M,R)-systems. Further explorations of this topic of fabrication will, again, have to wait for my next book. In relational biology, artificial life is about the artful fabrication of an (M,R)-system. It is most certainly not about making algorithmic simulations that can *deceive* us into believing that it is alive.

13.27 The Ontology of Biology   Biology is a subject concerned with organization of relations. A living system is a material system, so its study shares the material cause with physics and chemistry. But physicochemical theories are only surrogates of biological theories, because the manners in which the shared matter is organized are fundamentally different. Hence the

328

behaviours of the realizations of these mechanistic surrogates are different from those of realizations of (M,R)-systems that are organisms. The difference involved here is in kind, that of predicativity and impredicativity, that of the impermeable dichotomy of simplex and complex.

The reductionistic claim bears the false witness that if one has enough such surrogates, and knows enough about them, then the biological organization will follow as a corollary. It is not just a technical matter of the impossibility in human terms of acquiring a sufficiently large collection of surrogates. The inherent impredicativity of complexity cannot be analytically resolved. A typical example is that one cannot solve a classical N-body problem by solving N one-body problems.

Biology poses problems. Experimental and theoretical techniques, from molecular biology to quantum mechanics, provide methods that may be applied to attempts in solving these problems. Many of these techniques (realized as their practitioners) claim their methods are adequate, and some of them even claim genericity, that no other methods will do. Any question becomes unanswerable if one does not permit oneself a large enough universe to deal with the question. The failure of reductionism is that of the inability of a small surrogate universe to exhaust the real one. Equivocations create artefacts. The limits of mechanistic dogma are very examples of the restrictiveness of self-imposed methodologies that fabricate non-existent artificial 'limitations' on science and knowledge. The limitations are due to the nongenericity of the methods and their associated bounded microcosms. One learns something new and fundamental about the universe when it refuses to be exhausted by a posited method. The main lesson one learns from life itself is the troubles that arise when one tries to legislate a process, often to the exclusion of other processes and with a claim of objectivity besides, when the said process is, in the first place, neither a law of nature nor a law of mathematics.

Unus non sufficit orbis. Euouae.

Appendix
Category Theory

There is therefore only a single categorical imperative
and it is this: Act only on that maxim through which you
can at the same time will that it should become a
universal law.

— Immanuel Kant (1785)
Grundlegung zur Metaphysik der Sitten
(*Groundwork of the Metaphysic of Morals*)

Category theory is a formal image of the modelling process itself. It
is, indeed, the *general* theory of modelling relations, and not just some
specific way of making models of one thing in another. It thus generates
mathematical counterparts of epistemologies, entirely within the formal
realm. The definitive reference on this branch of abstract algebra is written
by one of its founders, Mac Lane [1978]. This Appendix is a concise
summary of the category-theoretic concepts that appear in this monograph.

Categories → Functors
→ Natural Transformations

Many problems in mathematics are not primarily concerned with a single object such as a mapping, a group, or a measure, but deal instead with large classes of such objects. The classes consist of *sets with a given structure* and of the *mappings preserving this structure*.

Thus one may be dealing with groups; the mappings preserving the group structure are the (group-)homomorphisms. When one turns to vector spaces, the appropriate mappings are the linear transformations. And when one studies topological spaces, continuous mappings arise naturally. Indeed, category theory arose as an organizing framework for expressing the *naturality* of certain constructions in mathematics.

A useful discussion of this situation can be given within a general framework that assumes very little about the mappings. All one needs is that they are closed under composition and include the identity mapping. But one need not even assume them to be mappings. The definition takes the following form:

A.1 Category A *category* **C** consists of

(i) a collection of *objects*;

(ii) for each pair of **C**-objects A, B, a set $\mathbf{C}(A,B)$, the *hom-set* of *morphisms* from A to B; [If $f \in \mathbf{C}(A,B)$, one may also write $f: A \to B$. Often for simplicity, or when the category **C** needs not be emphasized, the hom-set $\mathbf{C}(A,B)$ is denoted by $H(A,B)$.]

(iii) for any three **C**-objects A, B, C, a mapping

(1) $\qquad \circ : \mathbf{C}(A,B) \times \mathbf{C}(B,C) \to \mathbf{C}(A,C)$

taking $f: A \to B$ and $g: B \to C$ to its *composite* $g \circ f : A \to C$.

These entities satisfy the following three axioms:

(c1) $\mathbf{C}(A,B)\cap\mathbf{C}(C,D)=\varnothing$ unless $A=C$ and $B=D$. [Thus each mor-phism $f:A\to B$ uniquely determines its *domain* $A=\mathrm{dom}(f)$ and *codomain* $B=\mathrm{cod}(f)$. So the objects in a category $\mathbf{C}$ are actually redundant, and one can simply consider $\mathbf{C}$ as a collection of morphisms, or *arrows*.]

(c2) *Associativity*: If $f:A\to B$, $g:B\to C$, $h:C\to D$, so that both $h\circ(g\circ f)$ and $(h\circ g)\circ f$ are defined, then $h\circ(g\circ f)=(h\circ g)\circ f$. The composite $h\circ g\circ f:A\to D$ may be represented thus:

(2)

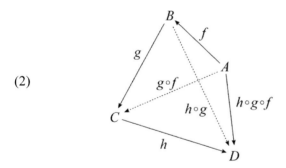

(c3) *Identity*: For each object A, there exists $1_A:A\to A$ such that for any $f:A\to B$, $g:C\to A$, one has $f\circ 1_A=f$, $1_A\circ g=g$. 1_A, which is demonstrably unique, is called the *identity morphism* on A.

A.2 Discrete Category Note that the only morphisms that are required to exist are the identities on the objects. When there are no objects, there are no identity morphisms. So trivially there is the empty category $\varnothing$, with no objects and no morphisms.

The next simplest category is one in which every morphism is an identity. In other words, one may have $\mathbf{C}(A,B) = \varnothing$ when $A \neq B$, and $\mathbf{C}(A,A) = \{1_A\}$. Such a category $\mathbf{C}$ is called *discrete*. Every set X is the set of objects of a discrete category (and each element $x \in X$ determines the identity morphism $1_x : x \to x$ on the object x). Every discrete category is so determined by its set of objects. Thus, discrete categories are sets. In particular, the one-object category $\mathbf{1}$ has one object (which may be called 0) and one (identity) morphism.

Now for something a little less trivial. The category axioms are usually interpreted within set theory, whence an object is a set with a prescribed mathematical structure, and a morphism is a mapping preserving this structure. When there are no additional structures to preserve, one has

A.3 The Category Set The category in which the collection of objects is the collection of all sets (in a suitably naive universe of small sets) and morphisms are mappings is denoted **Set**. Given two sets X and Y, one uses the notation Y^X for the set $\mathbf{Set}(X,Y)$ of *all* mappings from X to Y.

The etymology of this representation of $\mathbf{Set}(X,Y)$ as a 'power', or 'exponential', Y^X is the following. The number zero may be *defined as* the empty set, $0 = \varnothing$. Then a natural number may be defined as the set of nonnegative integers less than it; thus $1 = \{0\} = \{\varnothing\}$ (a set containing one element; i.e. a *singleton set*), $2 = \{0,1\} = \{\varnothing, \{\varnothing\}\}$ (a set containing two elements), etc. Next, if X is a set, the *power set* $\mathbf{P}X$ of X (*cf.* Definition 1.1(a)), the family of all subsets of X, may be identified as the set of all mappings from X to $2 = \{0,1\}$ using the *characteristic mapping*: for a subset $A \subset X$, its characteristic mapping is $\chi_A \in \mathbf{Set}(X,2)$ defined by

(3) $$\chi_A(x) = \begin{cases} 0 & \text{if } x \notin A \\ 1 & \text{if } x \in A \end{cases}$$

(note that $A = \chi_A^{-1}(1)$). This establishes the bijection $\mathsf{P}X \cong \mathbf{Set}(X,2)$. Now if X is a finite set with n members, then $\mathsf{P}X$ has 2^n members, which leads to the alternate notation $\mathsf{P}X = 2^X$ for *all* sets X, finite or infinite. Thus $2^X \cong \mathbf{Set}(X,2)$, whence generalizing to $Y^X = \mathbf{Set}(X,Y)$ for any co-domain Y. (This exponential notation Y^X further evolves into a category-theoretic construction called *exponential*, which I shall explain towards the end of this Appendix, in A.41.)

Note that, because of Axiom A.1(c1), the morphisms $f : X \to Y$ and $f : X \to Z$, where $f(X) \subset Y$ and $f(X) \subset Z$ but $Y \neq Z$, are considered *different* **Set**-morphisms. They have different codomains, and are therefore different mappings, even though as 'sets of ordered pairs' they are the same. Similar remarks apply to other examples of categories that follow.

A.4 Hom-sets involving the Empty Set   *By convention*, one sets $Y^\varnothing = \{\varnothing\}$. Thus there is exactly one mapping from the empty set to any set Y, namely the 'empty mapping' $\varnothing$. Note that the empty set $\varnothing$ is indeed a mapping. This is because $\mathrm{dom}(\varnothing) = \varnothing$, and $\varnothing \subset \varnothing \times Y$ is a set of ordered pairs (albeit with no elements). In order to show that $\varnothing$ is *not* a mapping, there must be $x \in \varnothing$ and $y, z \in Y$, such that $(x, y) \in \varnothing$ and $(x, z) \in \varnothing$ but $y \neq z$. Since $\varnothing$ has no elements, this is impossible. All arguments concerning the empty set follow this pattern: to prove that something is *true* about the empty set, one proves that it *cannot be false*. In mathematics, a proposition is said to be *vacuously true* when there is nothing to contradict it.

On the other hand, when $X \neq \varnothing$, $\varnothing^X = \varnothing$. This is because if $X \neq \varnothing$, then $f(X) \neq \varnothing$ for any mapping f with $\mathrm{dom}(f) = X$, whence there cannot be any mapping $f : X \to \varnothing$.

A.5 Isomorphism   Informally, two mathematical systems of the same nature are said to be *isomorphic* if there is a one-to-one correspondence between them that preserves all relevant properties, i.e. if there is a 'structure-preserving bijection'. Such a mapping is an *isomorphism*, and it usually coincides with the intuitively most natural concept of structural preservation. Categorically, one has the

Definition A morphism $f : A \to B$ is an *isomorphism* if there exists an *inverse morphism* $g : B \to A$ such that $g \circ f = 1_A$ and $f \circ g = 1_B$. [If such an inverse morphism exists it is unique, and may be denoted by f^{-1}.]

An isomorphism with the same object A as domain and codomain is an *automorphism* on A. If there exists an isomorphism from A to B then A is *isomorphic* to B, denoted by $A \cong B$. Isomorphic objects are considered abstractly (and often identified as) the same, and most constructions of category theory are 'unique up to isomorphism' (in the sense that two similarly constructed objects are isomorphic, if not necessarily identical). One may easily verify that the isomorphism relation $\cong$ is an equivalence relation on the collection of objects in a category. So in particular, instead of "A is isomorphic to B" one may simply say "A and B are isomorphic" by symmetry.

A.6 More Examples of Categories

(i) **Set** : sets and mappings as discussed in A.3. Isomorphisms in the category **Set** are, naturally, bijections (*cf.* 1.8). Automorphisms in **Set**, i.e. bijections of a set onto itself, are also called *permutations*.

(ii) **Set$_*$** : pointed sets and pointed mappings: A *pointed set* is a set X with a chosen distinguished element $*_X \in X$, called the *base point*. A pointed mapping $f : X \to Y$ of pointed sets is a mapping from X to Y such that $f(*_X) = *_Y$.

(iii) **Grp** : groups and homomorphisms.

(iv) **Vct** : vector spaces (over a fixed field) and linear transformations.

(v) **Top** : topological spaces and continuous mappings. **Top**-isomorphisms are homeomorphisms.

A.7 Subcategory Given categories **A** and **B**, one says that **A** is a *subcategory* of **B** if each **A**-object is a **B**-object, each **A**-morphism is a **B**-morphism, and compositions of morphisms are the same in the two categories. Thus for any two **A**-objects X and Y, one has $\mathbf{A}(X,Y) \subset \mathbf{B}(X,Y)$. If $\mathbf{A}(X,Y) = \mathbf{B}(X,Y)$ holds for all **A**-objects X and Y, **A** is a *full subcategory* of **B**.

The category of sets and injections is a subcategory of **Set** of sets and mappings, but it is not a full subcategory. The category **Ab** of abelian groups is a full subcategory of the category **Grp** of groups.

I often employ non-full subcategories of **Set**, and I use $H(X,Y)$ for appropriate subsets of $Y^X = \mathbf{Set}(X,Y)$ under consideration (e.g. when mappings $f : X \to Y$ represent metabolic functions). These subsets $H(X,Y)$ themselves, of course, still have to satisfy the category axioms.

A.8 Opposite Category Associated with each category **C** there is another category called its *opposite* (or *dual*), denoted by $\mathbf{C}^{\mathrm{op}}$, formed by 'reversing all the arrows'. Explicitly, $\mathbf{C}^{\mathrm{op}}$ has the same objects as **C**, but to each **C**-morphism $f : X \to Y$ there corresponds a $\mathbf{C}^{\mathrm{op}}$-morphism $f^{\mathrm{op}} : Y \to X$, so that $f^{\mathrm{op}} \circ g^{\mathrm{op}}$ is defined whenever $g \circ f$ is defined, and that $(g \circ f)^{\mathrm{op}} = f^{\mathrm{op}} \circ g^{\mathrm{op}}$. Evidently, $\left(\mathbf{C}^{\mathrm{op}}\right)^{\mathrm{op}} = \mathbf{C}$.

Top, the category of topological spaces and continuous mappings, is an example of a naturally occurring opposite category. Morphisms are mappings that preserve the mathematical structure of the objects. In most common categories, this preservation is in the 'forward' direction. For example, in **Grp**, the category of groups and homomorphisms, a group homomorphism $f : G \to H$ is such that " ' $z = x \cdot y$ in G ' $\Rightarrow$ ' $f(z) = f(x) \bullet f(y)$ in H ' ". But in **Top**, a continuous mapping preserves the topology (i.e. the collection of open sets) in the 'backward' direction: a mapping $f : X \to Y$ is continuous if each open subset V of Y has an open subset $f^{-1}(V)$ of X as its *inverse image*, i.e., " 'U open in X' $\Leftarrow$ '$f(U)$

open in Y ' ". The concept dual to a continuous mapping is an *open mapping*, one that sends open sets to open sets in the *forward* direction. In general topology, open mappings enter the picture occasionally (for example in connection with quotient spaces), but it is much more natural to involve the 'opposite' continuous mappings.

A.9 Product Category If **A** and **B** are categories, so is their *product* **A** × **B**, defined in the obvious fashion: **A** × **B**-objects are ordered pairs of **A**- and **B**-objects, and **A** × **B**-morphisms are ordered pairs of **A**- and **B**-morphisms, with compositions and identities defined componentwise. The product construction may be generalized to $\prod_{i \in I} \mathbf{A}_i$ of an arbitrary family $\{\mathbf{A}_i : i \in I\}$ of categories, and in particular one may form the *n*-ary product $\mathbf{A}^n = \prod_{i=1}^{n} \mathbf{A}$. I shall consider the concept of product *within* a category presently.

A.10 Functor Given a new type of mathematical structure, what are the corresponding morphisms preserving these structures? The idea of a 'structure-preserving mapping' may be extended to categories themselves. Let **A** and **B** be categories; then a *(covariant) functor* from **A** to **B** is a mapping $F : \mathbf{A} \to \mathbf{B}$ that assigns to each **A**-object X a **B**-object FX and to each **A**-morphism $f : X \to Y$ a **B**-morphism $Ff : FX \to FY$ such that

(f1) If $g \circ f$ is defined in **A**, then $Fg \circ Ff$ is defined in **B**, and $F(g \circ f) = Fg \circ Ff$.

(f2) For each **A**-object X, $F1_X = 1_{FX}$.

One may think of the functor F as giving a picture, indeed a *model*, in **B** of all the objects and morphisms of **A**.

Besides the covariant functors there is another kind of functor, which reverses the composition. A *contravariant functor* F from **A** to **B** assigns to each **A**-object X a **B**-object FX and to each **A**-morphism $f : X \to Y$ a **B**-morphism $Ff : FY \to FX$ such that

$(f1^{\text{op}})$ If $g \circ f$ is defined in **A**, then $Ff \circ Fg$ is defined in **B**, and $F(g \circ f) = Ff \circ Fg$.

$(f2)$ For each **A**-object X, $F1_X = 1_{FX}$.

A contravariant functor from **A** to **B** may be alternately described as a covariant functor from $\mathbf{A}^{\text{op}}$ to **B**. Consider a covariant functor $F : \mathbf{A}^{\text{op}} \to \mathbf{B}$. By definition it assigns to each $\mathbf{A}^{\text{op}}$-object X a **B**-object FX, and to each $\mathbf{A}^{\text{op}}$-morphism $f^{\text{op}} : Y \to X$ a **B**-morphism $Ff^{\text{op}} : FY \to FX$, with $F1_X = 1_{FX}$ and $F(f^{\text{op}} \circ g^{\text{op}}) = Ff^{\text{op}} \circ Fg^{\text{op}}$ whenever $f^{\text{op}} \circ g^{\text{op}}$ is defined. The functor F may be expressed directly in terms of the original category **A** if one writes $\bar{F}f$ for Ff^{op}: then $\bar{F} : \mathbf{A} \to \mathbf{B}$ is a contravariant functor, which assigns to each **A**-object X a **B**-object $\bar{F}X = FX$, and to each **A**-morphism $f : X \to Y$ a **B**-morphism $\bar{F}f : \bar{F}Y \to \bar{F}X$ (note the *reversal*), such that $\bar{F}1_X = 1_{FX}$ and $\bar{F}(f \circ g) = \bar{F}g \circ \bar{F}f$ whenever $f \circ g$ is defined. Thus one sees that $\bar{F}$ satisfies all the requirements of a contravariant functor.

Similarly, a contravariant functor from **A** to **B** may be described as a covariant functor from **A** to $\mathbf{B}^{\text{op}}$.

It is more convenient to speak of covariant functors than contravariant ones. Because of the equivalent alternate descriptions, one often replaces a contravariant functor with a covariant functor involving an opposite category.

A.11 Theorem *Let $F : \mathbf{A} \to \mathbf{B}$ be a (covariant or contravariant) functor. Then F maps **A**-isomorphisms to **B**-isomorphisms.*

A.12 Examples of Functors

(i) Trivially, for each category A, the *identity functor* $I_A : A \to A$, which sends each **A**-object X to itself and each **A**-morphism $f : X \to Y$ to itself, is covariant.   Dually, the *dual functor* $I_A^{op} : A \to A^{op}$, which sends each **A**-object X to itself and each **A**-morphism $f : X \to Y$ to $f^{op} : Y \to X$, is contravariant.   Note that $I_A^{op} \circ I_A^{op} = I_A$: an operation which when applied twice is equivalent to the identity is called an *involution*.

(ii) Define the *power set functor* $P : \mathbf{Set} \to \mathbf{Set}$ to assign to each set X its power set PX, and assign to each mapping $f : X \to Y$ the mapping $Pf : PX \to PY$ that sends each $A \subset X$ to its image $f(A) \subset Y$.   One has $P(g \circ f) = P(g) \circ P(f)$ (the mapping that sends $A \subset \mathrm{dom}(f)$ to $g(f(A)) \subset \mathrm{cod}(g)$) and $P1_X = 1_{PX}$, so P is a covariant functor from **Set** to **Set**.

   Dually, the *contravariant power set functor* $\overline{P} : \mathbf{Set} \to \mathbf{Set}$ assigns to each set X its power set PX, and to each mapping $f : X \to Y$ the mapping $\overline{P}f : PY \to PX$ that sends each $B \subset Y$ to its inverse image $f^{-1}(B) \subset X$.

(iii) The process that assigns to each vector space V its dual vector space V^* (the space of all linear functionals on V), and to each linear transformation $T : V \to W$ its dual $T^* : W^* \to V^*$ (defined by $T^*(g) = g \circ T$ for every $g \in Y^*$), is a contravariant functor from the category **Vct** of vector spaces to **Vct**.   Iterating the process, $V \mapsto V^{**}$ and $(T : V \to W) \mapsto (T^{**} : V^{**} \to W^{**})$ is a covariant functor from **Vct** to **Vct**.

(iv) There is a covariant functor from the category **Grp** of groups (or any category of 'sets with structure') to the category **Set**, which assigns to each group (or each set with structure) its underlying set, and regards each homomorphism (or each morphism that preserves the structure) as a mapping of sets. This functor is called the *forgetful functor*.

(v)   If **A** is a subcategory of **B**, then the inclusion of **A** in **B** is a functor, called the *inclusion functor*.

(vi) The *homology functors* H_n, from the category **Top** of topological spaces to the category **Ab** of abelian groups, that take a topological space X to its singular homology groups $H_n(X)$, and a continuous mapping $f : X \rightarrow Y$ to the homomorphisms $f_* : H_n(X) \rightarrow H_n(Y)$ are covariant functors. Similarly, one has the *cohomology functors* H^n. In fact, it is in the study of algebraic topology that the ideas of category theory originated. In algebraic topology, the topological spaces may be considered as being 'modelled' by various algebraic objects.

A very important class of functors are the

A.13 Hom-Functors For any category **C** and a **C**-object A, the *covariant hom-functor* $h^A = \mathbf{C}(A, \bullet)$ from **C** to **Set** assigns to each **C**-object Y the set $h^A Y = \mathbf{C}(A,Y)$, and to a **C**-morphism $k : Y \rightarrow Y'$ the mapping $h^A k : \mathbf{C}(A,Y) \rightarrow \mathbf{C}(A,Y')$ defined by

(4) $h^A k : f \mapsto k \circ f$ for $f : A \rightarrow Y$;

i.e. via the diagram

(5)

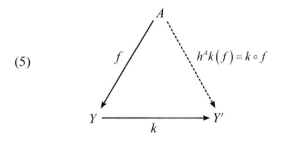

340

Note the action of $h^A k$ may be described as 'composition with k on the left'.

Dually, for a category $\mathbf{C}$ and a $\mathbf{C}$-object B, the *contravariant hom-functor* $h_B = \mathbf{C}(\bullet, B)$ may be described *covariantly* from $\mathbf{C}^{\mathrm{op}}$ to $\mathbf{Set}$ as follows: it assigns to each $\mathbf{C}$-object X the set $h_B X = \mathbf{C}(X, B)$, and to a $\mathbf{C}^{\mathrm{op}}$-morphism $g^{\mathrm{op}} : X' \to X$ (i.e. a $\mathbf{C}$-morphism $g : X \to X'$) the mapping $h_B g : \mathbf{C}(X', B) \to \mathbf{C}(X, B)$ defined by

(6) $\qquad h_B g(f) = f \circ g \quad \text{for} \quad f : X' \to B$;

i.e. via the diagram

(7) $\qquad h_B g(f) = f \circ g$

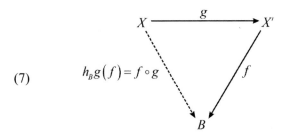

Note the action of $h_B g$ may be described as 'composition with g on the right'.

A.14 Multivariate Functor The definition of a functor may be extended naturally to involve several 'variables'. An *n-ary functor* F from a category $\mathbf{A}$ to a category $\mathbf{B}$ is a functor $F : \mathbf{A}^n \to \mathbf{B}$ that assigns to each n-tuple of $\mathbf{A}$-objects $(X_1, ..., X_n)$ a $\mathbf{B}$-object $F(X_1, ..., X_n)$, and to each n-tuple of $\mathbf{A}$-morphisms $(f_1 : X_1 \to Y_1, \ ..., \ f_n : X_n \to Y_n)$ a $\mathbf{B}$-morphism $F(f_1, ..., f_n)$, so that the functor axioms are satisfied componentwise. If an n-ary functor is covariant with respect to the i th argument, then the component FX_i appears in the domain of $F(f_1,...,f_n)$ and FY_i appears in the codomain of $F(f_1,...,f_n)$); dually, a contravariant ith argument means the component FY_i appears in the domain of $F(f_1,...,f_n)$ and FX_i appears in the codomain of $F(f_1,...,f_n)$.

For example, the *binary hom-functor* hom from a category **C** to **Set** assigns to each ordered pair of **C**-objects (X,Y) the hom-set $\hom(X,Y)=\mathbf{C}(X,Y)$, and to each pair of **C**-morphisms $f_1:X_1\to Y_1$ and $f_2:X_2\to Y_2$ the mapping

$$(8) \qquad \hom(f_1,f_2):\mathbf{C}(Y_1,X_2)\to\mathbf{C}(X_1,Y_2)$$

defined by

$$(9) \qquad \hom(f_1,f_2)(g)=f_2\circ g\circ f_1 \in \mathbf{C}(X_1,Y_2) \;\; \text{for} \;\; g\in\mathbf{C}(Y_1,X_2),$$

i.e., by the commutative diagram

(10)

One sees that the binary hom-functor is contravariant with respect to its first argument, and covariant with respect to its second argument. Indeed, $\hom(\bullet,B)=h_B(\bullet)$ and $\hom(A,\bullet)=h^A(\bullet)$.

As another example, the cartesian product of sets X and Y, defined by $X \times Y = \{(x, y) : x \in X, y \in Y\}$, forms a *bifunctor* (i.e., a binary functor, or a functor with two arguments) $\bullet \times \bullet : \mathbf{Set} \times \mathbf{Set} \to \mathbf{Set}$ with its action on morphisms defined componentwise. The product bifunctor is covariant in both arguments.

A.15 The Category Cat The idea of category may be applied to categories and functors themselves. Indeed, the slogan of category theory [Mac Lane, 1978] proclaims

> "With each type of mathematical object,
> consider also the morphisms."

When the objects are categories, the morphisms are functors.

Functors can be composed — given functors $F : \mathbf{A} \to \mathbf{B}$ and $G : \mathbf{B} \to \mathbf{C}$, the maps $X \mapsto G(FX)$ and $f \mapsto G(Ff)$ on $\mathbf{A}$-objects X and $\mathbf{A}$-morphisms f define a functor $G \circ F : \mathbf{A} \to \mathbf{C}$. This composition is associative. For each category $\mathbf{A}$ there is an *identity functor* $I_{\mathbf{A}} : \mathbf{A} \to \mathbf{A}$. So one may consider the category **Cat** having as objects all categories (i.e. all *small* categories in a suitably naïve universe), and as morphisms all functors between them.

An *isomorphism* $F : \mathbf{A} \to \mathbf{B}$ of categories is a functor that is a bijection both on objects and on morphisms. This is equivalent to the existence of an 'inverse functor' $F^{-1} : \mathbf{B} \to \mathbf{A}$.

A.16 Full and Faithful Functors A functor $F : \mathbf{A} \to \mathbf{B}$ is *full* if to each pair X, Y of $\mathbf{A}$-objects and to every $\mathbf{B}$-morphism $g : FX \to FY$, there is an $\mathbf{A}$-morphism $f : X \to Y$ such that $g = Ff$. A functor $F : \mathbf{A} \to \mathbf{B}$ is *faithful* if to each pair X, Y of $\mathbf{A}$-objects and to every pair of $\mathbf{A}$-morphisms $f_1, f_2 : X \to Y$, the equality $Ff_1 = Ff_2$ implies $f_1 = f_2$.

The two properties, full and faithful, may be defined in terms of hom-sets. For each pair of **A**-objects X and Y, the functor $F : \mathbf{A} \to \mathbf{B}$ assigns to each **A**-morphism $f \in \mathbf{A}(X,Y)$ a **B**-morphism $Ff \in \mathbf{B}(FX,FY)$, and so defines a mapping

(11) $\qquad F_{X,Y} : \mathbf{A}(X,Y) \to \mathbf{B}(FX,FY)$

with $F_{X,Y}(f) = Ff$. Then the functor F is full when each $F_{X,Y}$ is surjective, and faithful when each $F_{X,Y}$ is injective. Note, however, that if F is both full and faithful, then each such mapping $F_{X,Y}$ is bijective, but that does not mean that F is a **Cat**-isomorphism, because there may be **B**-objects that are not in the image of F.

If **A** is a subcategory of **B**, then the inclusion functor is faithful. It is full if and only if **A** is a full subcategory of **B**.

A.17 Natural Transformation   Suppose $F, G : \mathbf{A} \to \mathbf{B}$ are two functors between the same two categories. A *natural transformation* α from F to G, notated $\alpha : F \to G$, is defined by

(*t*1)   for each **A**-object X there is a **B**-morphism $\alpha X \in \mathbf{B}(FX,GX)$;

(*t*2)   for each **A**-morphism $f \in \mathbf{A}(X,Y)$ the following rectangle of **B**-morphisms commutes:

(12)

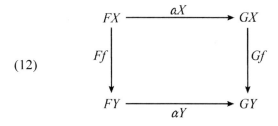

In other words,

(13) $Gf \circ \alpha X = \alpha Y \circ Ff$ for all $f \in \mathbf{A}(X,Y)$.

Note that all four morphisms Gf, αX, αY, and Ff, hence their compositions, are in **B**.

A natural transformation $\alpha : F \to G$ may be considered to be determined by the family of **B**-morphisms $\alpha X : FX \to GX$ (in the sense that when the **A**-object X is treated as a variable, the **B**-morphism $\alpha X : FX \to GX$ is "defined in the same way for each X"), whence $\alpha X : FX \to GX$ is said to be *natural in* X (which is the standard terminology of a more proper " $\alpha(\bullet) : F(\bullet) \to G(\bullet)$ is natural in its variable").

This notion of naturality may be generalized to n-ary functors. Let F and G be n-ary functors from a category **A** to a category **B**, and let

(14) $\mathsf{F} = \{\alpha(X_1,...,X_n) : F(X_1,...,X_n) \to G(X_1,...,X_n)\}$

be a family of arrows indexed by an n-tuple of **A**-objects $(X_1,...,X_n)$. If, for an index i, holding all the other arguments X_j with $j \neq i$ fixed, the resultant single-variable family

(15) $\alpha(\cdots,X_i,\cdots) : F(\cdots,X_i,\cdots) \to G(\cdots,X_i,\cdots)$

determines a natural transformation, then one says the family F is *natural in* X_i.

Since a functor $F : \mathbf{A} \to \mathbf{B}$ gives a picture (or model) in **B** for any collection of objects and morphisms of **A**, one may consider a natural transformation $\alpha : F \to G$ to be a translation (alternate description or model) of the picture F to the picture G. For example, picture (1), the commutative diagram of **A**-morphism commutativity, has the following translation from F to G:

(16)

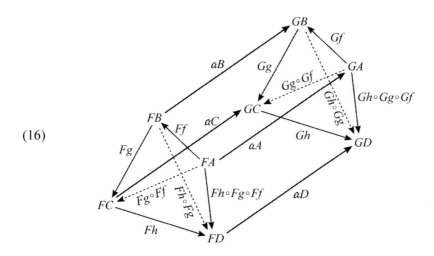

in which all triangles and parallelograms are commutative.

A.18 Functor Category The whole hierarchical process can be iterated. If **A** and **B** are categories, one can define the *functor category* $\mathbf{B}^{\mathbf{A}}$ to have as objects all (covariant) functors from **A** to **B**, to have as morphisms natural transformations, and to have composition and identities the 'pointwise' ones. It is easy to check that $\mathbf{B}^{\mathbf{A}}$ is indeed a category.

Isomorphisms in $\mathbf{B}^{\mathbf{A}}$ are called *natural isomorphisms* (also *natural equivalences*). The natural transformation $\alpha : F \to G$ is a natural isomorphism, denoted $\alpha : F \cong G$, if and only if for each **A**-object X, αX is an isomorphism (from FX to GX) in **B**. (There are actually several fine nuances of natural isomorphisms, but this characterization will serve our purpose here.)

A.19 Examples of Natural Transformations

(i) Recall (A.3) that for sets X and Y, Y^X is the set of all mappings from X to Y. The *evaluation* mapping $e:Y^X \times X \to Y$, defined, for $f:X \to Y$ and $x \in X$, by $e(f,x) = f(x)$, may be interpreted as a natural transformation as follows. For a fixed X, the map $Y \mapsto Y^X \times X$ extends to a functor $F:\mathbf{Set} \to \mathbf{Set}$ with, for $g:Y \to Z$, $Fg:Y^X \times X \to Z^X \times X$ defined by $Fg:(f,x) \mapsto (g \circ f,x)$ for $f:X \to Y$ and $x \in X$. Then, for this fixed X, $e:F \to I_{\mathbf{Set}}$ is a natural transformation from the functor F to the identity functor $I_{\mathbf{Set}}$, i.e., the following square commutes for any mapping $g:Y \to Z$:

(17)

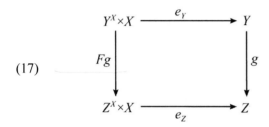

This reduces to the equation $g\big(e_Y(f,x)\big) = e_Z(g \circ f,x)$, which says simply that $g\big(f(x)\big) = (g \circ f)(x)$.

(ii) In the category **Vct** of vector spaces over a fixed field K, evaluation takes the following form. Each element $x \in V$ defines an *evaluation mapping* $\hat{x}:V^* \to K$ by $\hat{x}(f) = f(x)$ for every $f \in V^*$. $\hat{x}$ is a linear functional on V^*, hence it is a member of V^{**}, the second dual space of V. The mapping $\alpha_V:V \to V^{**}$, defined by $\alpha_V(x) = \hat{x}$, is an isomorphism (of vector-spaces) when V is finite dimensional. It is called the *natural isomorphism* between V and V^{**}. (Note this linear-algebraic terminology is part of the inspiration for its category-theoretic analogue.) For a linear transformation $T: V \to W$, one has $T^{**} \circ \alpha_X = \alpha_Y \circ T$, i.e., the diagram

(18)

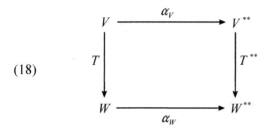

commutes, which says precisely that $\alpha : I_{\mathbf{Vct}} \to (\,\bullet\,)^{**}$ is a natural transformation.

(iii)   A mapping of two variables $t : X \times Y \to Z$ may be considered as a mapping $\varphi t : X \to Z^Y$ of one variable (in X), and the values of which are mappings with domain in the second variable (in Y) and codomain in Z:

(19) $\left[\varphi t(x) \right](y) = t(x,y)$ for $x \in X$ and $y \in Y$.

Equality (19) describes φ as a bijection (i.e. an isomorphism in **Set**)

(20) $\varphi : \mathbf{Set}(X \times Y, Z) \cong \mathbf{Set}(X, Z^Y)$

that is natural in X, Y, and Z. The isomorphism (17) may be written as

(21) $\mathbf{Set}(X \times Y, Z) \cong \mathbf{Set}(X, \mathbf{Set}(Y, Z))$

or

348

(22) $H(X \times Y, Z) \cong H(X, H(Y, Z)).$

The last bijection (22) is of particular importance in connection with (M,R)-systems.

Samual Eilenberg and Saunders Mac Lane, the two founders of category theory, first observed: 'category' has been defined in order to be able to define 'functor' and 'functor' has been defined in order to be able to define 'natural transformation'. In our context, the objects in our category are models, and morphisms are entailments; the encoding and decoding in the modelling relation are functors, while morphisms in the functor category of models, their comparison in terms of analogy and alternate descriptions, are natural transformations.

Universality

A.20 Universal Property In various branches of mathematics, many constructions are characterized by properties that require an object X to be 'special' among all other similar objects, in the sense that if another object Y satisfies similar conditions, then there exists a unique structure-preserving mapping between that other object Y and the special object X. These properties are called *universal properties*. In category-theoretic terms, one has the

Definition Let F be a functor from a category **A** to a category **B**, and let V be a **B**-object. A *universal morphism from F to V* consists of a pair (X, φ), where X is an **A**-object and $\varphi : FX \to V$ is a **B**-morphism, satisfying the following *universal property*: if Y is an **A**-object and $f : FY \to V$ is a **B**-morphism (i.e. if (Y, f) is another similar pair), then there exists a unique **A**-morphism $g : Y \to X$ (whence a unique **B**-morphism $Fg : FY \to FX$) such that the following diagram commutes:

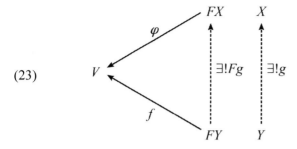

(23)

(The symbol $\exists$ is 'there exists' and the symbol ! is 'a unique'; while $\exists!$, 'there exists a unique', is strictly speaking not part of the commutative diagram, it is conventional in category theory to 'provide this additional information'.) Intuitively , the existence of the morphism g says that "X is general enough", while the uniqueness of the morphism g says that "X is not too general".

Defining a quantity does not guarantee its existence. The requisite universal morphism (X,φ) defined above may indeed not exist; but if it does, then it is *unique up to isomorphism*, in the sense that if (X',φ') is another universal morphism with the same properties as (X,φ), then (X,φ) and (X',φ') are isomorphic:

A.21 Lemma *Let F be a functor from a category* **A** *to a category* **B**, *and let V be a* **B**-*object. Any two universal morphisms from F to V are isomorphic.*

Stated otherwise, *any constructions in a category via universal properties are unique up to isomorphism.*

A.22 Product In set theory, the *product* of a family $\{A_i : i \in I\}$ of sets is the 'cartesian product set' $A = \prod_{i \in I} A_i$ of all I-tuples $(a_i : i \in I)$ with each

350

$a_i \in A_i$. (When the index is a finite set, say $I = \{1, 2, ..., n\}$, the product is more often denoted by $A_1 \times A_2 \times \cdots \times A_n$.) The mapping $\pi_j : A \to A_j$ that sends the I-tuple (a_i) to a_j is called the j th *projection* (or natural projection onto the jth coordinate). If B is a set and if there are mappings $f_j : B \to A_j$ for $j \in I$, then there exists a unique mapping $f : B \to A$ such that $\pi_j \circ f = f_j$ for all $j \in I$; namely, $f(x) = (f_i(x) : i \in I)$ for $x \in B$.

With the preceding motivation, one has the

Definition Given a family $\{A_i : i \in I\}$ of objects in a category **C**, a *product* of this family is a **C**-object A, denoted by $A = \prod_{i \in I} A_i$, with an I-tuple of **C**-morphisms (called *projections*) $(\pi_i : i \in I)$ where, for each $j \in I$, $\pi_j : A \to A_j$, possessing the universal property that whenever B is a **C**-object similarly equipped with I **C**-morphisms $f_j : B \to A_j$, there exists a unique **C**-morphism $f : B \to A$ such that for all $j \in I$, $\pi_j \circ f = f_j$; whence the commutative diagram

(24)

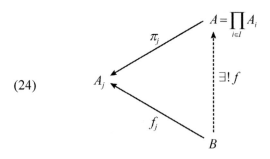

A category **C** *has products* if $\prod_{i \in I} A_i$ exists for every family $\{A_i : i \in I\}$.

A.23 Diagonal Morphism   The *diagonal morphism* for a **C**-object X is $\delta_X : X \to \prod_{i \in I} X = X^I$, such that $\pi_i \circ \delta_X = 1_X$ for each $i \in I$. This defines a natural transformation, natural in X.

A.24 Product as a Universal Construction   The product of a family of objects is essentially the 'most general' object *from* which a morphism exists to each object of the family. To cast the construction of product in the formulation of universal property, consider the index set I as a discrete category (i.e. the objects of the category I are the elements of the set I, and the only I-morphisms are identities; *cf.* A.2).   Then the functor category $\mathbf{C}^I$ has its objects the I-indexed families $\{A_i : i \in I\}$ of **C**-objects, and its morphisms the I-indexed families $\{f_i : i \in I\}$ of **C**-morphisms. Define the *diagonal functor* $\Delta : \mathbf{C} \to \mathbf{C}^I$ (not to be confused with the diagonal **C**-morphism $\delta_X : X \to X^I$) to send each **C**-object X to the 'constant family' (all entries in the I-tuple $= X$) and each **C**-morphism f to the 'constant family' (all entries in the I-tuple $= f$).   A universal morphism from Δ to $\{A_i : i \in I\}$ is the pair $\left(\prod_{i \in I} A_i, \{\pi_i : i \in I\} \right)$, where $A = \prod_{i \in I} A_i$ is the **C**-object and $\{\pi_i : i \in I\}$ is the $\mathbf{C}^I$-morphism (where $\pi_j : A \to A_j$ for each $j \in I$) with the requisite universal property.

By Lemma A.21, any two products of $\{A_i : i \in I\}$ are isomorphic. One may, therefore, refer to $A = \prod_{i \in I} A_i$ as *the* product rather than *a* product. The correspondence $f \leftrightarrow (f_i : i \in I)$ in the definition of product defines a natural isomorphism

(25) $$\mathbf{C}\left(B, \prod_{i \in I} A_i \right) \cong \prod_{i \in I} \mathbf{C}(B, A_i).$$

Here the product on the left denotes the product in **C**, while the product on the right, being a product of sets, is the cartesian product set in **Set**. Succinctly, the covariant hom-functor (see A.13) takes products to products.

A.25 Definition The product of the empty family in a category **C** is the *terminal object* of **C**.

Ω is the terminal object of **C** if and only if for every **C**-object X there is a unique **C**-morphism from X to Ω.

A.26 Examples of Product The category **Set** has products, the usual cartesian product sets as described above. The terminal object in **Set** is a singleton set. **Top** has products, the cartesian product sets with the product topologies. The terminal object is a singleton set with the only topology. **Grp** has products, the direct product of groups. The terminal object is the trivial group. One sees that products for 'sets with structure' are often — but not always — based on the notion for sets, and are thus 'cartesian product sets with product structure', in which case they are also known as *direct products*.

A.27 Power If the factors in a family $\{A_i : i \in I\}$ of **C**-objects are all equal (i.e., $A_i = Z$ for all $i \in I$), then the product $\prod_{i \in I} A_i = \prod_{i \in I} Z$ is called a *power*, and is written $\prod_{i \in I} Z = Z^I$. The equivalence

(26) $\qquad \mathbf{C}(X, Z)^I \cong \mathbf{C}(X, Z^I)$

is natural in X. Note that the power on the left hand side of the equivalence is that in **Set** (where every product, hence every power, exists); the power Y^I in **Set** is the set of all mappings from I to Y (*cf.* the discussion of the power notation $Y^I = \mathbf{Set}(I, Y)$ in A.3).

A.28 Finite Products To say that a category 'has products' requires the product to exists for *every* family, finite and infinite. Finite products of objects with a prescribed mathematical structure often preserve this structure, but infinite products sometimes do not. One may define a less stringent property: a category **C** *has finite products* if $\prod_{i \in I} A_i$ exists for every *finite* family $\{A_i : i \in I\}$. Since 'finite' includes 0 and 2, this means then **C** has a terminal object Ω (the product of the empty family) and a product of any two objects.

Having binary products is sufficient to guarantee, by iteration, the existence of products involving finitely many factors numbering three or more, but the existence of the product with no factors (i.e. the terminal object) has to be postulated separately:

A.29 Lemma *If a category* **C** *has a terminal object* Ω *and a product* $X \times Y$ *for every pair* X, Y *of its objects, then* **C** *has finite products.*

When **C** has finite products, the (binary) product objects define a bifunctor $\mathbf{C} \times \mathbf{C} \to \mathbf{C}$ by $(X,Y) \mapsto X \times Y$. The associativity law holds, in the sense that for three **C**-objects X, Y, Z, there is an isomorphism

$$(27) \qquad X \times (Y \times Z) \cong (X \times Y) \times Z$$

natural in X, Y, and Z. Also, for each **C**-object X, there are isomorphisms

$$(28) \qquad \Omega \times X \cong X \text{ and } X \times \Omega \cong X$$

natural in X.

A.30 Duality For each concept in a category **C**, there is a co-concept from its opposite category $\mathbf{C}^{\mathrm{op}}$. We have already encountered some examples. If $f : X \to Y$ is a **C**-morphism, then X is the *domain* of f in **C**;

now the $\mathbf{C}^{op}$-morphism $f^{op} : Y \to X$ is such that Y is the domain of f^{op} in $\mathbf{C}^{op}$, hence Y is the *codomain* of f in $\mathbf{C}$. Another dual pair is covariance/contravariance.

If $\Sigma(\mathbf{C})$ is a statement about an arbitrary category $\mathbf{C}$, let Σ^{op} be the statement defined by $\Sigma^{op}(\mathbf{C}) = \Sigma(\mathbf{C}^{op})$. For example, consider the statement

$\Sigma(\mathbf{C})$ = Products in a category $\mathbf{C}$ are unique up to isomorphism.

Then

$\Sigma(\mathbf{C}^{op})$ = Products in a category $\mathbf{C}^{op}$ are unique up to isomorphism.

Therefore

$\Sigma^{op}(\mathbf{C}) = \Sigma(\mathbf{C}^{op})$
$\qquad = $ *Coproducts* in a category $\mathbf{C}$ are unique up to isomorphism.

(Note that co-isomorphisms are isomorphisms, and I shall give an explicit definition of coproduct shortly.)

The Principle of Categorical Duality Σ^{op} *is universally true if* Σ *is.*

("Universally true" means that the statement is a consequence of the category axioms.) Duality cuts the work of proving theorems in half.

Note, however, that the economy only applies to theorems. As far as dual structures are concerned, their constructions are usually dramatically different, even though 'reversing all the arrows' seems mostly harmless. It is therefore illustrative to consider co-concepts explicitly.

A.31 Universal Property (Dual Definition) Let F be a functor from a category **A** to a category **B**, and let V be an **B**-object. A *universal morphism from V to F* consists of a pair (X, φ), where X is an **A**-object and $\varphi : V \to FX$ is a **B**-morphism, satisfying the following *universal property*: if Y is an **A**-object and $f : V \to FY$ is a **B**-morphism (i.e. if (Y, f) is another similar pair), then there exists a unique **A**-morphism $g : X \to Y$ (whence a unique **B**-morphism $Fg : FX \to FY$) such that the following diagram commutes:

(29)

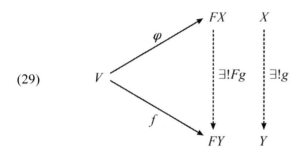

The dual of Lemma A.21 is

A.32 Lemma *Let F be a functor from a category **A** to a category **B**, and let V be a **B**-object. Any two universal morphisms from V to F are isomorphic.*

A.33 Coproduct A **C**-object A with **C**-morphisms $\iota_j : A_j \to A$ is the *coproduct* of the family $\{A_i : i \in I\}$ in **C** if, of course, $(A, \iota_j^{op} : A \to A_j)$ is the product of $\{A_i : i \in I\}$ in $\mathbf{C}^{op}$. Just as I refer to *the* product rather than *a* product because of the isomorphism, I have referred to *the* coproduct rather than *a* coproduct. Explicitly, one has the

356

Definition $\left(A, \iota_j : A_j \to A\right)$ is the *coproduct* of $\{A_i : i \in I\}$ in **C** if for $\left(B, g_j : A_j \to B\right)$ there exists a unique **C**-morphism $g : A \to B$ such that for all $j \in I$, $g \circ \iota_j = g_j$. The morphisms ι_j are called *injections* and the coproduct of $\{A_i\}$ is denoted by $A = \coprod_{i \in I} A_i$. (When the index is a finite set, say $I = \{1, 2, ..., n\}$, the coproduct is sometimes denoted by $A_1 + A_2 + \cdots + A_n$.) The commutative diagram is

(30)

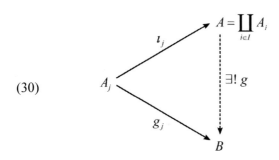

A category **C** *has coproducts* if $\coprod_{i \in I} A_i$ exists for every family $\{A_i : i \in I\}$.

A.34 Coproduct as a Universal Construction Dual to the case for product above, the universal morphism from $\{A_i : i \in I\}$ to Δ is the pair $\left(\coprod_{i \in I} A_i, \{\iota_i : i \in I\}\right)$, where $A = \coprod_{i \in I} A_i$ is the **C**-object and $\{\iota_i : i \in I\}$ is the $\mathbf{C}^I$-morphism (where $\iota_j : A_j \to A$ for each $j \in I$) with the requisite universal property. The coproduct of a family of objects is essentially the 'most general' object *to* which a morphism exists from each object of the family.

The correspondence $g \leftrightarrow (g_i : i \in I)$ in the definition of coproduct defines a natural isomorphism

$$(31) \qquad \mathbf{C}\left(\coprod_{i \in I} A_i, B\right) \cong \prod_{i \in I} \mathbf{C}(A_i, B).$$

Succinctly, the contravariant hom-functor (see Example A.13) takes coproducts to products.

A.35 Definition The coproduct of the empty family in a category $\mathbf{C}$ is the *initial object* of $\mathbf{C}$.

A is the initial object of $\mathbf{C}$ if and only if for every $\mathbf{C}$-object X there is a unique $\mathbf{C}$-morphism from A to X.

A.36 Examples of Coproduct The category **Set** has coproducts, the *disjoint union*

$$(32) \qquad \coprod_{i \in A} A_i = \prod_{i \in A} (\{i\} \times A_i) = \{(i,a) : i \in I, a \in A_i\}$$

and the jth injection ι_j sending $a \in A_j$ to (j,a). The unique initial object of **Set** is the empty set $\varnothing$. (Recall the convention $Y^\varnothing = \{\varnothing\}$ discussed in A.4.)

Top has coproducts, the disjoint union equipped with the 'direct sum topology' — a set G in $\coprod_{i \in I} A_i$ is open if and only if $G \cap A_i$ is open for each $i \in I$. The initial object is the empty space.

Unlike products, coproducts in many categories are *not* obviously based on the notion for sets, i.e. coproducts of sets with structure are often *not* 'disjoint union with structure'. This is because, essentially, unions do not behave well (as direct products usually do) with respect to preserving operations. For example, the union of two groups need not be a group.

The coproduct in **Grp**, called the *free product*, is, indeed, quite complicated.

There is, however, a class of categories in which the coproduct is an 'almost disjoint union': the object generated by the disjoint union of all 'nonzero' elements, together with a common 'zero'. For example, in **Ab**, the coproduct $\coprod_{i\in I} A_i$ is the subgroup of $\prod_{i\in I} A_i$ consisting of all I-tuples (a_i) such that $a_i = e_i = $ the identity of A_i for all but finitely many $i \in I$. (When the index set I is finite, therefore, the coproduct coincides with the product.) This coproduct $\coprod_{i\in I} A_i$ is usually referred to as the *direct sum* $\bigoplus_{i\in I} A_i$. For the universal property, $g : \bigoplus_{i\in I} A_i \to B$ is defined by

$$(33) \qquad g\big((a_i : i \in I)\big) = \sum_{i\in I} g_i(a_i).$$

Note that for all but finitely many $i \in I$, $a_i = e_i$ whence $g_i(a_i) = e_B = $ the identity of B, so there is no 'convergence' problem in the sum even when the index set I is infinite. The initial object of **Ab** is the trivial group, which is also the terminal object.

A.37 Definition In a category **C**, an object that is both initial and terminal is called the *zero object*.

Since the zero object is both A and Ω, it could have been assigned the ostentatious name 'God object'. The trivial group is thus the zero object of **Ab**. For another example, the singleton set $\{*\}$ (where $*$ is necessarily the base point) is the zero object of **Set**$_*$.

A.38 When Direct Sums and Direct Products Coincide The construction of the coproduct in **Ab** applies in a similar and obvious way to the category **Vct** of vector spaces and linear transformations, and indeed to many categories with an inherent 'additive structure'. Note that, as observed for **Ab** above, for a finite collection of vector spaces, the direct sum is the same as the direct product. This is indeed what a student learns in linear algebra, when the subject is finite-dimensional vector spaces. But one must note that

the equality $\coprod_{i \in I} A_i = \prod_{i \in I} A_i$ *only holds under special conditions,*

and is not true in general. The epistemology of these special conditions is an integral part of our study.

The term 'additive category', of which **Ab** and **Vct** are examples, has the following

A.39 Definition A category **A** is said to be *additive* if

(*a*1) Each hom set $\mathbf{A}(X,Y)$ is an abelian group.

(*a*2) The composition of morphisms $\circ : \mathbf{A}(X,Y) \times \mathbf{A}(Y,Z) \to \mathbf{A}(X,Z)$ is *biadditive*, i.e. for $f_1, f_2 : X \to Y$ and $g_1, g_2 : Y \to Z$,

(34) $g_1 \circ (f_1 + f_2) = g_1 \circ f_1 + g_1 \circ f_2$ and $(g_1 + g_2) \circ f_1 = g_1 \circ f_1 + g_2 \circ f_1.$

(*a*3) Each *finite* family of objects has a product and a coproduct.

Note that the three axioms (*a*1), (*a*2), (*a*3) are self-dual. Axiom (*a*3), when applied to the empty family of objects, says that an additive category has an initial object and a terminal object. It is actually enough to assume (*a*3) for pairs of objects and for the empty family; then the full strength follows by induction. Also, (*a*3) only assumes the *existence* of coproducts and products for finite families, but it is an immediate corollary that they are 'identical' (i.e. isomorphic):

A.40 Theorem *In an additive category the product and coproduct of any finite family are isomorphic.*

Morphisms and Their Hierarchies

A.41 Equalizers Let A and B be sets and $f, g : A \to B$ be two mappings. The inclusion map i of the subset $E = \{x \in A : f(x) = g(x)\}$ in A (*cf.* 1.8) can be characterized up to isomorphism by the following universal property: for every mapping $i' : E' \to A$ such that $f \circ i' = g \circ i'$, there exists a unique mapping $j : E' \to E$ such that $i \circ j = i'$ (since the image of i' is contained in E, j is defined by $j(x) = i'(x)$ for $x \in E'$).

Generalizing this idea, given morphisms $f, g : A \to B$ in a category **C**, an *equalizer* of (f, g) is an object E with a morphism $i : E \to A$ satisfying the following universal property:

(i) $f \circ i = g \circ i$;

(ii) given i' with $f \circ i' = g \circ i'$, there exists unique j such that $i \circ j = i'$.

(35)

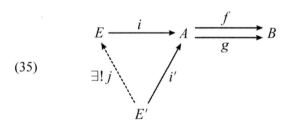

(An equivalent way of defining an equalizer is to say that it is a terminal object in the category of all **C**-morphisms that satisfy $f \circ i = g \circ i$.) As usual for 'universal property' definitions, equalizers are unique up to isomorphism and will be denoted by $\mathrm{eq}(f, g)$. A category **C** *has equalizers* if $\mathrm{eq}(f, g)$ exists for every pair $f, g : A \to B$.

A.42 Coequalizers $q: B \to Q$ in a category $\mathbf{C}$ is a *coequalizer* of $f, g: A \to B$ if, of course, $q^{\mathrm{op}} = \mathrm{eq}\left(f^{\mathrm{op}}, g^{\mathrm{op}}\right)$ in the dual category $\mathbf{C}^{\mathrm{op}}$.

Set has coequalizers. Given $f, g: A \to B$ let R be the equivalence relation on B generated by $A' = \{(f(a), g(a)) : a \in A\}$, i.e., let R be the intersection of all equivalence relations on B containing A'. Let $Q = B/R$ with canonical projection $q: B \to Q$. Then $q = \mathrm{coeq}(f, g)$ and $q \circ f = q \circ g$.

(36)

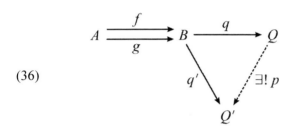

Suppose $q': B \to Q'$ and $q' \circ f = q' \circ g$; then $R' = \{(b_1, b_2) : q'(b_1) = q'(b_2)\}$ is an equivalence relation on B containing A' and hence contains R; p is thus defined by $p(b)_R = q'(b)$ and so $p \circ q = q'$.

A.43 Monomorphisms   There are many categorical definitions that characterize injective mappings in **Set**; we will content ourselves with three of them.

Let $f: A \to B$ in a category $\mathbf{C}$. The morphism f is *split mono* (also 'split monic') if there exists a $g: B \to A$ with $g \circ f = 1_A$, and *equalizer* if $f = \mathrm{eq}(g_1, g_2)$ for some pair $g_1, g_2: B \to C$, and *mono* (also 'monic') if for all pairs $g_1, g_2: X \to A$ with $f \circ g_1 = f \circ g_2$ one has $g_1 = g_2$.

It is a general theorem in category theory (the 'hierarchy theorem for monomorphisms') that split monos are equalizers and equalizers are monos. Also, if f and g are mono or split mono, so is $g \circ f$ (when composition is appropriate); if $g \circ f$ is mono or split mono, so is f. (The analogue for equalizers is not always true; it is true, however, when a category has epi-equalizer factorizations. See A.45 below.)

In **Set**, monos are the same as injective mappings, and it is easy to see that all monos are equalizers. If $f : A \to B$ is mono and A is nonempty, then f is split mono (let $g = f^{-1}$ on $f(A)$ and arbitrary elsewhere). Note, however, that the inclusion map of the empty set into a nonempty set is mono, but never split mono (because $B^{\varnothing} = \{\varnothing\}$ for sets B but $\varnothing^{B} = \varnothing$ for $B \neq \varnothing$; see A.4 above).

A.44 Epimorphisms The dual concepts to split mono, equalizer, and mono are, respectively *split epi, coequalizer,* and *epi*. Explicitly, $f : A \to B$ (in a category **C**) is *split epi* if there exists a $g : B \to A$ such that $f \circ g = 1_{B}$; f is a *coequalizer* if $f = \operatorname{coeq}(g_1, g_2)$ for some pair $g_1, g_2 : C \to A$; f is *epi* if for all pairs $g_1, g_2 : B \to X$, $g_1 \circ f = g_2 \circ f$ implies $g_1 = g_2$.

Dually, the hierarchy theorem for epimorphisms states that split epis are coequalizers and coequalizers are epis. Also, if f and g are epi or split epi, so is $g \circ f$; if $g \circ f$ is epi or split epi, so is g. (Again, the analogue for coequalizers is not always true, but is true when the category has coequalizer-mono factorizations; see A.45 below.)

In **Set**, all epis split and all three concepts mean 'surjective': since any mapping $f : A \to B$ composes equally with χ_{B} and $\chi_{f(A)} \in 2^{B}$, epis are surjective. The Axiom of Choice (1.37) entails that surjections are split epi.

A.45 Image Factorization The categorical view of the *image* of a mapping f is as a factorization $f = i \circ p$, where p is surjective and i is injective. Explicitly, let $f : X \to Y$. Then $p : X \to f(X)$, defined by $p(x) = f(x)$ for all $x \in X$, is a mapping from X onto $f(X)$. The inclusion map $i : f(X) \to Y$ of the range $f(X)$ of f in the codomain Y of f is one-to-one, and $f = i \circ p$.

Two of the many possible such views in an arbitrary category are as follows. Given a morphism $f : A \to B$ in **C**, an *epi-equalizer factorization* of f is $f = i \circ p$ with p an epi and i an equalizer. The dual concept is a *coequalizer-mono factorization* $f = i \circ p$ with p a coequalizer and i a mono. It is a general theorem that epi-equalizer [and coequalizer-mono] factorizations are unique up to isomorphism. As a corollary, f is an isomorphism if and only if f is both an equalizer and epi and if and only if f is both a coequalizer and mono. (Note that a morphism that is epi and mono need not, however, be an isomorphism.)

One says **C** *has epi-equalizer* [dually, *has coequalizer-mono*] factorizations if every morphism in **C** has an epi-equalizer [respectively, a coequalizer-mono] factorization. The category **Set** has epi-equalizer and coequalizer-mono factorizations and they both coincide with surjective-injective factorizations.

As a second example, the category **Top** of topological spaces and continuous mappings has epi-equalizer and coequalizer-mono factorizations. Given a continuous mapping $f : A \to B$ with image factorization $f = i \circ p$ at the level of **Set**, one can provide $f(A)$ with the subspace topology induced by i, then (p,i) is an epi-equalizer factorization, or one can provide $f(A)$ with the quotient topology induced by p, in which case (p,i) is a coequalizer-mono factorization. The two image factorizations are not in general homeomorphic. Note that although both the epi-equalizer and coequalizer-mono factorizations are unique up to isomorphism, the two factorizations are not necessarily isomorphic.

A.46 Subobjects In **Set** (and in most of the categories studied in linear algebra), since a mono splits and all three definitions of monomorphism coincide with injection, there is only one way to define a subobject — namely, one says A is a *subset* of B if there is an injection $f : A \to B$. (One sees that this category-theoretic definition of subset is consistent with the set-theoretic Definition 0.1.) In a general category **C**, one may define *subobject* in as many ways as there are distinct kinds of monomorphisms.

The hierarchy theorem for monomorphisms, that split monos are equalizers and equalizers are monos, implies split monos have the most stringent requirements as monomorphisms. This also entails that, therefore, split monos, among the various monomorphisms, preserve the most of the categorical structure of objects. So one most often define that A is a *subobject* of B (up to isomorphism, of course) if there is a split mono $f : A \to B$.

Adjoints

A.47 Natural Bijection Let us revisit the bijection $\varphi : \mathbf{Set}(X \times Y, Z) \cong \mathbf{Set}(X, Z^Y)$ in Example A.19(iii), defined by $[\varphi t(x)](y) = t(x, y)$ for $x \in X$ and $y \in Y$. If one holds the set Y fixed, one may define functors $F, G : \mathbf{Set} \to \mathbf{Set}$ by $FX = X \times Y$ and $GZ = Z^Y$, then the bijection takes the form

(37) $\qquad \varphi_{X,Z} : \mathbf{Set}(FX, Z) \cong \mathbf{Set}(X, GZ),$

which is natural in X and Z. To show the naturality in X for the equivalence (37), one must show that for each $h : X' \to X$ the diagram

$$
\begin{array}{ccc}
\mathbf{Set}(FX,Z) & \xrightarrow{\ \varphi_{X,Z}\ } & \mathbf{Set}(X,GZ) \\[2mm]
\Big\downarrow{\scriptstyle Fh} & & \Big\downarrow{\scriptstyle Gh} \\[2mm]
\mathbf{Set}(FX',Z) & \xrightarrow[\ \varphi_{X',Z}\ ]{} & \mathbf{Set}(X',GZ)
\end{array}
$$

(38)

commutes. (Note the contravariance: $h:X'\to X$ but $\mathbf{Set}(-X,\bullet)$ $\to \mathbf{Set}(-X',\bullet)$.) This requirement is realized by the definitions $Fh(t)$ $=t\circ(h\times 1_Y)$ and $Gh(\varphi t)=\varphi t\circ h$ for $t:X\times Y\to Z$:

(39)

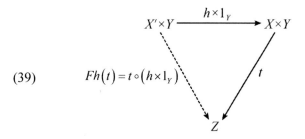

$$Fh(t)=t\circ(h\times 1_Y)$$

(40)

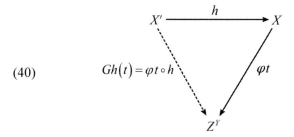

$$Gh(t)=\varphi t\circ h$$

366

Similarly, naturality in Z means that for each $k: Z \to Z'$ the diagram

(41)

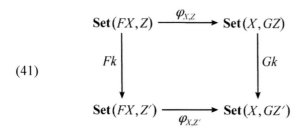

commutes. (Note the covariance: $k: Z \to Z'$ and $\mathbf{Set}(\cdot, -Z) \to \mathbf{Set}(\cdot, -Z')$.) This is realized by the definitions $Fk(t) = k \circ t$ and $Gk(\varphi t) = \varphi[k \circ t]$ for $t: X \times Y \to Z$:

(42)

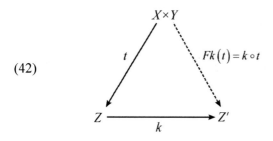

(43)

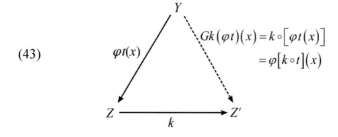

The bijection (37) may be rephrased thus: the functors $F:X\mapsto X\times Y$ and $G:Z\mapsto Z^Y$ uniquely determine each other by the bijection $t\leftrightarrow\varphi t$. Generalizing from **Set** to arbitrary categories, one has the following definition.

A.48 Adjunction An *adjunction* from a category **A** to a category **B** is a triple $\langle F,G,\varphi\rangle:\mathbf{A}\to\mathbf{B}$, where $F:\mathbf{A}\to\mathbf{B}$ and $G:\mathbf{B}\to\mathbf{A}$ are functors, and φ is a mapping (of sets) which assigns to each pair of **A**-object X and **B**-object Y a bijection of sets

$$(44)\qquad \varphi=\varphi_{X,Y}:\mathbf{B}(FX,Y)\cong\mathbf{A}(X,GY)$$

that is natural in X and Y. The functor F is called a *left adjoint* for the functor G, and G is called a *right adjoint* for F.

The left hand side $\mathbf{B}(FX,Y)$ of the equivalence (44) is the bifunctor

$$(45)\qquad \mathbf{A}^{op}\times\mathbf{B}\xrightarrow{F^{op}\times I_{\mathbf{B}}}\mathbf{B}^{op}\times\mathbf{B}\xrightarrow{hom}\mathbf{Set}$$

that sends each pair of objects (X,Y) to the hom-set $\mathbf{B}(FX,Y)$, and the right hand side $\mathbf{A}(X,GY)$ is a similar bifunctor $\mathbf{A}^{op}\times\mathbf{B}\to\mathbf{Set}$. The naturality of the bijection φ means that for all $k:Y\to Y'$ and $h:X'\to X$ both the diagrams

$$(46)\qquad \begin{array}{ccc} \mathbf{B}(FX,Y) & \xrightarrow{\varphi_X} & \mathbf{A}(X,GY)\\ \downarrow{(\cdot)\circ Fh} & & \downarrow{(\cdot)\circ h}\\ \mathbf{B}(FX',Y) & \xrightarrow{\varphi_{X'}} & \mathbf{A}(X',GY) \end{array}$$

368

and

$$\begin{array}{ccc} \mathbf{B}(FX,Y) & \xrightarrow{\;\varphi_Y\;} & \mathbf{A}(X,GY) \\[1em] {\scriptstyle k\circ(\bullet)}\downarrow & & \downarrow{\scriptstyle Gk\circ(\bullet)} \\[1em] \mathbf{B}(FX,Y') & \xrightarrow[\;\varphi_{Y'}\;]{} & \mathbf{A}(X,GY') \end{array}$$

(47)

commute.

We have, of course, already encountered the left-right adjoint pair $F:X \mapsto X \times Y$ and $G:Z \mapsto Z^Y$ from **Set** to **Set**. Another example of *adjunction* is from the category **Set** to the category **Vct**, the triple $\langle F,G,\varphi \rangle : \mathbf{Set} \to \mathbf{Vct}$ where $F:\mathbf{Set} \to \mathbf{Vct}$ sends a set X to the vector space FX with basis X (i.e., all formal linear combinations of members of X), $G:\mathbf{Vct} \to \mathbf{Set}$ assigns to a vector space V the set GV of all its vectors (i.e., G is the forgetful functor), and the bijection

(48) $\qquad \varphi : \mathbf{Vct}(FX,V) \to \mathbf{Set}(X,GV)$

is $\varphi : T \mapsto T|_X$ (sending a linear transformation T to its restriction on a basis). Note that the inverse φ^{-1} extends a mapping defined on a basis to the whole vector space, which is the linear-algebraic theorem that a linear transformation is uniquely determined by its values on a basis.

A.49 Adjointness as a Universal Property The statement that F is a left adjoint for G is equivalent to the following universal property for the functor $F:\mathbf{A} \to \mathbf{B}$. For each **A**-object X, there is a **B**-object FX and an **A**-morphism $\varphi : X \to GFX$, such that for any **A**-morphism $f:X \to GY$, there is a unique **B**-morphism $g:FX \to Y$ satisfying $Gg \circ \varphi = f$:

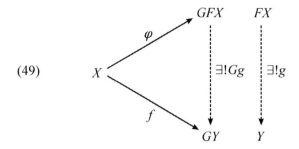

(49)

Many categorical structures may be described via adjoints.

A.50 Extremal Adjointness   For any category **C**, there is a unique functor U to the one-object category **1** (trivially sending every **C**-object to the only object 0 of **1**, and every **C**-morphism to the only morphism 1_0 of **1**). U has a left (respectively, right) adjoint if and only if **C** has an initial object A (respectively, a terminal object Ω). For every **C**-object X there is a unique **C**-morphism from A to X (respectively, a unique **C**-morphism from X to Ω). With $\{*\}$ denoting the singleton set, one has the bijection

$$(50) \qquad \mathbf{C}(A, X) \cong \{*\}$$

(respectively,

$$(51) \qquad \mathbf{C}(X, \Omega) \cong \{*\}).$$

A.51 Products and Coproducts as Adjoints   For a category **C**, the diagonal functor $\Delta : \mathbf{C} \to \mathbf{C} \times \mathbf{C}$ has a right adjoint if and only if **C** has binary products: for all **C**-objects X, Y, Z, one has the natural isomorphism

$$(52) \qquad \mathbf{C} \times \mathbf{C}(\Delta Z, (X, Y)) = \mathbf{C}(Z, X) \times \mathbf{C}(Z, Y) \cong \mathbf{C}(Z, X \times Y).$$

Dually, the diagonal functor $\Delta : \mathbf{C} \to \mathbf{C} \times \mathbf{C}$ has a left adjoint if and only if $\mathbf{C}$ has binary coproducts: for all $\mathbf{C}$-objects X, Y, Z, one has the natural isomorphism

$$(53) \qquad \mathbf{C}(X + Y, Z) \cong \mathbf{C}(X, Z) \times \mathbf{C}(Y, Z) = \mathbf{C} \times \mathbf{C}\big((X, Y), \Delta Z\big).$$

A.52 Exponential In Example A.19(iii) and A.47 we saw the natural isomorphism $\mathbf{Set}(X \times Y, Z) \cong \mathbf{Set}(X, Z^Y)$ for the category $\mathbf{Set}$. If a category $\mathbf{C}$ has (binary) products, then there is an induced functor $\bullet \times \bullet : \mathbf{C} \times \mathbf{C} \to \mathbf{C}$. In particular, fixing a $\mathbf{C}$-object Y, consider the induced functor $\bullet \times Y : \mathbf{C} \to \mathbf{C}$ which maps $\mathbf{C}$-objects $X \mapsto X \times Y$. Then, by definition, this functor $\bullet \times Y : \mathbf{C} \to \mathbf{C}$ has a right adjoint $G : \mathbf{C} \to \mathbf{C}$ if and only if one has the natural isomorphism $\mathbf{C}(X \times Y, Z) \cong \mathbf{C}(X, GZ)$. If one denotes this right adjoint $G(\bullet) = (\bullet)^Y$, then

$$(54) \qquad \mathbf{C}(X \times Y, Z) \cong \mathbf{C}(X, Z^Y).$$

The $\mathbf{C}$-object Z^Y is called an *exponential*.

Thus in **Set**, the exponential Z^Y is the set $\mathbf{Set}(Y, Z)$ of all mappings from Y to Z. In **Cat**, the exponential $\mathbf{Z}^Y$ is the functor category. So the exponential notation is consistent with previous usage in these two categories. Note that, in a general category, given $\mathbf{C}$-objects Z and Y, the exponential Z^Y does not necessarily exist. Even when it does exist, it is simply a $\mathbf{C}$-object; it does not necessarily correspond to the hom-set $\mathbf{C}(Y, Z)$. This is (roughly) because there is not always a 'good' way to define a $\mathbf{C}$-structure on the hom-set $\mathbf{C}(Y, Z)$ to turn it into a $\mathbf{C}$-object. Also note that the exponential Z^Y and the power Z^J (*cf.* Definition A.27) are very different $\mathbf{C}$-objects: in the former, both Z and Y are $\mathbf{C}$-objects; in the latter, Z is a $\mathbf{C}$-object but J is an index set (i.e. a **Set**-object).

Specifying the adjunction $\left\langle \bullet \times Y, (\bullet)^{Y}, \varphi \right\rangle : \mathbf{C} \to \mathbf{C}$ amounts to assigning to each pair of **C**-objects X and Z the **C**-morphism $e : Z^{X} \times X \to Z$, called the *evaluation morphism*, which is natural in Z and universal from $\bullet \times X$ to Z. In **Set**, it is, of course, the evaluation mapping (Example A.19.(i)) $e : (g, x) \mapsto g(x)$ for $g : X \to Z$ and $x \in X$.

In our synthetic continuation in relational biology, we mostly encounter the category **Set**, its subcategories, and other categories of sets with specified additional structures. We now have all the pieces in category theory to readily define one special case, a category that subscribes to the three natural isomorphisms (51), (53), and (54):

A.53 Cartesian Closed Category Let the category **C** have finite products. It is called *cartesian closed* when each of the following three functors

$$(55) \qquad \mathbf{C} \xrightarrow{U} \mathbf{1} \qquad \mathbf{C} \xrightarrow{\Delta} \mathbf{C} \times \mathbf{C} \qquad \mathbf{C} \xrightarrow{\bullet \times Y} \mathbf{C}$$

defined by

$$(56) \qquad X \mapsto 0 \qquad X \mapsto (X, X) \qquad X \mapsto X \times Y$$

has the specified right adjoints defined by

$$(57) \qquad 0 \mapsto \Omega \qquad (Z, Y) \mapsto Z \times Y \qquad Z \mapsto Z^{Y}$$

To summarize, the first right adjoint specifies the terminal object Ω of **C**. The second right adjoint specifies, for each pair of **C**-objects X and Z, a product object $X \times Z$ (along with its projections). The third right adjoint specifies the exponential object Z^{Y} for the **C**-object Z, with the corresponding bijection $\mathbf{C}(X \times Y, Z) \cong \mathbf{C}(X, Z^{Y})$, natural in X and Z.

Set and **Cat** are cartesian closed categories.

Exponentials in cartesian closed categories have the following properties (hence their name):

A.54 Lemma

(i) $Z^{\Omega} \cong Z$.

(ii) $Z^{Y \times X} \cong \left(Z^{Y}\right)^{X}$.

(iii) $Z^{Y} \times Y^{X} \to Z^{X}$ is a natural transformation, which agrees in **Set** with composition of mappings.

Bibliography

Aczel, Peter [1988] *Non-Well-Founded Sets.* Lecture Notes No. 14. Center for the Study of Language and Information, Stanford CA.

Brown, A. L. and Page, A. [1970] *Elements of Functional Analysis.* Van Nostrand, London.

Carroll, Lewis [1895] 'What the Tortoise said to Achilles', *Mind*, n.s., **4**, 278. [Reprinted in many Carroll collections, *e.g.*, 'The Complete Works of Lewis Carroll' (1976) Vintage Books, New York; and as *Two-Part Invention* in D. R. Hofstadter (1979) 'Gödel, Escher, Bach: An Eternal Golden Braid', Random House, New York.]

Bertalanffy, Ludwig von [1968] *General System Theory: Foundations, Development, Applications.* Fourth printing 1973. Braziller, New York.

Birkhoff, Garrett [1967] *Lattice Theory.* Third Edition. American Mathematical Society Colloquium Publications, Volume 25. AMS, Providence RI.

Danielli, James F. [1974] 'Genetic Engineering and Life Synthesis: An Introduction to the Review by R. Widdus and C. Ault', *International Review of Cytology* **38**, 1–5.

374

Euler, Leonhard [1736] 'The Seven Bridges of Königsberg', in *The World of Mathematics* (1956, Ed. J. R. Newman, Vol. 1, pp.573–580). Simon and Schuster, New York.

Gross, Jonathan L. and Yellen, Jay [1999] *Graph Theory and Its Applications*. CRC Press, Boca Raton FL.

Halmos, Paul R. [1958] *Finite-Dimensional Vector Spaces*, 2nd edn. Van Nostrand, Princeton, NJ.

Halmos, Paul R. [1960] *Naive Set Theory*. Van Nostrand, Princeton NJ.

Hoffman, Kenneth and Kunze, Ray [1971] *Linear Algebra*, 2nd edn. Prentice-Hall, Englewood Cliffs, NJ.

Kercel, Stephen W. [2007] 'Entailment of Ambiguity', *Chemistry and Biodiversity* 4, 2369–2385.

Kleene, Stephen Cole [1952] *Introduction to Metamathematics*. North-Holland, NY.

Louie, A. H., Richardson, I. W., and Swaminathan, S. [1982] 'A Phenomenological Calculus for Recognition Processes', *Journal of Theoretical Biology* 94, 77–93.

Louie, A. H. [1983] 'Categorical System Theory and the Phenomenological Calculus', *Bulletin of Mathematical Biology* 45, 1029–1045.

Louie, A. H. and Somorjai, R. L. [1984] 'Stieltjes Integration and Differential Geometry: A Model for Enzyme Recognition, Discrimination, and Catalysis', *Bulletin of Mathematical Biology* 46, 745–764.

Louie, A. H. [1985, CS] 'Categorical System Theory', in *Theoretical Biology and Complexity: Three Essays on the Natural Philosophy of Complex Systems* (Ed. R. Rosen), 69–163. Academic Press, Orlando FL.

Louie, A. H. [2007] 'A Rosen Etymology', *Chemistry and Biodiversity* **4**, 2296–2314.

Mac Lane, Saunders [1978] *Category Theory for the Working Mathematician*. Second Edition. Springer-Verlag, NY.

Richardson, I. W. and Louie, A. H. [1983] 'Projections as Representations of Phenomena', *Journal of Theoretical Biology* **102**, 199–223.

Richardson, I. W. and Louie, A. H. [1986] 'Irreversible Thermodynamics, Quantum Mechanics, and Intrinsic Time Scales', *Mathematical Modelling* **7**, 211–226.

Rosen, Robert [1958] 'A Relational Theory of Biological Systems', *Bulletin of Mathematical Biophysics* **20**, 245–260.

Rosen, Robert [1959] 'A Relational Theory of Biological Systems II', *Bulletin of Mathematical Biophysics* **21**, 109–128.

Rosen, Robert [1971] 'Some Realizations of (M,R)-Systems and their Interpretation', *Bulletin of Mathematical Biophysics* **33**, 303–319.

Rosen, Robert [1972] 'Some Relational Cell Models: The Metabolism-Repair Systems', in *Foundations of Mathematical Biology*, Vol. 2 (Ed. R. Rosen), 217–253). Academic Press, New York

Rosen, Robert [1973] 'On the Dynamical Realization of (M,R)-Systems', *Bulletin of Mathematical Biology* **35**, 1–9.

Rosen, Robert [1974] 'Planning, Management, Policies, and Strategies: Four Fuzzy Concepts', *International Journal of General Systems* **1**, 245–252.

Rosen, Robert [1978, *FM*] *Fundamentals of Measurement and Representation of Natural Systems*. North-Holland, New York.

Rosen, Robert [1985a, *AS*] *Anticipatory Systems*. Pergamon Press, Oxford.

Rosen, Robert [1985b, *NC*] 'Organisms as Causal Systems which are Not Mechanisms: An Essay into the Nature of Complexity', in *Theoretical Biology and Complexity: Three Essays on the Natural Philosophy of Complex Systems* (Ed. R. Rosen), 165–203. Academic Press, Orlando FL.

Rosen, Robert [1991, *LI*] *Life Itself*. Columbia University Press, New York.

Rosen, Robert [2000, *EL*] *Essays on Life Itself*. Columbia University Press, New York.

Rosen, Robert [2000] 'Autobiographical Reminiscences of Robert Rosen', *Axiomathes* **16**(1–2), 1–23.

Rubin, Herman and Rubin Jean E. [1963] *Equivalents of the Axiom of Choice*. North-Holland, Amsterdam.

Rudin, Walter [1973] *Functional Analysis*. McGraw-Hill, New York.

Rudin, Walter [1974] *Real and Complex Analysis*, 2nd edn. McGraw-Hill, New York.

Trudeau, Richard J. [1993] *Introduction to Graph Theory*. Dover Publications, Inc, Mineola NY.

Wigner, Eugene P. [1960] 'The Unreasonable Effectiveness of Mathematics in the Natural Sciences', reprinted in *Symmetries and Reflections* (1967), 222–237. University of Indiana Press, Bloomington IN.

Acknowledgments

I thank Roberto Poli and Margaret Schaeken for their critical readings of the manuscript. The number of errors has decreased as a result of their efficiency.

I would also like to thank Cynthia Chan, Tim Gwinn, Stephen Kercel, Luk Suk Fun, Donald Mikulecky, and Judith Rosen, for their substantial encouragement and motivation.

My sincere gratitude is due to my wife Margaret, and my other mentor, colleague, and friend I. W. Richardson, for their exertions on my behalf throughout the years. Their formative and precious support has been my shining light *de tenebris*.

In fine, may this monograph be my relational offering to my exemplar Robert Rosen, who would have received it with delight.

A. H. Louie
12 April, 2009

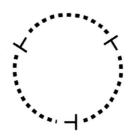

Index

382

384

388

More Than Life Itself:
A Synthetic Continuation in Relational Biology

A. H. Louie

MMIX

Categories

Editor
Roberto Poli (Trento)

Advisory board
John Bell (London, CA)
Mark Bickhard (Lehigh)
Heinrich Herre (Leipzig)
David Weissman (New York)

Aims and Scope

Four of the major areas of our concern are widely changing their nature. Philosophy, natural science, cognitive science and mathematics (i.e. the set of tools we have been able to develop for modelling fragments of reality) are definitely leaving the conceptual framework inaugurated by Galilei and Descartes and essentially adopted as possibly the main reference framework for scientific and philosophical investigations up to the end of Nineteenth century. Since then, investigations in philosophy, science and mathematics have experimented new paths, which proved to be substantially different from those previously followed. Many scientific results of the twentieth century, in different fields of research, seemingly converge on the conclusion that science is changing its nature. A number of problems that were labelled as extraneous to the realm of science by the modern vision of science have been attacked with some success. Quantum indeterminacy, computational limitations, complexity, chaos and turbulence, non-linear dynamics and far-from-equilibrium systems, defects in phase transitions, the far-reaching importance of intentionality, emergent properties and emergent objects, forward, upward and downward forms of causation are all facets of a general view claiming that we are approaching a new scientific agenda. Something similar is taking place in mathematics. After the second great unification based on set theory (the former unification obviously being analytic or Cartesian geometry), a new generalization and unification is under development since the Forties, under the name of Category Theory. As to philosophy, after two centuries of oblivion, ontology is now starting to win back the central place it was used to have, as witnessed by the reappearance of the very same term "ontology" in the titles of academic books and papers. Ten or fifteen years ago the situation was very different. The general understanding of ontological problems is still rather cursory (i.e. we cannot say that there is some generally accepted criterion for distinguishing ontology from metaphysics, or ontology from epistemology. Or for deciding which problems are ontological, as opposed to, say, logical or linguistic problems.) There is room for serious work, from both the historical (meaning, the best proposals from the past) and the systematic viewpoint (structure and tools of any well-rounded ontology). Moreover, a strong "ontological" movement has recently arisen in computer science. Here ontology is explicitly declared to be helpful when the problems of the acquisition, integration and sharing of knowledge are addressed. Generally speaking, ontology comes into play as a viable strategy with which, for example, to construct robust databases. An ontologically grounded knowledge of the objects of the world should provide general patterns making their codification simpler, more transparent and more natural. Indeed, ontology can give greater robustness to databases by furnishing criteria and categories with which to organize and construct them; and it is also able to provide contexts in which different databases can be embedded and recategorized to acquire greater reciprocal transparency. These different but non contrasting reasons seem to converge towards the conclusion that the four-centuries-old Galileian vision of science inadvertently but inexorably is giving way to a new one in which formal, material, mental and social sciences are developing new forms of interaction and are beginning to integrate with each other. Mathematics and philosophy are running through similar epoch-breaking changes. The idea that the four series of transformation are not unrelated arises spontaneously. Many aspects of this new scenario are still unknown; many others are emerging; and many blind alleys lie in wait, especially if we lack awareness of where we are and where we are heading. All the above supports the idea of a series wishing to publish (1) some the most relevant novelties in the mentioned fields, and (2) works trying to understand the processes under development. An increasing number of scholars from many different fields is becoming more and more aware of the fact that something has changed and continues to change in both their own field of expertise and in the other more or less close fields their know something of. This is a kind of general trend. It may be time to explicitly address the problem of the new scientific and philosophical paradigms under formation. Before presenting the last pieces of information, let me sum up the main features of the actual proposal. In as few words as possible, the core topics of the proposal are (1) ontology, (2) frontiers of science (from the point of view of a philosophically minded eye), (3) cognitive systems and (4) introductions to and applications of formal theories, with a particular bias towards category theory. It is worth noticing that nothing similar is offered by any other publishing house.

Publications

"Generic figures and their glueings - A constructive approach to functor categories", by Marie La Palme Reyes, Gonzalo E. Reyes, Houman Zolfaghari

"The Continuous and the Infinitesimal - in mathematics and philosophy", by John L. Bell